D1569942

WHOSE BODY IS IT ANYWAY?

Whose Body is it Anyway?

Justice and the Integrity of the Person

CÉCILE FABRE

CLARENDON PRESS • OXFORD

OXFORD
UNIVERSITY PRESS

Great Clarendon Street, Oxford OX2 6DP

Oxford University Press is a department of the University of Oxford.
It furthers the University's objective of excellence in research, scholarship,
and education by publishing worldwide in

Oxford New York

Auckland Cape Town Dar es Salaam Hong Kong Karachi
Kuala Lumpur Madrid Melbourne Mexico City Nairobi
New Delhi Shanghai Taipei Toronto

With offices in

Argentina Austria Brazil Chile Czech Republic France Greece
Guatemala Hungary Italy Japan Poland Portugal Singapore
South Korea Switzerland Thailand Turkey Ukraine Vietnam

Oxford is a registered trademark of Oxford University Press
in the UK and in certain other countries

Published in the United States
by Oxford University Press Inc., New York

British Library Cataloguing in Publication Data

Data available

Library of Congress Cataloging in Publication Data

Data available

Typeset by Laserwords Private Limited, Chennai, India
Printed in Great Britain
on acid-free paper by
Biddles Ltd., King's Lynn, Norfolk

ISBN 0–19–928999–9   978–0–19–928999–8

1 3 5 7 9 10 8 6 4 2

To Sam

Summary Contents

Detailed Contents

Acknowledgements

I began this book in the Winter of 2000—at a time when, having finished my earlier work on constitutional social rights, I was toying with ideas for a large project on global distributive justice as well as a smaller one on the legitimacy of inheritance and bequests. Frustrated by my inability to get anywhere with the former, I concentrated on the latter, and discovered, first (with some shock), that I did believe in the confiscation of cadaveric body parts, and, second (with even greater shock), that I also believed in the limited confiscation of *live* body parts.

At that time, the British public was up in arms about the Alder Hey scandal, which involved a respected pathologist taking away organs from dead children without parental consent. When asked to comment on such practice, the medical establishment, the media, and politicians all reiterated the widely held view that our bodies are ours to do as we wish provided we do not actively harm others: not a very promising context in which to muster the intellectual confidence to deploy controversial views on this issue. But as I presented my work at various seminars and conferences, and submitted it, at first entirely unsuccessfully, to various journals, I realized not only that I was increasingly committed to it, but also that although the vast majority of my readers and audiences strongly, sometimes vociferously, disagreed with me, they were sufficiently intrigued by my arguments to be willing to engage fully with them. It seemed, then, that my views were not so outlandish as to warrant complete dismissal.

And, indeed, three of the book's chapters finally appeared (in modified form) as journal articles: 'Justice and the Compulsory Taking of Live Body Parts', *Utilitas* 15 (2003): 127–50; 'Good Samaritanism and Justice', *Critical Review of International Social and Political Philosophy* 5 (2004): 128–44; and 'Justice and the Confiscation of Cadaveric Organs', *British Journal of Political Science* 34 (2004): 69–86. I thank Edinburgh University Press, Routledge, and Cambridge University Press for granting me permission to reprint this material here.

Never have I felt so privileged to be an academic as I did in the course of writing this book, for, in effect, I was paid to write and teach on issues which I have always found absolutely fascinating. Moreover, the written and oral discussions I have had with a number of people on the arguments deployed here have been extraordinarily rich and fruitful. I started this project at Nuffield College, Oxford, where I was a postdoctoral research fellow, but wrote the bulk of it at the London School of Economics where I took up a lectureship in September 2000. My colleagues in both institutions gave me steadfast support, even though they found my endeavours rather worrisome. I am particularly grateful to my political theory colleagues at the LSE, and to Dominic Lieven, then head of the Department of Government, for relieving me of teaching and administrative duties for six months, as well as to the Arts and Humanities Research Board for funding additional research leave. For their helpful insights and oral comments, I also want to thank my graduate students, as well as seminar participants at the LSE, Nuffield College (whose Political Theory Workshop has provided me with invaluable intellectual support for the last ten years), the Université de Montreal, the Philosophy Department at Bristol University, the Government Department at Essex University, the 2002 APSA Conference, and the 2002 Annual Conference of the UK Association for Social and Legal Philosophy.

I have run up a particularly large debt of gratitude to a number of individuals. Catriona Mackenzie, Hillel Steiner, and Suzanne Uniacke reviewed the typescript for Oxford University Press and gave me the kind of written feedback—probing, demanding, constructive, and thoughtful—one dreams of receiving from reviewers. In particular, I am grateful to Hillel for providing the book's main title. I should also like to express my heartfelt thanks to friends and colleagues who provided comments and assistance of various kinds on draft chapters: Rodney Barker, Garrett Brown, Daniel Butt, Clare Chambers, John Charvet, Miriam Cohen-Christofidis, Richard Dagger, Jurgen de Wispelaere, Anneliese Dodds, Keith Dowding, François Fabre, Katrin Flikschuh, Ori Golan, Axel Gosseries, Keith Graham, Nick Humphrey, George Jones, Paul Kelly, Matthew Kramer, Cécile Laborde, Alex Leveringhaus, Christian List, Haidee Lorrey, Andrew Mason, Dan McDermott, Susan Mendus, Søren Mitgaard, Eva-Maria Nag, Serena Olsaretti, Jonathan Seglow, Peter Vallentyne, Vassos Vassou, Alex Voorheve, Albert Weale, and Andrew Williams. In addition, Rebecca Bryant, Rupert Cousens, Helen Gray, and Peter Momtchiloff efficiently steered the book through the publishing process and Jeremy Williams helped me with the index—for which I am thankful.

It is to David Miller and Jerry Cohen, however, that I owe the most: David read the entire draft; Jerry read several of the chapters more than once. Their support and advice have proven invaluable for the last thirteen years: for that, and, more importantly for their friendship, I am profoundly thankful.

Finally, my son, Sam, was born two years before I finished this book. Watching him learn how to use his body in all the ways we take for granted, and sharing his delight in the autonomy his new-found mobility gave him, helped me put the words that follow into much-needed perspective. Still, I dedicate them to him, with unbounded love.

London, January 2006

Introduction

In the prevailing liberal ethos, if there is one thing that is beyond the reach of others, it is our body in particular, and our person in general. Thus, there is a very strong presumption, in liberal societies, that unprovoked assaults are impermissible and should be punished by the state. Likewise, the Anglo-American political and legal tradition is unsympathetic to the view that we have a stringent moral duty to be Good Samaritans and that such duty should be enforced by the state. Similarly, in the USA, the Uniform Anatomical Gift Act of 1968 and its revised version of 1987 provide that organs cannot be removed from a dead body unless the deceased has given her consent. In Canada, where those issues are dealt with by provincial legislatures, the relevant statutes stipulate (with minor divergences) that no organ can be removed from a dead body unless the deceased had prehumously given his consent or, absent such consent, unless the next-of-kin consents to it. In the UK, the Human Tissue Act of 1961 states that if any person has expressed the wish, orally in front of two witnesses or in writing, that his body or any of its parts be used after his death, doctors are allowed to remove them. They are not required by law to ask the next-of-kin whether they object. Needless to say, no law (that I know of) allows for the mandatory taking of *live* body parts.

To the extent that our legal and philosophical tradition forbids the confiscation of personal resources on the grounds that individuals have a fundamental interest in controlling what happens to their person, one might think that it would allow for their commercialization, precisely on those very grounds. Not so, though: in fact, most liberal legal systems hold that we cannot renounce our right to control what happens to our person in exchange for money. And so we cannot, for example, prostitute ourselves, sell our kidneys, or rent our womb for nine months. In the UK, the Human Transplant Act of 1991 explicitly forbids organ sales. In the USA, although the sale of blood and sperm is allowed, the National Organ Transplant Act of 1984 makes the interstate commercial transfer of organs a federal crime, and the Public Health Code makes it illegal to acquire, receive, or transfer human organs against payment (indeed, to do so is subject to a hefty fine and a jail sentence). Concerning prostitution and surrogacy, neither the UK nor the USA is sympathetic to the view that prostitutes and surrogate mothers should be regarded as workers. In the UK, whereas the act per se of engaging in prostitutional sex is not a criminal offence, soliciting, pimping, kerb-crawling, and advertising for sexual services are. In the USA, some states, such as Vermont, prohibit the act of prostitutional sex itself, whilst others adopt the British approach. 'Reformist movements' in both countries focus on lifting all penalties on prostitutes and imposing harsher ones on their pimps and clients: on that view, clients would be disallowed to buy sex, which in effect would place considerable restrictions on the prostitutes' ability to sell it, and thus to use their body as they wish. Finally, although most countries desist from criminalizing surrogacy contracts, they do not acknowledge them as legally valid, with the effect that surrogate mothers' moral right to hire their body out for reproductive purposes, and commissioning parents' moral right to avail themselves of that reproductive route, are weakened by being left legally unprotected.

In a nutshell, then, our legal and political tradition is such that we have the right to deny others access to our person, even though doing so would harm those who need such access; however, we lack the right to use ourselves as we wish in order to raise income, even though we do not necessarily harm others by doing so — even though we might in fact benefit them by doing so. My aim in this book is to show that, at the bar of the principles of distributive justice which inform most liberal democracies, both in practice and in theory, it should be exactly the other way around: that is, if it is true that we lack the right to withhold access to material resources from those who need them, we also lack the right to withhold access to our person from those who need it; but we do, under some circumstances, have the right to decide how to use it in order to raise income. Moreover, although it is true that, in some cases, we lack the right to access other people's body and person without their consent, we nevertheless have the right to avail ourselves of them, in cases where they consent to it, subject to payment.

Thus, I argue for a highly qualified right to control what happens to our person — that is to say, a highly qualified right to personal integrity. In so far as those who might need our body parts and personal services sometimes have a right to them, our right to personal integrity does not include a right to the exclusive use of our person; however, it does include, under some conditions, a right to sell some of our body parts, and lease ourselves out for sexual and reproductive purposes. In so arguing, I also defend a qualified right to control what happens to other people's person. For, notwithstanding my argument in support of confiscation, in so far as individuals who need body parts and personal services do not *always* have a right to them, the right to control what happens to others' persons does not include a right to its exclusive use. But it does include, under conditions to be specified later, a right to buy parts of their body as well as to hire them for the aforementioned purposes, provided they consent to it.

My remarks so far are reminiscent of a well-known debate between egalitarian liberals and libertarians. In their overwhelming majority they both hold, implicitly or explicitly, that we have the right to control what happens to our body, and that others therefore lack a right that we give them any of its parts (however great their need for organs, blood, and tissue might be). But they sometimes disagree about the legitimacy of coerced taxation and its implications. Egalitarian liberals argue that we do not have an exclusive right to the income we get from using our body through labour; in contrast, some libertarians claim that if others have a right against us that we give them part of our income, then, by the same token, they have a right against us that we make our body available to them—and that, they think, is a powerful reason to reject coercive taxation for distributive purposes.[1]

Ronald Dworkin's reply to the libertarian argument is a perfect example of egalitarian liberals' strategy at this point: according to Dworkin, we can stave off the libertarian challenge by drawing around the body 'a prophylactic line that comes close to making [it] inviolate, that is, making body parts not part of social resources at all'.[2] In this book, however, I argue, against egalitarian liberals and in agreement with libertarians, that being committed to coercive taxation for the purpose of distributive justice *does* entail that we cannot be committed to a full right to personal integrity. Contra libertarians, I also argue that rejecting the view that individuals have such a right does *not* entail sacrificing one of liberalism's core values—the importance of which underpins many libertarian concerns about taxation—to wit, individual autonomy, and this for two reasons.[3] First, the duty to help by way of providing personal resources is subject to a number of conditions which preserve some space for duty-holders to frame and pursue a meaningful conception of the good. Second, such duty is compatible with the view that individuals have the right to sell parts of their body and to lease it for sexual and reproductive purposes, and thereby to raise the income they need to implement such conception. By implication, it is also compatible with the view that individuals who are under a duty to make themselves available to others may also have the right to buy body parts and to hire other people's bodies for sexual and reproductive purposes with the latter's consent, and thereby to implement their conception of the good.

Note, however, that, although the conclusion I reach with respect to the confiscation of body parts echoes the libertarian claim about the implication of

[1] See, e.g., R. Nozick, *Anarchy, State and Utopia* (New York: Basic Books, 1974); J. Narveson, 'On Dworkinian Equality', *Social Philosophy and Policy* 1 (1983): 1–23. I say 'some libertarians', for the position I describe here is endorsed by, e.g., R. Nozick, but is rejected by, e.g., P. Van Parijs and P. Vallentyne, who nonetheless are, or at least call themselves, libertarians.

[2] R. Dworkin, 'Comment on Narveson: In Defence of Equality', *Social Philosophy and Policy* 1 (1983): 24–40, at 39.

[3] That individual autonomy is a central value of liberalism is hardly in dispute. That it is central to libertarianism is more controversial, in so far as libertarians seek to derive their principles from the thesis that we own ourselves—a thesis which differs from the claim that we are autonomous beings. As G. A. Cohen has shown persuasively, however, the self-ownership thesis makes sense in so far as it serves individual autonomy. See his *Self-Ownership, Freedom and Equality* (Cambridge: Cambridge University Press, 1995), ch. 10.

coercive taxation, my explicit aim is not to take part in the aforementioned dispute. In particular, I do not take self-ownership to be the organizing principle of a theory of justice. But nor do I deny that it can be deemed, in a qualified form, to be such a principle. In fact, none of my arguments in this book turns on whether it is appropriate, or not, to conceive of our body as something over which one can have property rights. As we shall see, given that there are many analogies between material and personal resources, and given that we do have property rights over the former, it may indeed make sense to talk of property rights over the latter. But perhaps it does not make sense: perhaps, as some have argued against libertarians, our person is not something which it is appropriate to think of as property, even though some of the rights we have over it are similar to those we have over things.[4] Whatever the outcome of this particular debate, what matters, for my purpose here, is whether we have the right to control what happens to our person, as well as to other people's persons, and if so, to what extent.

Before making my case for a qualified right to personal integrity, I set out, in Chapter 1, the relationship between persons and their body, as well as the conception of justice which underpins it. Justice, or so I claim there, requires that two principles be satisfied. According to the *principle of sufficiency*, individuals have rights to the resources they need in order to live a minimally flourishing life. According to the *principle of autonomy*, once everybody has such a life, all individuals should be allowed to enjoy the fruits of their labour in pursuit of their conception of the good.

Chapter 2 defends the first of four duties to help others by providing personal services, to wit, the duty to help someone in peril—in short, to be a Good Samaritan. Neglect of such duty is standardly regarded as a failure to perform a duty of charity, or as a failure to be appropriately altruistic. By contrast, a failure to give the poor the material resources they need is standardly condemned as a violation of a duty of justice. Yet, if liberals are committed to the view that the needy have a right, as a matter of justice, to some of the material resources of the comparatively well off, they have to accept that the imperilled have a right, as a matter of justice, to the personal services of those who are in a position to help. In short, Good Samaritan duties appear to be neither a matter of charity nor a matter of altruism; rather, they firmly fall within the purview of justice—more specifically, of the principle of sufficiency—and should be legally enforced.

This is also the case with duties to provide personal services other than rescue services, such as, for example, working with the handicapped, troubled children,

---

[4] There is a long tradition of thinking of the body as property. Locke's *Second Treatise of Government* is the *locus classicus* for that view in classical political thought; more contemporary examples include R. Nozick's *Anarchy, State and Utopia*, and G. A. Cohen's *Self-Ownership, Freedom and Equality*. For a hostile take on this view, see J. Harris, *Property and Justice* (Oxford: Oxford University Press, 1996), pp. 284ff. In fact, it is sometimes said that it is precisely because we cannot alienate our body as we can alienate things that it is inappropriate to think of it as something which we own.

or the homeless. Typically, tasks of that kind are performed either through the market or through government services. However, there are cases where neither the market nor governments do, or indeed can, provide such services. As I argue in Chapter 3, sufficiency requires that all able-bodied individuals provide personal services to the needy so as to enhance their prospects for a minimally flourishing life. More specifically, it requires that every able-bodied eighteen-year-old perform what I shall call a 'civilian service', and work for one year, against a subsistence wage, in schools, hospitals, or similar institutions.

In Chapters 2 and 3, it is claimed that personal services can be owed to the imperilled and the needy, as a matter of justice. What about body parts? After all, medically needed body parts are scarce, with devastating consequences for thousands of people, whose quality of life, indeed whose life *tout court*, depends on getting blood, bone marrow, or an organ. Chapter 4 argues the following: if one thinks that the needy's interest in leading a minimally flourishing life, and a fortiori in remaining alive, is important enough to confer on them a right to some of the material resources of the well off, by way of taxation and, in particular, through restrictions on bequests and inheritance, one must think that that very same interest is important enough to confer on the sick a right to the organs of the now-dead able-bodied. Objections grounded in non-conscientious and conscientious reasons to the effect that organs, unlike wealth, are such that they simply cannot be taken away from individuals without their consent, are unconvincing.

Some liberals might be ready to accept the foregoing claims. But the overwhelming majority of them would deny that one can have a right to someone else's body parts while they are alive. And yet, as I show in Chapter 5, if one thinks that the needy have a right to the material resources of the better off, to the personal services of the able-bodied, and to the organs of the dead, on grounds of their neediness, then under some circumstances one is committed to conferring on them a right to the body parts of the living. As I also show, arguments grounded in the importance of personal integrity and individual autonomy are mistaken. In fact, one can advocate the confiscation of some live body parts without compromising the autonomy of the able-bodied to an unacceptable extent.

Chapters 2 to 5 defend the view that the principle of sufficiency is satisfied only if those who need others' personal services and body parts so as to lead a minimally flourishing life have a moral right to them, and that it can be satisfied without undermining individual autonomy. But justice does not merely require that sufficiency be satisfied. To reiterate, it also comprises the principle of autonomy, whereby once the needy lead a minimally flourishing life, all individuals, including those who have so helped them, should be allowed to enjoy the fruits of their labour in pursuit of their conception of the good.

Now, at the bar of autonomy, or so I argue in Chapter 6, individuals, including the able-bodied, have the right to sell their body parts, provided others do not need those body parts in order to lead a minimally flourishing life; conversely, they have the right to buy them from those willing to sell, as a means towards implementing their own conception of the good. Reasons standardly advanced in support of the moral wrongness of organ sales, such as the putatively exploitative character of such transactions and the relationship between person and body which they bespeak, are flawed. And even if organ sales are morally wrong for those reasons, it does not follow—or so I argue—that individuals lack a right to engage in them.

Chapter 6, thus, defends the claim that individuals have the right to sell and buy organs. Do they have the right to lease and hire their, and other people's, bodies for sexual and reproductive services? That they have the former right does not suffice to show that they have the latter. Indeed, it is important to distinguish organ selling from surrogacy and prostitution. For a start, whereas individuals are (under some circumstances) under a duty of justice to make their organs available to those who need them (as Chapters 4 and 5 demonstrate), they are not under a duty of justice to make themselves available for sexual and reproductive services (as Chapter 5 also shows). Thus, the issues of prostitution and surrogacy on the one hand, and of organ sales on the other hand, arise against very different backgrounds. Furthermore, selling a resource, unlike leasing it, results in its complete loss. Yet, when we sell a kidney or a cornea, we admittedly do not engage as intimate a part of ourselves as we do when we have sex or carry a child: to a considerable extent, thus, those transactions differ from one another in their implications for the seller's person. Finally, prostitution and surrogacy, unlike organ sales, raise gender issues which need addressing. Notwithstanding such differences between all three practices, I argue in Chapters 7 and 8 that individuals do have the right to lease, and hire, one another's bodies for sexual and reproductive services.

Before I start, six remarks are in order. First, as I have made clear, my aim is to show that if one thinks that the needy have a right against the better off that they give them material resources, one *must* endorse the view that they, and the imperilled, have rights to the personal services and body parts of those in a position to help. Sometimes I shall put that point differently, and claim that the proponent of welfare rights *is committed* to rights to personal resources. By 'must', and 'is committed to', I shall mean that the set of premises which yields the conclusion that the needy have welfare rights also yields the conclusion that they, and the imperilled, have rights to personal resources. I sketch out an argument for the former conclusion in Chapter 1, which takes the following form:

(1) Individuals have an equal fundamental interest in having a minimally flourishing life for which autonomy is a privileged condition.

(2) Individuals have equal rights against others that they respect this interest and its privileged condition.

(3) If some of their needs are not met—typically, for housing, minimum income, and health care—individuals cannot have a minimally flourishing life. Therefore:

(4) Individuals have equal rights to housing, minimum income, and health care.

My aim, in Chapters 2 to 4, is to show that claims (3) and (4) apply not merely to material resources, but also to personal resources. That is, individuals have needs for personal resources which, if unmet, prevent them from leading a minimally flourishing life, from which it follows that, under conditions to be specified, they have rights to those resources.

Second, the contrast I draw between, on the one hand, providing material resources, and, on the other hand, providing personal resources is somewhat misleading. For in some cases, what is needed is a combination of both, as when a swimmer in peril needs someone to throw him a lifebelt. Duties of Good Samaritanism as I understand them are duties to provide a rescue service, but in this particular example the service consists, at least in part, in giving *a thing* to the imperilled. What I call 'a duty to provide material resources', in fact, consists in a duty to contribute to standard resource transfers such as taxation, and is to be contrasted with a duty to act in a particular way—which may involve giving something, such as a lifebelt—as well as a duty to transfer some of one's body parts. For the sake of stylistic convenience, however, I shall continue using the terminology I have employed so far, and contrast material versus personal resources.

Third, my concern is with the rights we have over our, and other people's, body parts and personal services, or what I shall call personal resources, in so far as those resources are needed in order to live a minimally flourishing life and, beyond that, to implement our conception of the good. On the view I defend here, to be a Good Samaritan, or to help a disabled person with her shopping and bathing seven days a week, consists in providing a personal service. By contrast, to transfer one of our organs to a patient on a transplant waiting list, or indeed to sell our blood, consists in providing a body part. To be sure, the distinction between providing a personal service and providing a body part is not as clear-cut as I may have implied so far, simply because personal services cannot but be provided through the body. There is a sense, then, in which to claim that, for example, one has the right to sell sexual services is tantamount to claiming that one has the right to hire out whatever body part is needed under the terms of the transaction (for example, and to put it bluntly, one's penis, vagina, hands, mouth, and so on). Similarly, there is a sense in which to claim that the able-bodied are under a duty to help a drowning swimmer to the shore is tantamount to claiming that they are under a duty to use their legs, arms, and hands as required by the situation—which is to say, in turn, that they lack the right to use their body as they wish. When I talk of a right to personal integrity, thus, I have in mind a right to control what happens to our person, whether such a right is understood as a right to divest oneself of, or to withhold, parts of one's body, or whether it is understood as a right to provide, or withhold, personal services *through* the use of our body.

Fourth, theories of distributive justice divide into ideal theories, which assume that individuals fully comply with their obligations towards one another, and non-ideal theories, which assume that they do not comply (or do so only partially) with those obligations. My arguments throughout this book are located in ideal theory. Thus, I assume that individuals' needs for material resources are already met, so that no one lacks, through no fault of their own, access to housing, minimum income, or the kind of health care which does not necessitate body parts. My aim is to assess whether, from the point of view of an ideal theory of justice, a society is just where the needy have rights to some of the resources of the materially better off, but not to the personal resources of the able-bodied, and where individuals have freedom of occupational choice but cannot raise money by selling parts of their body or sexual and reproductive services.

That I should like to examine organ sales, prostitution, and surrogacy contracts in ideal theory may seem odd, for standard objections against those practices are meant to take on board the fact, precisely, that individuals do not comply with their obligations towards one another, as a result of which some individuals are so desperately poor (and unjustly so) that they have no recourse but to prostitute themselves or sell a kidney. As we shall see, however, while those practices might become less prevalent in a just society than they are now, there are good reasons to believe that they will still exist. Accordingly, the question of the legitimacy of organ sales, prostitution, and surrogacy contracts does not become moot once individuals have the material resources to which they are entitled at the bar of justice.

Fifth, my argument is about the rights individuals have over one another's body parts and personal services in a just society. It is worth stressing, though, that there are other kinds of arguments for the view that individuals are under a moral duty to rescue the imperilled or to relinquish their body parts. For example, some religions encourage, indeed in some cases prescribe, organ donation as one way to exercise the virtues of compassion and charity towards needy members of one's community. I shall not address those arguments here. Rather, in appealing to rights to defend my proposal, I aim to show that those who are committed to distributive justice and who take rights as a fundamental category of moral and political philosophy would be mistaken in thinking that individuals have the right to withhold their personal services and organs from the imperilled and the sick, but lack the right to sell their body parts and sexual or reproductive services to those willing to buy them. As I argue here, they would be mistaken in thinking so precisely in virtue of their commitment to rights-based principles of distributive justice.

Last, but not least, some of the views I defend here will come across as very controversial to many, and hard to implement to quite a few. On the first count, I surmise, quite plausibly, that no existing democratically elected government wishing to implement my proposals for the confiscation of organs would get enough public support to do so. And it is not clear at all that it would get enough public support to commercialize them or to legislate in favour of treating prostitutes and surrogate mothers on a par with other workers. Be that as it may, it remains the case, or so I argue here, that *justice* requires conferring on the sick a right to the organs of the dead and, in some cases, of the living; and that it also requires conferring on individuals a right to buy and sell organs, sex, and reproductive services. Assessing whether one should bring about justice or defer to the wishes of citizens is beyond the scope of this book. However, assessing the extent to which the proposals I defend here are practically feasible is, up to a point, within its remit, which is why I sketch out some of their policy implications. I say 'sketch', rather than 'spell out' in detail, as this is neither an endeavour in social policy nor a party manifesto: rather, it is a philosophical inquiry on the rights justice confers on us over others', and our own, person.

1

A Rights-Based Theory of Justice

1.1 SETTING THE PROBLEM

To reiterate, my aim, in this book, is to show the following to be true: *if*, as many believe, we lack an exclusive right to the income we earn from our labour, then we lack an exclusive right to control what happens to our person, although we do have a right, under some circumstances, to sell some of the parts of our body and lease ourselves out for sexual and reproductive services.

Notice that the conditional is phrased in such a way that it can be endorsed not only by radical egalitarians, who believe that justice requires an equal distribution of (depending on which metric they endorse) resources, welfare, access to advantage, primary goods, and so on, but also by advocates of more modest distributive policies whose aim is to ensure that we all have the resources necessary for us to lead a minimally flourishing life. In fact, throughout this book, I shall assume that justice does not require radically egalitarian policies, but rather, that those of us who lack the resources needed to lead such a life have rights that those in a position to help should do so. My concern, thus, is to show that a fairly uncontroversial stand on the requirements of justice with respect to the distribution of material resources yields fairly controversial conclusions with respect to our rights over our own, and other people's, person.

Now, a theory of distributive justice must give an account of the following three elements: the *scope* of the principles which it defends, to wit, to whom justice is owed and on whom it is incumbent to act justly; the *content* of those principles, to wit, what must be distributed as a matter of justice; and the *strength* of those principles, to wit, the degree to which it is imperative that such distribution should occur. Regarding its scope, justice is owed to persons, and it is persons on whom it befalls to act justly.[1] Regarding its strength, whatever justice requires that persons should receive and distribute, it requires that they do so as a matter of rights. I give an account of the notions of personhood and rights in section 1.2. Having thus sketched two of the book's central assumptions, with respect to the scope and strength of principles of justice, I devote section 1.3

---

[1] There are other issues of scope, of course, such as whether duties of justice are owed to members of one's national community only, or to foreigners as well. I need not address them here.

to articulating my fairly standard view on the content of those principles with respect to the distribution of material resources.

1.2 PERSONHOOD, JUSTICE, AND RIGHTS

1.2.1 Personhood and Justice

It is central to persons' flourishing that they respect themselves as persons. This requires that they can successfully pursue some of their important projects, plans, goals, and interests, and in turn requires not merely that others respect them as persons—that is, not actively prevent them from implementing their goals by denying them fundamental freedoms—but also that they not deny them the resources (personal and material) they need. To put the point differently, a just society is one where persons respect one another as such, that is, give one another opportunities for self-respect.

I shall expand on some of these claims in sections 1.2.2, 1.2.3, and 1.3, and argue for the confiscation of personal resources in Chapters 2 to 5. I shall also defend the view, in Chapters 6 to 8, that—under conditions to be specified there—individuals have the right to sell parts of their body as well as personal services. Many reject those two views, on the grounds that the body is part of the person, so that the coercive redistribution of its parts undermines persons themselves, and that in selling parts of one's body, or some services such as sex and reproduction where the body is central, one is in fact selling one's person.

I shall examine those claims at some length in the relevant chapters. However, they and, indeed, my forthcoming rebuttal of them, rest on a particular account of personhood, and more specifically on a particular understanding of the relationship between person and body, which stands in need of elaboration. At the most abstract level, it is often said that a person is a being who is 'self-conscious, aware of its identity and its continued existence over time'.[2] Were those features understood as sufficient conditions for personhood, it would imply that a being without the capacity for moral and rational agency is a person, which rather strains normal uses of that word. I shall take it, then, that in order to be a person one must have the capacity for moral and rational agency as well as awareness of one's identity and continued existence over time.

On that account, the question is left open of what must be the case for a given person to have continued existence over time (diachronic personal identity). In answering that question, we shall go some way towards giving an account of personhood itself. My intention, here, is not to toil over the voluminous body of work which has been done on diachronic personal identity. Rather, I shall describe two competing criteria for it—the psychological criterion and the bodily

[2] D. Parfit, *Reasons and Persons* (Oxford: Clarendon Press, 1984), p. 202.

criterion—and sketch out the implications of each for my arguments about individuals' rights to their, and one another's, person, explaining why, throughout this work, I assume that the bodily criterion is correct.

Derek Parfit is one of the best-known advocates of the psychological criterion, which he defines as follows: 'X today is one and the same person as Y at some past time if and only if ... X is psychologically continuous with Y, this continuity has the right kind of cause, and it has not taken a branching form.'[3] Psychological continuity in turn consists in 'the holding of overlapping chains of *strong connectedness*', i.e. of chains of 'direct psychological connections'.[4] Thus, if X remembers something because Y experienced it, or does something because Y intended to do it, then X and Y are psychologically connected. If there are many such connections between X and Y, then X and Y are strongly connected. And if X and Y are strongly connected in overlapping chains, then one can say that they are psychologically continuous, that is, that X is the same person as Y.

On that view, spatio-temporal continuity of the body (bodily continuity, for short) is neither necessary nor sufficient for X to be the same person as Y. For all that matters is that X and Y be psychologically continuous in the way just suggested. Consider the following well-known and often-discussed scenario: suppose it becomes possible to remove a person's brain from her head, to examine and operate on it, and then to put it back into that person's body. Imagine now two individuals, Brown and Robinson, who both have a brain tumour, and whose brain is removed from their body by the surgeon for treatment purposes. Unfortunately, after the operation, the surgeon puts Brown's brain in Robinson's body, and vice versa. One of these patients dies, but the one who has Robinson's body and Brown's brain survives. Who is he? He recognizes Brown's family as his, displays the same psychological features as Brown, has memories of what Brown did previously, and so on. On the psychological criterion, it seems clear that this person is Brown, although he now has Robinson's body.

Some philosophers disagree. Thus, in his discussion of body transplants—or body interchange, as he calls them—Bernard Williams objects that in order to remain the same person, one must retain one's specific bodily skills. Accordingly, if you transplant the brain of a peasant's into an emperor's body, and vice versa, neither individual will remain peasant and emperor. For the individual with the emperor's body and the peasant's brain will have the emperor's vocal cords and will not sound at all like a gruff peasant; conversely, the individual with the peasant's body and the emperor's brain will not sound at all like a polished and well-read emperor, and so on.[5]

[3] Parfit, *Reasons and Persons*, p. 207.   [4] Ibid., p. 206.

[5] B. Williams, 'Personal Identity and Individuation', in his *Problems of the Self* (Cambridge: Cambridge University Press, 1973), pp. 11–12. For other criticisms of the psychological criterion, see S. Shoemaker, *Self-Knowledge and Self-Identity* (Ithaca, NY: Cornell University Press, 1963); C. Korsgaard, 'Personal Identity and the Unity of Agency: A Kantian Response to Parfit', *Philosophy and Public Affairs* 18 (1989): 101–32.

Williams's objection implies that someone who, as a result of an accident, becomes so seriously impaired that he cannot do with his body what he used to do is no longer the same person. But that seems wrong: a tetraplegic clearly is the same person he used to be, even though he has lost all the skills he used to have; similarly, someone whose voice, as a result of throat cancer, becomes absolutely unrecognizable, clearly is the same person he was before the cancer struck.

If the psychological criterion for personal identity is correct, then, a person is a being who is aware of himself as psychologically connected with other beings in the past, as having memories of their experiences, as carrying out projects they intended to carry out, and so on. On that view, although 'a person's existence just consists in the existence of a brain and body, and the occurrence of a series of interrelated physical and mental events',[6] her *continued* existence does not consist in the continued existence of her brain and body.

It is easy to see why the psychological criterion for personal identity is friendly to my argument, in subsequent chapters, that individuals are (sometimes) under a duty of justice to make their personal resources available to those who need them, and (sometimes) have the right to sell or hire out their body parts or personal services to those willing to pay for them. For it seems, then, and relevantly to our purposes here, that body transplant is simply the limit case of organ transplants: if someone can get a new heart, new lungs, new kidneys, new limbs, and new corneas, and remain the same person, then it would seem that he can go through a whole-body transplant and remain the same person.[7] It also seems that if psychological continuity is a necessary *and* sufficient condition for diachronic personal identity, then someone can lose, or sell, a great many of his body parts, and yet remain the same person.

The psychological criterion is endorsed by most philosophers, but although, I believe it to be correct, I shall not offer a defence of it. Rather, I shall focus, more fruitfully for my purposes here, on the bodily criterion for personal identity, precisely because that criterion, and the account of personhood which it informs, are the most inimical to my case for a qualified right to control what happens to our, and other people's, person. As I aim to show, even if the bodily criterion for personal identity is the right criterion, one can (sometimes) hold individuals under a duty to divest themselves of parts of their body for the sake of helping others, without destroying them as persons; one can also (sometimes) confer on them the right to sell parts of their body, or personal services, to those who are willing to pay, without exposing them to the risk that they will destroy themselves as persons.

In its strong variant, the bodily criterion holds that it is a necessary and sufficient condition for X to be the same person as Y that Y occupies the same body as X. On that view, then, the person who, after the body transplant operation,

---

[6] Parfit, *Reasons and Persons*, p. 211.
[7] See Shoemaker, *Self-Knowledge and Self-Identity*, pp. 22–5.

has Robinson's body, is Robinson, even though his psychological connections are Brown's. But that variant seems too strong: for it is implausible that someone who is not at all like Robinson, who has memories of Brown's experiences, and who acts on Brown's intentions, could still be Robinson simply by virtue of having Robinson's organs, limbs, hair, voice, and so on. It cannot be sufficient for someone to remain the person he was that he occupies the same body.

The weak variant, then, is more plausible, whereby continued occupancy of the same body is a necessary, but not sufficient, condition for diachronic personal identity: some degree of psychological continuity is necessary too, and both kinds of continuities together are sufficient for diachronic personal identity. More needs to be said, however, on the bodily criterion. For a start, although continuous occupancy of Y's body is necessary for X today to be the same person as Y at some past time, continuous occupancy of his *whole* body is not: for, if it were, someone who loses a limb or an organ would not remain the same person, which is manifestly absurd; likewise, someone who loses one of his organs and acquires a new one, thanks to a transplant operation, would not remain the same person either, which is equally absurd. Thus, for X today to be the same person as Y at some past time, X must occupy enough of Y's body. How much exactly is enough need not be settled here.

Relatedly, the claim that X need not occupy the whole of the body occupied by Y at some past time in order to be the same person as Y implies that even if Y's body were wholly human, X's need not be. Thus, someone who loses both arms and legs in an accident and is fitted with artificial limbs, or someone whose heart and lungs are failing and who is given artificial replacements instead of real organs, will nevertheless remain the same person he was before the operation. This suggests that body parts are fungible, in that it is possible to replace them with other body parts or (in some cases) prostheses, without loss of significant value. Of course, just as the bodily criterion for personal identity stipulates that X must occupy enough of Y's body in order to be the same person as Y at some past time, it also stipulates that X's body must retain enough of his human character in order to be the same person as Y at some past time; indeed, in order to be a person *tout court*. Again, how much is enough need not be settled here.

Finally, although X must occupy the same body as—and must be psychologically continuous with—Y in order to be the same person as Y at some past time, X's body need not be distinct from that of other human beings. There is no doubt that a dicephalic being, that is, a being which has one body but two heads, in fact consists of two distinct persons, each with her own thought processes, desires, memories, intentions, and so on.[8]

To recapitulate: X today is the same person as Y at some past time if and only if X occupies enough of the same body as Y, whether or not that body is distinct

---

[8] For a discussion of dicephalism, see J. McMahan, *The Ethics of Killing: Problems at the Margins of Life* (Oxford: Oxford University Press, 2002), pp. 35–9.

from that of other human beings, *and* if X is psychologically continuous with Y. Accordingly, X is a person if he is an embodied and individualized being, is conscious, is aware of his continued existence (that is, is aware that he occupies the same body as, and is psychologically continuous with, some individual at some past time), and, finally, has the capacity for rational and moral agency.

1.2.2 Interests, Rights, and Powers

If principles of justice apply to anyone, then they certainly apply to persons so defined. This is not to say that justice cannot apply to beings other than persons: it might well be, for example, that human beings who are so mentally disabled that they will never be rational and moral agents are owed support as a matter of justice; it might also be that beings who do not have a human body but nevertheless have the capacity for moral and rational agency can—should they turn out to exist—be held under obligations of justice. Be that as it may, I focus on persons: such is the scope of the principles of justice I defend in this book.

As I noted above, a theory of justice must give an account not merely of the scope of those principles, but also of their strength and content. Regarding the former, I assume (uncontroversially, I believe) that the requirements set by those principles should be understood as rights. To claim that X has a right to a particular good G or to perform some particular act A is not simply to say that it is desirable that X should get G or be left free to do A; it means that those against whom the right is held, who may in fact have current use of G, or have an interest in X's non-performance of A, do not have a choice in the matter: G *must* be made available to X, and doing A must be allowed to him.

This, of course, only gives us an incomplete picture of the nature of rights. As Hohfeld notes in his important essay on rights in legal reasoning, there are in fact four kinds of rights: claims, powers, liberties, and immunities. To have a claim against someone else means that that person is under a duty not to interfere with you or a duty to help you; to have a power against someone else means that you can, in virtue of some legal rule, change your legal relation to that person by conferring on her claims, duties, liabilities, and immunities; to have a liberty against someone else means that she lacks a claim against you that you behave in a particular way; finally, to have an immunity against her means that she lacks the power to change your relation to her.[9] Although Hohfeld's classification is of legal rights, it applies, *mutatis mutandis*, to moral rights.

The foregoing points only tell us that when one asserts that X has a right, one may in fact be describing one or several of those relations between X and other parties; it does not tell us what must be the case for X to stand in those relations. Throughout this book, I adopt the interest theory of rights. As that theory is

---

[9] W. N. Hohfeld, *Fundamental Legal Conceptions as Applied in Judicial Reasoning* (New Haven, Conn.: Yale University Press, 1919).

standardly articulated, it pertains to claims, and holds that for X to have a claim, it must be the case that this claim protects one or more of his interests. It pays to note, though, that the interest theory of rights can apply to liberties, powers, and immunities, as well as to claims.[10]

In what follows, I shall focus on claims and powers—that is, on statements of the form 'X has a claim to a good G, or to perform some act A, against some third party P', and 'X has a power to do A vis-à-vis some third party P'. First, though, a point of terminology. Although claims and powers are distinct, most philosophers and jurists call them rights, indiscriminately. And, indeed, depending on the context, it should be clear whether the rights at issue are claims, or powers. Henceforth, I shall follow standard usage and, unless I specify otherwise will refer to 'claims' when setting out persons' rights against others that they provide them with resources, and to 'powers' when setting out their rights to enter contractual agreements with one another.

1.2.2A Interests: In order fully to understand the kind of relationship which rights capture between those who hold them and those who have to respect them, it is necessary to get to grips with the concept of interest. Some philosophers believe that interests always and only refer to what their holders want, independently of their good; others, by contrast, claim that interests are all those things that contribute to their holders' good, irrespective of their wants.[11] Neither view is plausible, at least not as an account of the interests of persons. The interests-as-wants view is vulnerable to the charge that it rules out, counter-intuitively, the possibility of saying that someone can be mistaken as to where his interests are. By contrast, the interests-as-contribution-to-the-good view is vulnerable to the charge that it allows, counter-intuitively, for the possibility of defining someone's good without making any reference at all to that person's own understanding of it.

Those problems are particularly serious in the light of the conception of personhood developed in section 1.2.1 above, and of the requirements of justice articulated in section 1.3 below. For, as we saw earlier, someone, X, is a person if (among other things) he has the capacity for moral and rational agency. More explicitly, X is a person if he has the capacity to formulate, revise, and pursue long-term as well as short-term projects and goals, and if he is aware that the fact

[10] For variants and defences of the interest theory of rights, see, e.g., M. Kramer, 'Rights without Trimmings', in M. Kramer, N. E. Simmonds, and H. Steiner, *A Debate over Rights: Philosophical Enquiries* (Oxford: Clarendon Press, 1998); J. Raz, *The Morality of Freedom* (Oxford: Clarendon Press, 1986).

[11] For the first view, see, e.g., B. Barry, *Political Argument* (London: Harvester Wheatsheaf, revised edition, 1990). For the second view, see, e.g., G. Wall, 'The Concept of Interest in Politics', *Politics and Society* 5 (1975): 487–510. My necessarily sketchy account of interests in the following paragraphs owes much to C. Swanton's, as deployed in her 'The Concept of Interests', *Political Theory* 8 (1980): 83–101.

that he coexists with other such agents imposes constraints on the kinds of goals and projects he can pursue, as well as on the steps he can take to implement them. To claim that whatever he wants is in his interest implies that we should assent to the drug addict's claim that it is in his interest to get heroin, even though heroin undermines his capacity for rational and moral agency, and thus is not good for him as a person. I cannot think of any plausible conception of interests that could allow us to do that.

On the other hand, and to anticipate section 1.3.1, X is owed respect by persons precisely because he has the capacity for rational and moral agency. Now consider the claim that only those things which contribute to the good of individuals, regardless of their own, subjective, understanding of their good, are in their interests. If that claim is correct, it implies that we should reject the hunger striker's view that it is *not* in his interest to get food, on the grounds that, in so far as survival is to the good of individuals, anything that contributes to it is in their interests. But that would be incompatible with the requirement that to respect individuals as persons is sometimes to defer to their own understanding of what is good for them. Any plausible conception of interests must make space for that requirement.

The challenge, thus, is to construct an account of interests which is consistent with making X the final judge of what contributes to his good as a person and with allowing for the possibility that he may not always be in a position to make such judgement. The latter point suggests that X's judgement about his good is subject to two conditions: X must think rationally about alternatives to his current conception of the good, and be willing to subject such conception to critical scrutiny. With those conditions in place, something, G, is in his interest if either of the following two propositions is true: either (a) G contributes to X's pursuit of some goal or project of his, and there is no other goal that X would rather have if he thought rationally about alternatives; or (b) G contributes to X's acquiring that other goal.

To understand interests in such a way enables us to make sense of the claim that it is not in the drug addict's interest to get heroin, as well as of the claim that it is not in the interest of the hunger striker to get food. Getting heroin is not in the addict's interest, however much he wants it, because the addict, in the grip of his addiction as he is, is not in a position to reflect rationally about alternatives to an existence bedevilled by drugs, and it therefore cannot be said that there is no other goal that he would rather pursue. Getting food is not in the hunger striker's interest, however close he is to death, to the extent that there is no other alternative which, having thought long, hard, and rationally about it, he would rather pursue.

To say then that rights, be they claims or powers, protect interests, and to say it of rights held by persons, is to say that there are certain things that contribute to the good of persons as they understand that good, subject to the aforementioned conditions, and that those things are important enough to warrant protection. Which interests have, and which lack, that kind of importance is, in fact, the question that will occupy us in the remainder of the book, once I have brought out, as I shall do presently, the differences and connections between claims and powers.

1.2.2B Claims: Let us start with claims. To reiterate, X has a moral claim to do A, or to get G, against P, if an interest of his is deemed so important that he should be able to do A without P's interference, or that he should get G from P. This *in itself* does not imply that the state must protect X from P's interference or from his decision not to give him G. Put differently, it does not imply that all moral claims ought to be turned into legal claims. Consider claims acquired through certain kinds of promises. If you promise me, absent any witness, to feed my cat while I am away, I acquire a claim against you that you do so. But if you fail to fulfil your obligation to me to feed my cat, the state will not enforce my claim and punish you, since it will not find any reliable evidence in support of my claim. Enforcing that promise would be, in practice, absolutely impossible. Assuming that enforcing it would be possible, it would nevertheless be morally costly, since it would undermine the role played by trust in our personal relationships.

This suggests that there are two distinct kinds of considerations—purely practical and moral ones—which dictate against enforcing some claims.[12] Delineating which conditions a claim must meet in order to be enforceable amounts to delineating the limits of the criminal law—a task which lies well beyond the scope of this book. Briefly, though, a claim is enforceable if enforcement would not undermine some important interest(s) of the claim-holder, and would be purely and practically possible. Thus, by way of a counter-example, were it unlawful not to respect promises made verbally and without witnesses, we would not be able to trust, in general, that others will respect their promises whether or not they are bound by law to do so, for which our personal relationships would irretrievably suffer. Our interest in maintaining such relationships is important enough for the state not to step in when promises are breached. Moreover, in so far as those promises are made verbally and without witness, it would be purely and practically impossible to get evidence that they were made, and thus to enforce them.

That a claim is enforceable does not imply that the state ought to enforce it here and now; for there are considerations which might dictate against

---

[12] I call the first kind of considerations 'purely practical' to distinguish them from practical reasons which dictate against enforcement because they carry a moral cost. Thus, the claim 'we ought not enforce this right because the majority of people are so much against it that enforcement will be very difficult' adverts to a practical consideration, but ultimately gives weight to that consideration in virtue of a normative principle, to wit, that the majority should have its way in virtue of being the majority.

enforcement, and which would not apply at a later stage, or under different circumstances. It is coherent to argue, for example, on the one hand that homosexuals have a moral claim to adopt children, and on the other hand that changing adoption rules against the wishes of a very homophobic public opinion would create a serious backlash against homosexuals. This is not tantamount to arguing that homosexuals' claim to adopt is not enforceable, for the reason why adoption rules ought not to be changed is not that it would be practically impossible to change them, or that the majority's interest in discriminating against homosexuals outweighs the latter's claim: the reason is that another interest of homosexuals themselves would be jeopardized. The claim, then, is that the state ought to turn homosexuals' moral claim to adopt children into a legal claim as soon as doing so would not adversely affect their position in society.

From now on, I shall focus on enforceable moral claims, to wit, claims which the state can, and indeed ought to, turn into legal claims, although perhaps not here and now. Thus, when I say that X has a claim against third parties to do A, or to the provision of G, I mean that X's interest in doing A or getting G is important enough that others—be they private individuals or the state—not interfere with X's doing A, or that they provide G to X. For ease of exposition, I shall sometimes say that third parties are under a duty to X not to interfere with his doing A, or to provide him with G—by which I shall mean exactly the same thing.

1.2.2C Powers: Whereas moral claims are rights against others that they let us do something or that they give us something, moral powers are abilities, as granted by a moral or legal rule, to change one's relation to someone else. Transactions whereby someone agrees to sell a good or a service to someone else paradigmatically involve the exercise of a power. Thus, if Anne happens to have some good, G, in her possession, it is appropriate not merely to ask whether she has a claim that others let her use G as she sees fit, but also whether she has the power to change her moral relationship to others in respect of G, that is, to transfer to them, upon payment, all her claims, powers, and liabilities over G, if they consent to it.

It is sometimes said that for someone to have a power to do A vis-à-vis someone else implies that he also has a claim to exercise it, that is, that this person ought not to be interfered with when exercising that power, even though they might be adversely affected by it.[13] But that is not so: someone may have the power to change his relationship with Anne in respect of G by stealing G and selling it to a bona fide third party, as a result of which the latter will acquire rights over G. But this does not imply that Anne is under a duty not to interfere with the

---

[13] See. R. Flathman, *The Practice of Rights* (Cambridge: Cambridge University Press, 1976), p. 54.

thief's exercise of his power. Quite the contrary in fact: she has a claim to do so, in so far as she is G's legitimate owner.[14] Powers, in short, need not be protected by claims.

It is also sometimes said that for someone to have a power to do A means that he is at liberty to do so. As we shall see in section 1.2.3B, just as one can have a claim to act wrongly, one can have the power to act wrongly. As we shall also see, though, just as some wrongs are such that they cannot be protected by a claim, some wrongs are such that we cannot have the power to commit them.

In those cases where one does have the power to do A, *and* where whoever is liable to that power's exercise does not have a claim against us that we not exercise it, powers ought to be protected by claims so as to have any force. Anne's moral power to change her moral relationship to Ben in respect of G would be very fragile indeed if it were not protected by two claims against third parties, to wit, a claim that they not interfere with the transaction, and a claim that they not regard it as legally void. Granting Anne the former amounts to denying that the state can treat a transaction involving G as a criminal offence. Granting her the latter amounts to demanding that the state acknowledge the transaction as legally valid—that it recognize, that is, that parties have acquired rights, duties, powers, and liabilities vis-à-vis one another. In general, a transaction which is regarded as legally valid is one which the state can enforce against either party at the request of the other party. However, as we shall see in Chapter 8 when dealing with the issue of surrogacy contracts, it is possible on the one hand to consider a transaction as legally valid and on the other hand to regard it as voidable (in the sense that its parties can withdraw from it at any time but may have to pay damages to the other for so doing).

To recapitulate, then, a claim to the effect that Anne has the moral right to sell G to Ben standardly involves the following four claims: (a) she has the moral power to change her relation to Ben by making him, against payment, G's new owner; (b) she is at liberty to do so; (c) she has a moral claim against the state that it not prevent her from doing so; and (d) she has a moral claim against the state that it recognize the transaction as legally valid.

Note that the fact that Anne has a claim that the state not interfere with her transaction with Ben does not, in itself, imply that she had the power to make that transaction in the first instance. Thus, and to anticipate by way of an example some of the claims made in Chapter 8, it is sometimes argued that entering surrogacy contracts is morally wrong, that it nevertheless ought not to be treated as a criminal offence, but that such contracts ought to be regarded as null and void. This is another way of saying that parties in those contracts lack the power to change their relationship with one another, but have a claim that the state not make surrogacy contracts unlawful. My treatment of those claims

---

[14] See M. Kramer, 'Rights without Trimmings', p. 105.

in Chapter 8, and indeed of similar claims made in connection with organ sales and prostitution in Chapters 6 and 7 respectively, will depend on whether or not there can be such a thing as a power to enter a morally wrong transaction, and on the state's appropriate response to such transactions. I shall turn to this issue in section 1.2.3B. Suffice it to say for the time being that, unless otherwise stated, when I talk of the power to sell and buy body parts and personal services, I shall mean the (enforceable) power to do so, as well as claims against the state to non-interference and legal recognition.

1.2.2D Conditions for having rights: So much, then, for an analysis of the relationship between rights-holders and those against whom those rights are held—an analysis which does not tell us *who* can have claims and powers. On the interest theory of rights, you recall, X has a right if an interest of his is protected by that right. From this it follows that it is a necessary condition for having rights that one is the kind of being that can have interests. In so far as only beings with the capacity for sentience can have interests, it follows, in turn, that the capacity for sentience is a necessary condition for having rights.

The foregoing point implies that the concept of a posthumous right does not make sense.[15] For consider: if, in order for us to have rights it is a necessary condition that we are capable of having interests, then a necessary condition for us to have posthumous rights is that we are capable of having posthumous interests—interests, that is, which survive us and can be thwarted after we die. At first sight, that condition seems to be met: it does seem to make sense to say that I have an interest whilst alive (and, thus, whilst sentient) in my children's flourishing after I die, and that, should my will, whereby they stand to inherit my property, not be honoured, this interest of mine would be thwarted. It therefore seems plausible to claim that I can now have a right that my will be honoured after my death (although whether I do indeed have it is another matter).

Yet, further scrutiny casts doubt on the coherence of conferring on people claims that states of affairs obtain posthumously. Consider the claim that I now have a right that my will be honoured once I am dead. Whoever is under a duty to honour it—the state, anyone I did not designate as my heir—will have to fulfil their duty only upon my death. But they can be held under such a duty *to me then* only if it is *still* the case, once I am dead, that I have a right that they do so, and by implication only if it is still the case that I have an interest in their doing so. Put generally, one can confer on individuals a right that a state of affairs, *S*, obtain once they are dead only if they have, once dead, an interest in *S*. Now, the statement 'When dead I have an interest in *S*' makes sense only if one can give an account of who the interest-bearer is. It cannot be the corpse, or the ashes, of

---

[15] For a defence of posthumous rights, see, e.g., J. Feinberg, *Harm to Others* (Oxford: Clarendon Press, 1984); B. Levenbook, 'Harming the Dead, Once Again' *Ethics* 95 (1985): 162–4.

the deceased; and so it can only be the person who was and no longer is, or, as Feinberg puts it, the *antemortem* person.[16] But the *antemortem* person, in fact, is the person while she was alive, in other words, the living under another name: it is not the dead person. And so to claim that the *antemortem* person has an interest in *S* amounts to claiming that the person, while alive, had an interest in *S* obtaining after her death. It does not deliver the claim that we have interests once we are dead, and it thus does not allow us to conclude that we can have claims or powers once we are dead.[17]

1.2.3 Is there a Right to do Wrong?

So far I have given an account of the kind of demands claims and powers represent, as well as of the conditions one must fulfil in order to have them. Before outlining, in the next section, some of the specific claims one has against others, let us consider whether one can have a claim and a power to act wrongly. Some philosophers argue that selling and buying organs, sex, and reproductive services are morally wrong. On that view, if there is no such thing as a power to act wrongly, then there are no such things as the powers to buy and sell the aforementioned resources. To be sure, this would not suffice to confer on the state the claim to interfere with parties in those transactions, since although *ex hypothesi* those parties' interests in making the transactions would not be important enough to warrant a prohibition on state interference, other considerations (such as the difficulties attendant on enforcing the prohibition) might. Still, if there is no such thing as a power to do wrong, and if selling and buying organs, sex, and reproductive services are morally wrong, then a just society is not one in which individuals have the power to take part in those transactions.

Accordingly, in order to defeat the claim that organ sales, prostitution, and surrogacy are morally wrong and therefore should not be protected by powers and claims, one can either show that they are not morally wrong, or concede that they are and show (a) that there is such a thing as a power to do wrong and (b) that organ sales, prostitution, and surrogacy are not so wrong that they ought not to be protected by powers and claims. In Chapters 6 to 8, I shall argue that those transactions are not always morally wrong, and that, even in those cases where they are, they sometimes ought to be protected by claims and powers. My arguments there will depend on showing here that one can have a claim and a power to act wrongly.

[16] Feinberg, *Harm to Others*, p. 89.

[17] Note that my argument to the effect that posthumous rights are incoherent is compatible with the widely held view that one can be harmed even if one is not aware of it. For there is a crucially important difference between someone who is not aware of what happens because he is dead, and someone who is not aware of what happens through sheer ignorance, or because others are skilled at keeping secrets from him. The former, I have argued, cannot be an interest-bearer; the latter, however, can, because he exists and is sentient.

1.2.3A The claim to act wrongly: According to many philosophers, there is nothing incoherent in conjointly asserting the following two propositions:[18]

(1) X's doing A is morally wrong.
(2) X has a moral claim to do A, that is, others are under a moral duty not to interfere with X's doing A.

To give a couple of examples: it is perfectly possible, or so it is argued, to think on the one hand that it is morally wrong to read pornographic magazines or to join the Neo-Nazi party, and on the other hand that X has a moral claim to do so; in other words, that others are under a moral duty not to interfere with X's reading of pornography or joining the Neo-Nazi party.

Now, if the interest theory holds that the basis for granting X a claim to do A is the importance of that very interest, it seems to preclude a claim to act wrongly. Suppose for the sake of argument that reading pornographic magazines is morally wrong, and suppose that this is what X wants to do. It is very unclear what one would mean by asserting that X's interest in reading pornographic magazines is important enough *in itself* to be protected by a claim. It is equally unclear what one would mean by asserting that X's interest in reading pornographic magazines is important enough *to* X that it should be protected by a claim. For how could X's interest in doing something which is morally wrong be important enough in itself, or to him, to be protected by a claim, that is, to hold someone else under a duty not to interfere with him? As we saw in section 1.2.2A, something G is in X's interest if one of the following two propositions is true: either (a) G contributes to X's pursuit of some goal or project of his, and there is no other goal that X would rather have if he thought rationally about alternatives; or (b) G contributes to X's acquiring that other goal. It seems implausible that X, having thought rationally and with critical distance about his project, namely, reading pornography and realizing that it is actually morally wrong, could not find any other sexual goal which he would rather have. And this, in turn, would seem to suggest that X does not have a claim to be allowed to read pornography.

However, on the formulation I offered at the outset of section 1.2.2, whereby for X to have a claim it must be the case that the claim protects one or more of his interests, the basis for granting X a claim to do A need not be his interest in doing A: it may be some other interest of his. On that view, X can have a claim to do A, even though A is morally wrong, if an interest of his other than his interest

[18] See, for example, R. Dworkin, *Taking Rights Seriously* (London: Duckworth, 1978), p. 188; D. Enoch, 'A Right to Violate One's Duty', *Law and Philosophy* 21 (2002): 355–94; J. Raz, *The Authority of Law: Essays on Law and Morality* (Oxford: Clarendon Press, 1979), p. 274; J. Waldron, 'A Right to do Wrong', *Ethics* 92 (1981): 21–39. For the view that there cannot be such a thing as a right to act wrongly, see J. Mackie, 'Can there be a Right-Based Moral Theory?', in J. Waldron (ed.), *Theories of Rights* (Oxford: Oxford University Press, 1984).

in doing A warrants protection. For example, interfering with X by censoring pornographic magazines and punishing those who nevertheless manage to get them might foster a moralistic ethos which would also condone censoring Ingres' *Odalisque* and D. H. Lawrence's *Lady Chatterley's Lover*, at considerable costs, then, to freedom of artistic expression. This in turn would harm X's interest in living in a society where there is such freedom. And it is that consideration which justifies granting X a claim to read pornography.

Obviously, there are some kinds of wrong which individuals do not have a claim to do. Accordingly, one needs a criterion for distinguishing cases where a morally wrong act is not protected by a claim from cases where it is. In so far as my focus, in this book, is on what distributive justice requires of us and allows us to do, this amounts to determining when we have a claim at the bar of justice to act wrongly, and when we lack it. In so far as a just society is one where we treat one another as moral equals who are deserving of equal respect (or so I shall argue in section 1.3 below), failing to treat others with equal respect without their consent is not the kind of wrong that can be protected by a claim.

What about cases where we fail to treat *ourselves* as equally deserving of respect?[19] Is that morally wrong, and, if so, do we then lack the claim to do it? I believe that it is morally wrong so to treat ourselves, but that we nevertheless have a moral claim against others that they do not interfere with us. Acts of self-abasement take place in the geographical privacy of one's home and in the emotional privacy, so to speak, of one's relationships. Consequently, a law which would forbid acts of self-abasement could not be enforced except at the unacceptable cost of undermining the value of privacy in general. Moreover, assuming that it might be possible to identify acts of self-abasement without intruding on the life of their performers to an unacceptable extent, subjecting them to punishment (as would be the case if self-abasement were to be turned into a criminal offence) would not be the appropriate answer, in so far as they might, rather, need help for the condition which led them to lack self-respect to such an extent. In addition, punishing them might make them even more vulnerable than they currently are and prevent them from finding their way on the road to self-respect. In so far, then, as the basis for non-interference is an interest of the self-abaser (namely, his interest, precisely, in acquiring self-respect), one can conclude that he has the claim so to act, even though he is guilty of wrongdoing.

To be sure, many a liberal would argue that the state can and ought to prevent the occurrence of moral wrongs on grounds other than the fact that they harm those who commit them or that they harm or offend third parties. Thus, most people would claim that gladiatorial shows, where well-paid gladiators are willing

---

[19] I shall address cases where people agree to have others treat them as less than equal in section 1.2.3B.

to risk their life in front of thousands of spectators, should not be allowed, not necessarily on paternalistic grounds (that is, out of concern for the welfare and long-term autonomy of the gladiators), but rather on the grounds that for thousands of people to derive pleasure from watching two individuals maim and kill one another is simply evil.[20] It is hard, I admit, to resist the force of that example. Be that as it may, the fact that in such extreme cases moral evilness might constitute a reason for interfering does not show that the state should interfere with individuals when they are guilty of lesser wrongdoing—such as the wrongdoing involved in treating oneself as less than a person.

1.2.3B The power to act wrongly: Is there such a thing as power to act wrongly? As we saw earlier, a paradigmatic example of a power is the power to sell: for Anne to have that power is for her to have an ability, as granted by a moral rule, to change her moral relation to Ben by transferring to him her claims, powers, and liabilities over some good G, against payment. And Anne has such a power if one or several interests of hers are important enough to be so protected.

At first sight, it seems that there cannot be such a thing as a power to act wrongly. For, if it is wrong for Anne to make Ben the new owner of G, so it is hard to see how her interest in transferring G to Ben could be important enough to be protected by a power. However, just as a claim to do A need not be grounded in the importance of doing A for the claim-holder, a power to do A need not be grounded in the importance of doing A for the power-holder. Accordingly, if denying Anne the power to make that transaction jeopardizes some other important interest of hers—other, that is, than her interest in making that specific transaction with Ben—then she has that power.

Obviously, there are cases where we do not have the power to do wrong, that is, where the wrong involved in transferring some claims, powers, and liabilities over some good is such that, no matter how important our interests are which would be protected by that power, they are not important enough to warrant such protection. Knowingly contributing to the infliction of serious harm on others is one such case: for example, we lack the power to sell a gun to someone if we know that he will use it to kill someone else (and even if we do not intend him so to use it). Allowing others not to treat us as worthy of equal respect by granting them a number of claims and powers over ourselves is another such case.

That very last point may sound odd, for, if, as I argued in section 1.2.3A, we have a claim to treat ourselves as less than worthy, why do we lack the power to let others so treat us? The distinction between not respecting oneself and destroying opportunities for self-respect is crucial here. When someone fails to respect herself, she is failing to take up opportunities for self-respect. But when she allows

---

[20] On gladiatorial shows and state interference, see J. Feinberg, *Harmless Wrongdoing* (Oxford: Oxford University Press, 1988), pp. 128–33.

others not to treat her with the respect she deserves, she destroys those opportunities in the first instance. Suppose, for example, that you need to cross the road to get to the beach. My forbearing to interfere with you by blocking the road affords you an opportunity to get to the beach; should you decide not to cross the road after all, you would simply fail to take that opportunity. By contrast, should you allow me to block the road and thereby to interfere with you, you would remove that opportunity itself.

I believe that we almost always lack the power to deny ourselves opportunities for self-respect. This is because, although we have the right to treat ourselves in such a way, others cannot do it to us: as I argued two paragraphs ago, they lack the power to change their relationship with us when doing so amounts to inflicting serious harm on us. Not treating us as moral equals is one such harm; and they therefore lack the power to do so, *whether or not we consent to such treatment*. The italicized phrase is crucial, for someone who consents that others not treat her with respect, thereby destroying her opportunities for self-respect, has a distorted view of herself as unworthy, which it is grievously wrong to exploit for one's own benefit.

In so far, then, as individuals cannot acquire claims and powers over another person when so doing destroys her opportunities for self-respect, that person herself lacks the power to transfer those claims and powers to them: at the bar of justice, individuals owe one another equal respect, whether they want it or not. Note, however, that there is an exception to that rule, and that is when someone destroys her opportunities for self-respect as the only way for her to meet her basic needs, since once that person is lifted out of extreme neediness, she is then in a position to avail herself of future opportunities for self-respect.

Does the claim that individuals lack the power to allow others to desist from treating them with respect entail that they also lack a claim not to be interfered with when entering that kind of agreement? In section 1.2.2C, I noted that a power to enter a transaction with someone else ought to be protected by two claims against the state, to wit, a claim that it not make the transaction unlawful, as well as a claim that it recognize the transaction as valid. It would be tempting to infer that denying someone the power to enter a given transaction implies not only that that person lacks a right that the transaction be regarded as valid (which is surely the case), but also, more strongly, that the exercise of that power should be made unlawful—which is another way of saying that parties in the transaction lack a claim that the state not interfere with them. However, it does not follow from the fact that the party (parties) lack the moral power to enter a transaction that it should be made unlawful, for there might be very good reasons not to subject either or both parties to criminal sanctions: criminal sanctions might make them more vulnerable, might not work and would elicit contempt for the law, and so on. When those reasons pertain to some important interest of one or both parties in those transactions, to aver that the state ought not to interfere with the transaction, even though it is morally wrong, amounts to conferring on the parties a claim against the state that it not interfere with them.

1.3 WHICH THEORY OF JUSTICE?

I began this chapter by noting that a theory of distributive justice must give an account of the following three elements: the *scope* of the principles which it defends, to wit, to whom justice is owed and on whom it is incumbent to act justly; the *content* of those principles, to wit, the kind of goods which must be distributed as a matter of justice; and the *strength* of those principles, to wit, the strength of the requirement that those goods be distributed. So far, I have out-lined an account of the first and third elements: in reverse order, the requirements of justice have the strength of rights, and those rights, although they can be held by persons and non-persons alike, impose duties on persons only. In this section, I sketch the content of the principles of justice I defend in this book with respect to the distribution of material resources.

1.3.1 Self-respect and Justice

At the close of section 1.2.1, we saw that X is a person if he is an embodied being, is conscious, is aware of his continued existence, and, finally, has the capacity for rational and moral agency. The last point is particularly important in the context of this book. Indeed, persons have plans, projects, goals, and interests, on which they are capable of reflecting, and which they want to pursue. Failure to pursue those projects, either because of some particular trait of theirs, or because of other people's behaviour, prevents them from flourishing in at least three ways. First, to the extent that those plans and projects are absolutely central to their under-standing of the good life, they will not lead such a life if they cannot implement any of them. Second, to the extent that such failure originates in them, it will dent their self-respect, which in turn will make it impossible for them to flour-ish. Third, to the extent that such failure is due to, or shaped by, other people's behaviour, it will dent their perception of themselves as someone to whom others grant proper respect, and that too will make it that much more difficult for them to flourish.

Thus, self-respect is central to how someone's life is going: accordingly, a just society is one where individuals respect one another as persons, that is, where they give one another opportunities to act on the basis of the weight which they give to the fact that they are persons—opportunities, in fact, to live as self-respecting persons. Note that the relationship between being respected by others and respecting oneself is important but contingent. For, while not being respected by others often contributes to one's lack of self-respect, one can main-tain one's self-respect in the face of others' disrespectful treatment. Conversely, it is also possible for someone not to respect herself as a person, notwithstanding others' respectful treatment. Moreover, justice, as a property of our relationship to another, sets out what we owe one another. Accordingly, in virtue of the principle that 'ought' implies 'can', it cannot place us under an obligation to do that which we cannot do. In so far as we cannot make people respect themselves, we cannot, at the bar of justice, ensure that they do so. Thus, it is not necessary for a society to be just that persons actually do respect themselves: it is enough that they have *opportunities* for doing so.

The claim that a just society is one where individuals give one another opportunities to live as self-respecting persons invokes what some philosophers call *recognition* respect, as opposed to *evaluative* respect.[21] To respect someone as a person, in the recognition sense, is to take the fact that they are a person as imposing moral constraints on one's behaviour. On the recognition conception of respect, in so far as the mere fact that someone is a person dictates how we should behave towards her, respect is owed to all persons, and is not a matter of degree—which is why, in a just society, persons owe one another *equal* respect. By contrast, to have evaluative respect for someone is to appraise him positively on the basis of some of his features; accordingly, to have evaluative respect for someone as a person is to appraise him positively on the basis of those features which are positive features of persons. On the evaluative conception of respect, in so far as the fact that someone has those features dictates how one should appraise him, respect is not owed to everyone, and can be a matter of degree. Obviously, the distinction I have just drawn between recognition respect and evaluative respect applies to self-respect. To have recognition respect for oneself as a person is to give appropriate weight, when deciding how to act, to the fact that one is a person, and in particular to the fact that one is a moral and rational agent. To have evaluative respect for oneself as a person is to appraise oneself positively on the grounds that one has the positive features of a person.

Now, whilst it is a requirement of justice that we have recognition respect for one another, it is not a requirement that we evaluatively respect one another. To be sure, if others do not appraise us for engaging in the kinds of pursuits that display characteristics of persons—pursuits which we rationally pursue over the course of our life, which are not subsumed under those of others, and which constitute our ends—or, indeed, if they disapprove of us for so doing, we will not flourish.[22] However, justice stipulates how we should act, and not how we should feel, towards one another. In so far as giving evaluative respect to others

---

[21] For the distinction between recognition respect and evaluative respect, see S. L. Darwall, 'Two Kinds of Respect,' *Ethics* 88 (1977): 36–49; R. S. Dillon, 'Self-Respect: Moral, Emotional, Political,' *Ethics* 107 (1997): 226–49.

[22] Nor will we flourish if we lack evaluative self-respect, if we fail to feel pride for living a life worthy of a person or feel that our achievements count for nothing. For a good analysis of lack of evaluative self-respect in that sense, see R. S. Dillon, 'Self-Respect: Moral, Emotional, Political', at 232–3.

as persons is to have some relevant mental disposition towards them, it lies beyond the scope of justice. Accordingly, throughout this book, and unless otherwise stated, recognition respect, not evaluative respect, is at issue.

1.3.2 A Sufficientist Theory of Justice

We have seen in the last section that a just society is one where persons respect one another as persons, that is, where the fact that they are persons constitutes in their eyes a compelling reason to act, or to forbear to act, in certain ways towards one another. Principles of justice delineate how persons should act towards one another, in the light of that fact about themselves. Principles of *distributive* justice delineate how they should distribute available resources amongst themselves, in the light of that very same fact.

Now, one of the most influential theories of justice is that articulated by so-called radical egalitarians. For radical egalitarians, to treat one another with equal respect requires that no one be worse off than others through no fault of his own. To be a person, you recall, is amongst other things to be a self-aware, individualized being, with the capacity for rational and moral agency. Persons, thus, have a reflective interest in their life going well, and act accordingly. But if I allow your life to go badly, thus allowing you to be worse off than others, through no fault of your own, I fail to give you equal respect as a person, since in pondering how to act towards you I give weight to a fact about you (namely, your misfortune) which, in so far as it is beyond your agency, is not a fact about persons. Or so do radical egalitarians claim.

On that view, then, justice requires that individuals be given equal amounts of certain goods, for example, resources, opportunity for welfare, or access to advantage, provided they are not responsible for having a lesser amount of such goods than others.[23] I shall return to the no-responsibility proviso below. For now, let us focus on the requirement that individuals should be given equal amounts of *x*. It is an extraordinarily demanding requirement, for it mandates eradicating all inequalities for which individuals are not responsible. In so delineating the obligations of the well off, it prevents them from giving priority to many of their most cherished projects, goals, and attachments. For example, it disallows transfers of resources from parents to children, since such transfers produce inequalities between children whose parents are able and willing to give them resources and children whose parents are unable, or unwilling, to do so—inequalities for which the latter children cannot be held responsible. In the

---

[23] For a defence of equality of resources, see R. Dworkin, 'What is Equality? Part II: Equality of Resources', *Philosophy and Public Affairs* 10 (1981): 283–345; for a defence of equality of opportunity for welfare, see R. Arneson, 'Equality and Equal Opportunity for Welfare', *Philosophical Studies* 56 (1989): 77–93; for a defence of equality of access to advantage, see G. A. Cohen, 'On the Currency of Egalitarian Justice', *Ethics* 99 (1989): 916–44.

light of those considerations, many people, I believe, would argue that egalitarian justice is too demanding on the well off.

Many of those who reject radical egalitarianism tend to argue, as if it were the only alternative, that the well off are only under an obligation to help meet the basic needs of the poor. However, to reject the view that people should have equal amounts of resources or welfare does not commit one to the view that *only* their basic needs should be met. The central assumption which underpins basic needs theories of justice is that human beings have the capacity to live a life worthy of persons. Its central argument is that if we are to respect human beings for having that capacity, we must ensure that they are in a position to exercise it, and we must, thus, give them the possibility of meeting their basic needs, since they cannot hope to live a life worthy of a person if those needs are not met.

The problem with the basic needs theory of justice is that simply to give people access to what they need at a basic level does not do justice to what motivates the duty to help in the first instance. For in order to lead a life worthy of a person, or a minimally flourishing life, as I shall now call it, we do not only need enough food and water not to die, shelter and clothes to protect ourselves, and minimum health care. As I argued elsewhere, we lead such a life if we are autonomous.[24] More specifically, we must be able to frame, revise, and pursue a conception of the good with which we identify, where to be able to do so means not only that we have relevant personal capacities, but also a range of opportunities to choose from as well as access to those opportunities. Someone who has enough food to survive and a shelter, but who needs to work fifteen hours a day in order to subsist, might very well be in a position to frame a conception of the good, for example, to formulate what he would rather do if he had time and money. But he will not be able to *pursue* his chosen conception of the good, precisely for lack of time and money; in fact he most probably will not be able, for those very same reasons, to pursue *any* conception of the good which does not involve working fifteen hours a day. Under those conditions, I submit, he is not leading a minimally flourishing life. In failing to recognize that, basic needs theories of justice do not fulfil their promise to ensure that individuals can lead lives worthy of a person.

In criticizing radical egalitarianism for overlooking the importance of values such as individual autonomy, and in criticizing the basic needs principle for over-looking the importance of leading a minimally flourishing life as opposed to merely subsisting, I have brought out, by implication, two necessary features that a principle of distributive justice must have: on the one hand, it must make space for individual projects, but, on the other hand, it cannot make so much space for them that individuals who are excluded from those projects (for example, because they belong to a poorer community) cannot lead a flourishing life.

---

[24] See my *Social Rights under the Constitution* (Oxford: Clarendon Press, 2000), pp. 9–11.

I argued above that we lead a minimally flourishing life if we are capable of framing, revising, and implementing a conception of the good with which we identify, which in turn requires that we have the personal capacities to do so, a range of opportunities to choose from, and access—time and resources—to some of those opportunities. Justice so understood, thus, does not make the implausible claim that we should be given the wherewithal to implement the conception of the good of our choice; it only says that we should be able to implement a conception of the good which gives some meaning (although perhaps not the *most* meaning) to our life. The difficulty, of course, consists in delineating what constitutes an acceptable range of opportunities, as well as acceptable access to those opportunities, and thus in finding the right course between the two pitfalls which we identified when delineating an account of interests in section 1.2.2A. On the one hand, we should not fall into the trap of constructing a measure of acceptability which defines what is in persons' interests without making any reference to their understanding of what counts as a flourishing life. For, were we to do so, we would fail to respect them as potential authors of their life. On the other hand, we cannot wholly defer to those understandings. For, were we to do so, we would fail to recognize that those understandings may be shaped, indeed misshapen, by lack of information, false beliefs, adaptive preferences, and so on.

The notion of capabilities provides us with the right compass to navigate between those two pitfalls. We saw a few paragraphs ago that a minimally flourishing life does not merely consist in subsisting. In fact, it consists in being able to exercise those capabilities which are truly human. Broadly speaking, there are four kinds of such capabilities.[25] First, we are capable of relating to other human beings in a rich and multifaceted way, of feeling and expressing a whole range of emotions, good or bad, within a whole range of relationships. Second, we are capable of aesthetic experiences, either actively, as creative individuals, or passively, as recipients of other people's creativity. Third, we are capable of engaging in more directly intellectual activities of various kinds. Fourth, we are capable of developing, and exercising, a whole range of physical and manual skills.

In order to exercise those capabilities, we must have basic physical and mental abilities, and therefore have our basic needs met. In that sense, the principle of justice defended here overlaps with the basic needs theory. However, it goes further, as we must also have opportunities to exercise *all* the aforementioned capabilities, as well as access to those opportunities. Let us suppose, for example, that X has the capability for being a good pianist. To give him the opportunity to exercise this capability consists in providing for music schools, and in not preventing him from attending them. To give him access to such an opportunity consists in giving him the money he might need in order to pay for piano lessons at that school.

[25] For a longer, and more controversial, list, see M. Nussbaum, *Women and Human Development* (Cambridge: Cambridge University Press, 2000), pp. 78–9.

The foregoing example is only meant to clarify the distinction just drawn between having opportunities and having access to them: it is not meant to suggest that X should be provided with the opportunity to exercise the capability of his choice at exactly the level at which he wants to exercise it. X may want to be, and have the talent for being, a world-class pianist, but that in itself only entails that X should not be barred from attending a musical school for reasons unrelated to his pianistic talents. It does not entail that those who are better off than he is ought to set up, via taxation, a high-level music school, or give him a scholarship to go to such a school if it does exist. The fact that resources are scarce, together with the claim (which I defend a few paragraphs below) that there is a limit to the sacrifices one can expect the better off to make for the sake of the needy, imply that there should 'only' be some opportunities either to play music (albeit not necessarily at a professional level) or to listen to it, and that we should have reasonable access to them.

What I have said so far may have sounded both breathtakingly banal and disappointingly abstract. Yet, however breathtakingly banal the ideal of a minimally flourishing life principle may be as setting out the requirements of justice, it is so seldom defended in the literature on distributive justice that it is worth articulating as a plausible alternative to the egalitarian and the basic needs principles. Moreover, however abstract it may be, it is not so abstract as to be useless: for it is possible, within the framework it provides, to formulate more specific requirements on the better off, via the government. Steps to provide individuals with the means to lead a minimally flourishing life may consist, but not exclusively so, in the following: meeting the basic needs of very poor people by providing them with enough food, safe water, decent shelter, adequate transport, and minimum health care; ensuring that individuals have access to markets and financial services, are able to borrow money and to trade their goods; providing social services such as health and family planning clinics, and so on.

Whereas the view that individuals have rights against third parties to the enjoyment of civil freedoms and political powers is widely accepted, the claim that they have rights against them to material resources is more controversial. Yet, if the reason why one is committed to conferring on individuals rights of non-interference lies in the value of autonomy, and ultimately of leading a minimally flourishing life, one must be committed, on pain of arbitrariness, to conferring on them rights to the all-purpose resources they need in order to lead such a life, namely, adequate income, housing, and health care. Measures such as those described in the previous paragraph and which give effect to those rights are called for, by what I shall call, from now on, the *principle of sufficiency*.

Clearly sufficiency cannot be met unless the autonomy of some people — those who earn more than is necessary to lead a minimally flourishing life — is curtailed through distributive policies. However, once everybody has such a life, individuals should all be allowed to enjoy the fruits of their labour in pursuit of their conception of the good. They should, in other words, be allowed to maximize their autonomy, as a matter of right. This I call the *principle of autonomy*. The connection between the sufficiency and the autonomy principles on the one hand, and the ideas of respect and self-respect on the other hand, should be obvious: to deny individuals the material resources they need in order to lead a minimally flourishing life, and to deny them the freedom to pursue their own conception of the good, is a failure of respect, in that it is a failure to give them the opportunity to act on the basis of the weight they give to the fact that they are rational and moral project-pursuers.

Note that autonomy, as I define it, is a matter of degree: the greater our physical and mental capacities, the greater the range of options we can choose from, and the more access we have to those options, the more autonomous we are. My concern is to try to capture an 'autonomy-threshold' below which we are not minimally autonomous. Where *precisely* to set the threshold is one of the hardest tasks philosophers can set themselves, and I will not enter the fray here.[26] It suffices, for my present purpose, that there is a sense in which arguments for the coercively directed distribution of material resources invoke the view that there is a threshold of deprivation, abstractly described here, below which we cannot let individuals fall without their consent, and above which we can allow them to maximize their autonomy.

Let me put this very last point in another way: the book supposes that consequentialism, in its extreme form, is false. It is false, that is, that one must always act so as to bring about the greater good: after all, we do have projects and attachments of our own, to which it is our prerogative to devote some of our resources, even though, if we gave those resources to others, they would benefit to a greater degree than we would in withholding them.[27] As stated, this hybrid view does not specify how much priority agents can give to their own projects and interests. I contend, somewhat dogmatically, that agents can confer greater weight on their own prospects for a minimally flourishing life than on other people's similar prospects. But if they already lead a minimally flourishing life, and if helping the needy would not deprive them of their prospects for such a life, then they are under a duty to help. The hardest task, when assessing whether they are under a duty to help, is to determine whether their claim that they would no longer live a minimally flourishing life were they called upon to help is valid. Now, there are two kinds of claims one might invoke in order not to help. One

---

[26] A usefully cognate issue is that of legal competence, for which it is necessary that one reach a threshold of natural abilities such as intelligence. See J. Feinberg, *Harm to Self* (Oxford: Oxford University Press, 1986), p. 29; and D. Wikler, 'Paternalism and the Mildly Retarded', *Philosophy and Public Affairs* 8 (1979): 377–92.

[27] For classic statements of that view, see T. Nagel, *Equality and Partiality* (Oxford: Oxford University Press, 1991); S. Scheffler, *The Rejection of Consequentialism* (Oxford, Oxford University Press, 1982), and *Human Morality* (Oxford: Oxford University Press, 1992); B. Williams, 'Persons, Characters, and Morality', in his *Moral Luck* (Cambridge: Cambridge University Press, 1981). For objections to that view, see S. Kagan, *The Limits of Morality* (Oxford: Clarendon Press, 1989).

might claim that, if one were to help, one would no longer have the all-purpose means necessary to lead a minimally flourishing life; or one might claim that, if one were to help, one would lose the means necessary to implement one's conception of the good, and that in turn would render one's life less than minimally flourishing.

As should be clear, the first claim would succeed: if giving material resources to those who are needier would make one fall below the poverty threshold, one is not under a duty to do so. By contrast, being unable to implement one's preferred conception of the good would not, without further ado, count as good enough a reason to be exonerated from helping. For, as we saw above, justice does not require that persons have the wherewithal to implement the conception of the good which gives most meaning to their life; it only requires that they have the wherewithal to implement a conception of the good which gives some meaning to it. If that applies to the needy, it must also apply to those in a position to help them. In order to show, then, that they should be exonerated from a duty to help, the latter must show that, having thought rationally and with critical distance about alternatives to their current conception of the good, the latter is the only one which would give meaning to their life.

Some philosophers would reject the moderate view of morality which my argument presupposes, on the consequentialist grounds that there is a *pro tanto* reason to promote the good, even at the cost of our personal projects and attachments. I cannot hope to show, within the scope of this book, that the moderate view of morality is correct. But I do hope to show that, if one subscribes to it, one can accept that the needy and the imperilled have a right against the able-bodied that the latter provide them with personal resources, without jeopardizing one's commitment to individual autonomy.

Consequentialist opponents of standard morality might be tempted to point out that their conclusion is similar to mine, that is, that they can advocate some degree of confiscation of personal resources without jeopardizing individual autonomy. Thus, in *The Limits of Morality*, Shelly Kagan makes the following point: the extremist consequentialist opponent of standard morality 'would be the first to urge that mindlessly driving oneself to exhaustion or recklessly dispensing one's goods can be counterproductive. Far from being required, such behaviour is forbidden. What each agent is required to do is to act in such a way that she can make her greatest possible contribution to the overall good (given her own particular talents).'[28] If I would make a greater contribution to the overall good by withholding one of my cornea from a blind person than by giving it to him, I am not under a duty to do the latter; in fact, I am forbidden to do the latter. It could very well be, then, that the able-bodied will enjoy a similar degree of personal integrity under an extremist consequentialist view and under a standard view of morality.

[28] Kagan, *The Limits of Morality*, pp. 7–8.

Against the extremist consequentialist, though, not only is the rationale for maintaining the personal integrity of the able-bodied very different depending on which view of morality one adopts, but, in some cases, an extremist consequentialist will demand sacrifices from the able-bodied that the standard view would not. Suppose I am in a position to make a contribution to the overall good to the tune of x; suppose, further, that by killing myself and making my organs available, I could save the life of five people who, if fully healthy, could each contribute x to the overall good. If I do not kill myself, the overall good will be increased by x; if I do kill myself, it will be increased by $5x$. I do not know how Kagan would deal with this case (nor do I know, for example, how he would deal with cases such as those of seriously mentally disabled people who are otherwise physically healthy and who could provide non-disabled patients with much needed organs). It seems clear, however, that the extremist view holds that I am under a duty to kill myself, whereas the standard view no less clearly allows me not to do so.

To recapitulate, then, a just society is one where the principles of sufficiency and autonomy obtain. Now, you recall that, according to radical egalitarians, individuals should be given equal amounts of x provided they are not responsible for being worse off. If they are responsible for their predicament, they have no claim for compensation at the bar of justice. A sufficientist theory of justice could also attach a no-responsibility provision to the receipt of material assistance: such a theory would hold that a just society is one where individuals receive help towards meeting their material needs provided they are not responsible for being needy.

The no-responsibility condition is thought to be important by many philosophers because it trades on the widely and deeply held intuition that it is unfair for individuals to ask others to pay for the cost of their choices. However, it has attracted a fair amount of criticisms: it does, after all, imply that a just society is one which lets individuals live in abject poverty if they refuse to take a job, which denies them state-funded medical treatment for, and possibly lets them die of, AIDS if they failed to practise safe sex. And so on.

It is my contention that a just society, requiring as it does that persons give one another opportunities for self-respect, cannot endorse the no-responsibility condition across the board. As we saw, the requirement that persons respect one another as such states that when deciding how to act towards someone, we ought to regard the fact that she is a person as a compelling reason for us to behave in certain ways towards her—ways which are appropriate to her being a person. More specifically, this means that we must give proper weight to the fact that she has a conception of how her life should go and the capacity, as a rational and moral agent, to implement that conception, that she is aware of herself as having both that conception and that capacity, and that she is conscious of the ways in which others treat her.

In order to implement the no-responsibility condition when allocating resources, we would have to find out how exactly the needy found themselves in that predicament; this in turn would require that they disclose potentially shameful things about themselves.[29] Those who are in need because they cannot get a job would have to show, in order to get benefits, that the reason they cannot work is that they have no useful talent. Likewise, those who are ill and need medical treatment would have to reveal intimate details about themselves, some of which they might find shameful or embarrassing, in order to show that they are not responsible for their illness. But, in asking those who are not responsible for their predicament to reveal shameful things about themselves, we lead them to believe that they are not given the respect they are due and that in turn is likely to weaken their self-respect. Moreover, simply in *requiring* of them that they demean themselves (if in their eyes only), we deny them an opportunity for self-respect. If, then, respect for persons as such is central to a just society, the no-responsibility condition cannot hold, at least not in those cases—and there are many—where it would be impossible to implement it without jeopardizing respect.

Now, at this juncture, some radical egalitarians sympathetic to the no-responsibility condition might be tempted to object as follows: respect for persons as such in fact *requires* that we hold on to the no-responsibility condition. For, if to respect someone as a person means that in deciding how to behave towards him we take the fact that he is a person seriously, then we must take seriously the fact that he is a rational and moral agent. In so far as being such an agent means making choices reflectively and in awareness (as far as possible) of their consequences, for someone to demand that he be given that kind of respect should carry weight with us only if he is willing to bear responsibility for his choices; that in turn means that he should not expect others to pay for their cost.

I am not denying, of course, that if X demands that others respect him as a person, he must be willing to bear responsibility for, and to pay the cost of, his choices. And, to be sure, in dropping the no-responsibility condition in those cases where its implementation is incompatible with recognition respect, one would allow for a world where some individuals who are responsible for their predicament are given recognition respect undeservedly. But it is better, I believe, to err on that side, than to deny those who are not responsible for their neediness opportunities for self-respect. Moreover, as I have already intimated, I am not claiming that we should drop the condition altogether. There might be situations where we can see whether individuals are responsible for their neediness without getting them to reveal shameful facts about themselves, for example, in the context of health care, through diagnostic tests. In those cases, then, it is possible

---

[29] My argument in this paragraph is drawn from Jonathan Wolff's article 'Fairness, Respect, and the Egalitarian Ethos', *Philosophy and Public Affairs* 27 (1998): 97–122.

to implement the no-responsibility condition without failing to give proper respect to individuals who are not responsible for their condition.[30]

What does all this mean, in practice? I argued above that a just society is one where individuals have rights to minimum income, housing, and health care. I believe that it is not possible to implement the no-responsibility condition, when deciding to whom one should give minimum income and financial help towards housing, without failing to give proper respect to those who are not responsible for their predicaments; this suggests that welfare and housing benefits should be given unconditionally. However, it might sometimes be possible to implement the no-responsibility condition when delivering housing benefit in-kind, by way of a council flat, as well as health care. Someone who remains homeless because he has turned down three offers of perfectly acceptable council housing can, it seems to me, be deemed responsible for his plight and lose his entitlement to help. Similarly, someone of whom diagnostic tests show that he is clearly responsible for his predicament loses his entitlement to receive medical treatment.

One final point: to apply the no-responsibility condition when it is possible to assess that a needy person is clearly responsible for her predicament without getting her to make shameful revelations about herself is to say that, in those cases, and at the bar of justice, we are morally allowed, and have the right, not to do anything. But it is not to say that we are, all things considered, allowed not to help. For, when faced with someone who might incur serious harm unless we help them, there really would be something monstrous in not doing anything. In those cases where the needy are responsible for their predicament, and where we can know them to be so without failing to respect them, although our failure to help is not, indeed, a failure of justice, it is nevertheless a failure, in terms of showing basic compassion. Whether we have the right, all things considered, not to help, given that it is morally wrong on our part to abstain, in other words, whether the state lacks the power to force us to act, is a question which I shall not address here, focusing as I do on what *justice* requires of us and allows us to do.

1.4 CONCLUSION

At the outset of this chapter, we saw that a theory of justice must give an account of the scope, strength, and content of the principles which it defends. In this

---

[30] Against the view I deploy here, some might be tempted to press the following objection: 'look, justice does require that those who are responsible for their predicament lack a claim for help; but, as you say, implementing the responsibility condition will undermine opportunities for self-respect. However, this does not mean that justice dictates that we should drop the condition in those cases where we are in doubt. Rather, it means that there is a conflict between justice and respect, and that the latter outweighs the former.' My claim, though, is that it is central to justice that individuals be provided with opportunities for self-respect, so that a society where they are not so treated is unjust. Accordingly, it is unjust to implement the responsibility condition in those cases where, as we are in doubt, we cannot do so unless we ask people to make shameful revelations about themselves.

chapter, a number of points were made about all three dimensions of justice, the most important of which bear restating here.

1. A just society is one where *persons* give one another opportunities for self-respect. By persons, I mean embodied and individualized beings who consist in more than their brain and body, are conscious, are aware that they occupy the same body as, and are psychologically continuous with, some individual at some past time, and, finally, have the capacity for rational and moral agency.

2. Persons so understood have a number of rights against one another, more specifically, liberties, claims, and powers, where those rights protect some interests of theirs, including (within certain conditions) their interest in doing something which is morally wrong, even if they might harm themselves in so acting. Note, however, that they lack the power to let others treat them without the respect they are owed as persons.

3. According to the sufficiency principle, a just society is one where persons have prima facie rights against the comparatively well off to the material resources they need in order to lead a minimally flourishing life. According to the autonomy principle, once everybody has those resources, all individuals are allowed to enjoy the fruits of their labour in pursuit of their conception of the good.

To assessing the implication of those claims for the rights we have over our, and other people's, person, I now turn.

2

Good Samaritanism

2.1 INTRODUCTION

We have just seen that someone who leads a less than minimally flourishing life can claim the required material resources against the well off, provided the latter would not jeopardize their own prospects for such a life by providing help. Now, in many cases, the needy need things other than material resources. For example, they might need a kidney, or some blood, which may require not only that the well off channel part of their income towards (something like) a national health system, but also that someone make their kidney or their blood available to them. I shall deal with such cases in Chapters 4 and 5. In this chapter, I look at a different kind of need which material resources cannot meet, to wit, individuals' need for other people's personal services which arises when, for example, they are in danger of drowning, collapse on the pavement following a heart attack, and so on. I argue that those who are in a position to provide such help are under a duty to do so at the bar of justice.

Liberal theorists of justice hardly ever study duties of Good Samaritanism. As I noted in the Introduction, the Anglo-American political and legal tradition within which those theorists write is unsympathetic, on the whole, to the view that our moral duty to be a Good Samaritan (the existence of which it does not deny) is stringent enough to be enforced by the state. By contrast, most European countries have adopted so-called Bad Samaritan laws—laws, that is, which make it a crime for someone not to help the imperilled, when he could help them at very little cost to himself.[1] This is not to say that Anglo-American liberals regard a failure to be a Good Samaritan as morally acceptable: indeed, most of them think that it is morally wrong. But they tend not to think—or at least they do not

---

[1] In the USA, Massachusetts, Minnesota, Rhode Island, and Vermont have passed such laws. In Wisconsin, one is required to provide aid to, or to summon aid for, crime victims who have suffered bodily harm. In Europe, France, Germany, Belgium, the Netherlands, Portugal, and Russia have passed Bad Samaritan laws. Russia was the first country to do so, as early as 1889 (see A. Tunc, 'The Volunteer and the Good Samaritan'; and A. W. Rudzinski, 'The Duty to Rescue: A Comparative Analysis', in J. M. Ratcliffe (ed.), *The Good Samaritan and the Law* (Gloucester, Mass.: Peter Smith, 1981)). Note that *Bad* Samaritan laws, which criminalize failures to rescue, must not be confused with *Good* Samaritan laws, which prevent people from suing their rescuers on the grounds that the latter occasioned them some harm in the course of the rescue.

explicitly argue—that it constitutes a violation of a duty of justice. Rather, they condemn it as a failure to perform a duty of charity.

A standard argument to that effect takes the following form:

(1) One can only be under a duty of justice not to harm someone.
(2) Withholding emergency aid from someone does not cause them to suffer a harm. Therefore:
(3) one cannot be under a duty of justice to give emergency aid.[2]

It is not my intention to take a stand on that particular argument. Rather, in assuming that the needy have welfare rights, I assume that the well off are under an obligation to confer on them some benefits. Whether this is because not benefiting them would in those instances harm them, or for some other reason, is irrelevant to this chapter's central aim, which is to show the following: the same considerations which support the view that the needy have a right, as a matter of justice, to some of the material resources of the well off also support the view that the imperilled have a right, as a matter of justice, to the personal services of those who are in a position to help. Moreover, the state has the moral power to enforce that right or, to put it differently, Bad Samaritan laws are legitimate.

In section 2.2, I examine and reject a defence of the duty to rescue as a duty which we owe to society as a whole to support just institutions. In section 2.3, I argue that the duty to rescue is owed to the imperilled themselves and ought to be legally enforced.

Beforehand, though, three preliminary remarks are in order. First, a Good Samaritan, for my purpose here, does not stand in a special relationship to the person in peril; nor does he have a professional or contractual obligation to help those in need. A Good Samaritan, in short, is not a parent, a friend, a physician, or a policeman: he is a stranger who happens to be at the critical place, at the critical time, and who is asked to perform an action which he is not asked to do in the course of his professional life.

Second, I focus on needs which cannot be met through ordinary methods of resource transfers such as taxation. A Good Samaritan, here, is not someone who discharges his duty by giving money to the beggar; he is someone who discharges his duty by providing personal services to those who need them here and now, such as the child who is drowning in a shallow pond, or the man who suffers a heart attack and collapses on the pavement.

Third, we saw in Chapter 1 that to insist on the no-responsibility condition when allocating material resources violates the requirement that individuals be

---

[2] For the view that withholding emergency aid does not cause harm, see, e.g., E. Mack, 'Bad Samaritanism and the Causation of Harm', *Philosophy and Public Affairs* 9 (1980): 230–59; A. McIntyre, 'Guilty Bystanders? On the Legitimacy of Duty to Rescue Statutes', *Philosophy and Public Affairs* 23 (1994): 157–91. For the view that it does, see, e.g., J. Feinberg, *Harm to Others*, ch. 4; and J. Kleinig, 'Good Samaritanism', *Philosophy and Public Affairs* 5 (1976): 382–407, at 393–4.

treated with respect, except in those cases where we can assess who is responsible for their predicament and who is not, without relying on those who are needy having to make shameful revelations about themselves. When duties of Good Samaritanism are at issue, however, the no-responsibility condition ought not to come into play. For, in so far as those duties are owed to strangers, rescuers will not know the extent to which, if at all, the imperilled are responsible for their plight, unless they ask them some rather detailed questions about themselves. In so doing they would risk wasting time better spent in actually rescuing them.

2.2 GOOD SAMARITANISM: A DUTY OF JUSTICE TO SUPPORT JUST INSTITUTIONS?

Before I offer my own defence of the duty to rescue as a duty of justice, I should like to examine, and refute, a standard argument to that effect. On that view, our duty to provide emergency assistance is owed, not to the imperilled, but to society writ large. Thus, Alison McIntyre claims that there is a connection between a Good Samaritan's duty to obtain assistance and the organization of emergency services. Take the case of firefighters. As a community we want them to operate efficiently, for they maximize the general welfare; yet they cannot do so unless citizens assist in reporting fires. As she writes, 'one's duty to report a fire is a public duty, just as the fire-fighter is carrying out his duty to the community that employs him, rather than a duty to the individual whose property needs protection.'[3]

McIntyre is not alone in thinking along those lines. Arthur Ripstein, for example, also believes that a duty to rescue is a duty to support a just institution. In that sense, or so he claims, it is analogous to a duty to help via taxation, which is owed to social institutions and not to the needy themselves. On his view, the reason why we are under a duty to rescue others lies in the value of reciprocity: 'Reciprocity requires that the misfortunes which stand in the way of each person being able to live a self-directing life be held in common, so that all have the wherewithal to participate as full and equal members of society.'[4] And the reason, in turn, why we owe that duty not to those in need but to society writ large is that relational duties of that sort would make a mockery of liberals' cherished view that we should all bear some responsibility for the way our life goes. For me to be under a duty to *you* if you are in danger undermines my freedom, since the

---

[3] A. McIntyre, 'Guilty Bystanders?', at 181–2; A. Ripstein, 'Three Duties to Rescue: Moral, Civil, and Criminal', *Law and Philosophy* 19 (2000): 751–79.

[4] Ripstein, 'Three Duties to Rescue', at 765.

conditions of our interaction are laid down unilaterally by your need for help. By contrast, for me to be under a duty to the community to get out of the way of the ambulance that takes you to the hospital does not undermine my freedom, since it simply amounts to helping a just institution—the ambulance services—to do their job properly.

There are several problems with Ripstein's and McIntyre's line of argument. First, it justifies not so much duties to rescue as duties to help emergency services; in so doing, it justifies a weaker kind of Good Samaritanism—albeit one which could save lives—than its proponents explicitly recognize. And this is troublesome: for, after all, most instances of Good Samaritanism are ones where the rescuer needs to do something *before* the emergency services get to the scene (such as administering CPR, helping someone get up after a heavy fall, helping a swimmer in difficulty swim ashore, etc.), and, assuming that they will be needed at all, to get out of the way once they are there.

Second, and more importantly, the claim that we are under a duty to report a fire because we ought to support just institutions is implausible. Suppose that I see a fire breaking out in the house next door, that there are no emergency services (the government has run out of money), and that I can very easily, at no cost to myself, help its inhabitants to get out. It is unclear what McIntyre and Ripstein would say here. Should they hold that I am not under a duty to rescue, they would be vulnerable to the charge that the absence or existence of emergency services cannot determine my moral duty, at least when the rescue is easy. Should they hold that I am under a duty to rescue but that it is not a duty of justice, they would be vulnerable to the charge that the absence or existence of emergency services cannot determine whether my moral duty is one of justice or not.

Third, in so far as my duty is grounded in my neighbour's interest in survival (whether or not there are emergency services), that duty is owed *to him*. Given that to have a right means that an interest of one person is important enough to hold some other person under a duty, this in turn implies that my neighbour himself, and not society at large, has a right against me that I rescue him.

Fourth, and relatedly, assuming for the sake of argument that the duty of Good Samaritanism is a duty to assist emergency services, it nevertheless does not follow that it is a duty owed to society as whole. Consider a firefighter employed by the city council. To claim that he is under a duty to help to his employer—the community—and not to the imperilled, does not account for the fact that the latter are, in some cases, and rightly so, allowed to sue firefighting services themselves, but not the city council, for gross negligence. In any event, even if emergency services are under a duty to help to their employer and not to the imperilled themselves, it does not follow that those whom they deputize to act—namely, civilians—are not *themselves* under a duty to act to the imperilled.

2.3 THE DUTY TO RESCUE: AN ENFORCEABLE DUTY OF JUSTICE

In this section, I show, first, that we owe it to the imperilled, as a matter of justice, to rescue them (section 2.3.1), and, second, that duties of Good Samaritanism should be enforced by the state (section 2.3.2).

2.3.1 Defending the Duty to Rescue

On what grounds, then, do we owe it to others to help them if they need emergency assistance? I am assuming, you recall, that the needy have a right, as a matter of justice, to some of the material resources of the well off; that is, that they have rights to minimum income, housing, and health care. As we saw in Chapter 1, the rationale for holding the well off under that kind of duty is this: individuals have a fundamental interest in leading a minimally flourishing life, and self-respect is central to leading such a life. Accordingly, a just society is one where persons give one another opportunities for self-respect. This in turn requires that the comparatively well off provide the needy with the resources they require in order to respect themselves, and ultimately to lead a minimally flourishing life.

By the same token, one must also accept that individuals' interest in leading a minimally flourishing life is important enough to hold others under a duty not simply to give them material resources, but also to provide them with emergency assistance, in cases where, absent such assistance, they would not be able to lead a minimally flourishing life. The fact that in the former case material resources are needed, whilst in the latter personal services are, is not weighty enough to justify holding the well off under a duty to distribute and exonerating would-be rescuers from the task of helping. Consider the counterclaim that that fact is weighty enough. In effect, that counterclaim would be that the interest of the starving person in remaining alive is important enough to hold the well off under a duty to transfer resources to him, standardly by way of taxation, but that the interest of the imperilled swimmer in remaining alive is not important enough to hold other swimmers under a duty to help him out of the water. The only way to defend that counterclaim that I can think of is the following: being called upon to give material resources to those who need them is not onerous enough to justify not doing so, whereas being called upon to do something for the sake of the imperilled is onerous enough to justify not doing so.

The claim that giving material resources by way of taxation is not unacceptably onerous but that performing a rescue act is, must be disambiguated somewhat: for it could mean either (a) that the *process* of giving material resources is not unacceptably onerous whereas the process of rescuing is, or (b) that the *costs* arising from having given such resources are not unacceptably onerous whereas the costs arising from rescuing are, or (c) both. Now, it is true that the process of contributing to helping the needy by way of taxation can be absolutely costless in terms of time and energy, as when taxes are deducted from one's salary automatically. In many instances, however, one has to spend considerable time and effort completing a tax return—more time and effort than, in some cases, helping an imperilled swimmer to the shore. Moreover, it is unclear that the costs arising from having given a share of one's income through taxation (to wit, loss of disposable income) are always higher than those arising from having helped someone in peril (to wit, time, energy, etc.).

In sum, the contrast just drawn between giving something to someone and doing something for them is not strong enough to bear the weight it is asked to bear. But this is not meant to suggest that the duty to provide material resources is strictly analogous to the duty to provide emergency rescues. In fact, there are two differences between those duties, although neither of them, I now argue, undermines my case. First, although the duty to rescue is not always more demanding in effect than the duty to pay taxes, it imposes an additional burden which the latter does not. When a needy person calls upon the well off to give him material resources, he is (merely) imposing a cost on them, to wit, the cost of losing a share of their income. When someone in peril calls upon would-be rescuers to help him, not only is he imposing on them the cost of not being able to do what they want on that particular occasion; he is also imposing on them a risk of incurring a further cost, to wit, the cost of suffering some injury, in some cases death, in the course of the rescue attempt. Is he entitled to do so?

At this juncture, some might be tempted to hold the following principle (P) to be true:[5]

(P) One is under a duty to help and thereby incur a risk of cost C (R_c) only if one is under a duty to help and thereby incur C.

On that view, one determines whether imposing a risk of a particular cost is legitimate merely by determining whether imposing that cost itself is legitimate. This has the merit of simplicity as well as, unfortunately, the disadvantage of implausibility. For consider; suppose that S has been knocked unconscious by a falling branch into a shallow pond and that Q happens to pass by. S is quite heavy, and if Q lifts her out of the pond, there is a risk, but an absolutely minuscule one (much, much lower, say, than the similar risk Q incurs by cycling to work everyday) that he will have a heart attack. As should be clear by now, Q ought to lift S out of the pond. If (P) is true, though, then it follows that one cannot hold the following two claims to be true:

(1) One is not under a duty to die for the sake of someone else.
(2) Q is under a duty to lift S out of the pond.

[5] In this paragraph and the next two, I draw from J. J. Thomson, *Rights, Restitution, and Risk* (Cambridge, Mass.: Harvard University Press, 1986), ch. 11.

For, if Q lifts S out of the pond, and suffers a heart attack, from which he dies, then in so far as (1) is true (which it surely is), it seems that Q was not, in fact, under a duty to lift S out of the pond. But that strikes us as rather unacceptable. Consider another example. S is very ill, in bed, and needs some medicine: she asks Q to go to the chemist's, a five-minute walk which involves crossing a traffic-heavy thoroughfare. Surely Q ought to go, even though he risks being run over. Consider a final, contrastive, example: S is drowning in very stormy seas; Q is not a very good swimmer, and if he goes in to try to get S out, there is a 30 per cent risk—a very high risk by all accounts—that he will drown himself. In that case, surely Q is not under a duty to attempt to rescue S.

In order to claim, in the first two cases, that Q is under a duty to rescue S and thereby to put himself at risk of dying, and, in the third case, that Q is not under such duty, one must accept that proposition (P) is not *always* true, and that every single instance of it must be justified, or denied, separately, on its own merit. To defend such a principle in detail is beyond the scope of this chapter. I suggest, though, that a reasonable risk, as incurred in the course of a rescue, is one no greater than the risks most individuals routinely incur, and impose on others, in their everyday life, when driving, cycling, and so on. When engaging in those activities, they both run and impose risks of death and serious injuries. Accordingly, they are under a moral duty to help out of the water someone who is drowning, or, in the absence of ambulance services, to drive to the hospital someone who is in serious pain, and so on.

To sum up, although duties to rescue raise the question of risk-imposition and are thereby not strictly analogous to duties to provide material help, that particular disanalogy does not threaten my case for holding would-be rescuers under a duty of justice to provide personal help to those who need it. Having said that, those two kinds of provision differ in yet another, potentially problematic, respect. In the case of welfare assistance, the burden of helping the needy can be spread fairly amongst all would-be contributors, through taxation. Not so with emergency rescues, since whether or not one is under a duty to help depends on whether one finds oneself in the right place at the right time. It seems unfair, or so one might be tempted to argue, that some people, and not all, are under a duty to provide emergency rescues, simply out of the bad luck of being present when someone is in peril.

Now, there is no way, obviously, to spread the burden of rescuing amongst everybody. I do not think, though, that this undermines the view that duties to rescue are relevantly analogous to duties to provide welfare provision. For, just as one can spread the cost of expropriation by compensating expropriated property owners through general taxation, one can spread the (small) costs incurred by rescuers through a compensation scheme also funded through general taxation. And, just as the fact that expropriated property owners may sometimes find that compensation does not fully make up for their loss is not a good reason to deem expropriation illegitimate, the fact that rescuers may sometimes find that compensation does not make up for the costs incurred in the rescue attempt is not a good reason to exempt them from a duty to rescue.[6]

The imperilled, thus, have a right that those in a position to rescue them do so. None of my points to that effect, however, shows that the duties of Good Samaritanism, perfect and rights-correlated as they are, are duties *of justice* in the sense in which duties to provide material resources are. For not all rights-correlated duties are duties of justice: my moral duty not to lie to you is perfect and can conceivably be thought to be grounded in your right not to be lied to; however, it would not be appropriate to say that in lying to you, I would act unjustly towards you. One standard argument to that effect is that a principle for the regulation of individual behaviour counts as a principle of justice if it solves conflicts between individuals over the distribution of moderately scarce resources. In so far as the principle 'one ought not to lie to others' cannot in any way be taken to settle such conflicts, the duty not to lie is not a duty of justice.

It is unclear that justice by definition only deals with conflicts about resources. However, it still remains the case that, as I noted in the introduction to this book, arguments about *distributive* justice are (nearly always) arguments about the distribution of goods, such as money, housing, and health care, which are scarce, and distributable, resources. In so far as my case for duties of Good Samaritanism as duties of justice rests on an analogy between the provision of rescue services and the provision of material resources, it needs to establish not only that performing a rescue service consists in providing a resource, but also that it consists in providing a scarce resource, and, moreover, one of which it makes sense to say that one can have a right to it.

A resource is something which we need to pursue our ends, but not all the things for which we have such a need count as resources. I may need my son's love in order to lead a fulfilling life, yet to characterize that love as a resource would be inappropriate, for, in so considering my son's love, I would distance myself from him in a way which would be incompatible with the nature of my need for it.

---

[6] Two points. First, it is important to bear in mind that I am thinking in terms of expropriation for the sake, not of securing a public good, but of helping some needy individuals. In the former case, property owners can be said to benefit, in some way, from being expropriated; in the latter case they cannot. This strengthens their complaint that the compensation they receive does not really make up for their loss. However, it does not render it bulletproof, since it is simply not true, or so I imply in Chapter 1, that we are under an obligation to do something for the sake of others only if we benefit from doing it. (For the view that expropriation can be used by the state to realize any goal on which the legislative has authority to legislate, which may include bringing about distributive justice, see B. Ackerman, *Private Property and the Constitution* (New Haven, Conn.: Yale University Press, 1977)).

Second, my argument in this paragraph applies to cases where there is only one potential rescuer, as well as to cases where there are several. In the latter cases, the question arises of how to spread the burden of rescuing: suppose that Q_1 and Q_2 are equally good swimmers. Should they both rescue S? Probably, unless too many rescuers would spoil the broth. Suppose that Q_1 is not quite as good as Q_2: should he be exonerated from helping? Probably, unless two rescuers would improve the broth. And so on. I need not address those allocation issues here in order to make my case in favour of duties of Good Samaritanism as duties of justice.

This is because my need for his love is not a need for any child's love; in fact, it is not even a need for the love any child of mine could give me. It is a need for the love which this particular child of mine, with his traits of character, quirks, qualities, and flaws, can give me. To put the point differently, it is not a need for my son's *love*, but for *my son's* love, a love which cannot be replaced by anything else or anyone else's love.

This example indicates that a resource is a fungible means for the pursuit of our ends—of which money and goods are paradigmatic instances. We need them to pursue our ends, and each of their instances is fungible: I need a can of buttermilk paint to redecorate my living room, but any such can will do; I need a number of banknotes to pay my builder, but any such notes will do. Indeed, the provision of a service too can be a resource in that sense: not only do I need paint to have a nice living room, I also need my builder's service. Crucially, the service of any other (good) builder will do.[7] And, in so far as we provide a service when rescuing the imperilled, the provision of rescue services consists in the provision of a resource.

To many, the foregoing will sound odd. They would maintain that providing services is simply not like providing money or things; for, in providing a service, they would say, one responds as a whole person to the situation at hand: one does not make available a resource which happens to be at one's disposal.[8] As applied to Good Samaritanism, this suggests that the lifebelt I throw to someone who is drowning counts as a resource, but that the labour I perform by using my arms to throw it does not. I fail to see why this should be so. To be sure, I do not relate to the lifebelt I throw to the imperilled in the same way I relate to my labour. The latter, in so far as it is performed through the use of my body, is something which I do, whereas the lifebelt is something which I give. As we saw earlier, however, the contrast just drawn between giving something and doing something is overdrawn in the present context. In addition, when doing something for the imperilled, I cannot but be aware that someone else would do just as well, indeed that a robot might do just as well. Although *I* rescue you, what matters is that you receive that particular service in order to remain alive, from whomever is in a position to give it. In that sense, my service is entirely fungible.

There is nothing inappropriate, therefore, in regarding personal services—and more widely the use of the body to provide such services—as a resource. Moreover, personal services are a scarce resource, in so far as they are provided by persons through the use of their whole body: as I only have two arms and two legs, I cannot rescue you from the river *and* prune my flower beds at the same

---

[7] If my builder happens to be a good friend of mine, it may matter to me a great deal that he, rather than any other builder, should decorate my living room (it may also matter a great deal that another builder do the job, as I might be worried that hiring my friend as my builder would jeopardize the friendship). But the fact that in that particular case I will not really regard his service as a mere resource does not impugn my claim that personal services can be so regarded in many other cases.

[8] I owe this objection to C. Mackenzie.

time. Even if I had enough limbs to perform both tasks at the same time, I could not do so, since I cannot be in two different places at the same time. You have an interest in controlling the use of my arms and legs, as well as the location of my body, in such a way as to be rescued; but I have an interest in controlling them in such a way as to tend to my flower beds. If that is not a conflict over a scarce resource, I do not know what is. In fact, while it is possible to imagine a world of abundant material resources (abundant, that is, in the sense that there are enough of them to satisfy everybody's needs and wants); indeed, while it is possible to imagine a world of abundant body parts (thanks to stem-cell research and cloning), it is impossible to imagine a world of abundant personal services, precisely because such services cannot but be performed by individuals who have to be in the right place at the right time, and yet may not be, and who have to use their body as required by the needs of the imperilled, and yet may not want to.

Not only, then, are personal services a scarce resource: in addition, it is possible to conceive of them as resources the provision of which can be protected by rights. For consider: the provision of a good G can be protected by a right if it meets two conditions, which are singly necessary and together sufficient. First, G must be such that to be under a duty to transfer it to someone else does not change its nature. Suppose that you fall in love, unrequitedly, with your neighbour, become clinically depressed as a result, and will find your way back to mental health only if she reciprocates that love. As it stands, you arguably are not leading a minimally flourishing life. Yet, were we to claim that you have a right against her that she give you her love, we would fail to understand that love, just like friendship, must be freely given in order to count as such. To hold her under a duty to love you would therefore be incoherent.

Second, G must be such that the act of either transferring it to someone else or receiving it from someone else does not violate one's personhood. For, in so far as justice is a property of acts committed by persons (as we saw in Chapter 1), it could not require, on pain of defeating itself, that someone transfer a good to someone else and thereby cease to be a person.

Personal services in general, and rescue services in particular, meet both conditions. They remain services whether they are provided voluntarily or not; and one can be held under a duty to provide them without ceasing to be a person. To recapitulate, then, it makes sense to hold that the imperilled have a right to rescue services against potential rescuers. Moreover, a principle which delineates duties grounded in rights and which pertains to the provision of such services can be regarded as a principle of justice.

To recap, if one thinks that the needy have a right, as a matter of justice, to some of the material resources of the well off, one is committed to the view that the imperilled have a right, as a matter of justice, to the personal services of would-be rescuers. However, recall that, in Chapter 1, I posited that when someone leads a less than minimally flourishing life, he can claim the required material resources against the well off, *provided the latter would not jeopardize their prospects for such a life by providing help*. Clearly, the claim for help of the imperilled against rescuers is subject to the same proviso. For, just as it would be arbitrary to exonerate would-be rescuers from a duty to help whilst holding the materially well off under that duty, it would be arbitrary *not* to exonerate them from it when their prospect for a minimally flourishing life would be jeopardized whilst releasing the latter in similar circumstances.

2.3.2 From a Moral to a Legal Right to Rescue

That we have a moral right to emergency rescue clearly does not entail that the state ought to enforce that right, any more than my having a right that you meet me at five o'clock, as you promised, entails that the state ought to force you to do so. As we saw in section 1.2.2B, not all rights are enforceable. However, my concern in this book is with enforceable rights; accordingly, I should like to show, in this section, that the rights of the imperilled against potential rescuers ought to be turned into legal rights. If one agrees that obligations of Good Samaritanism are obligations of justice, and if one thinks, with liberal proponents of coercive taxation for distributive purposes, that the state has the moral power to make it compulsory to contribute to the provision of welfare services, then one cannot dismiss Bad Samaritan laws on the grounds that the state does not have the moral power to enforce positive rights to be helped. However, there might be other reasons as to why advocating legal welfare rights does not commit one to legal rights of rescue. Indeed, many commentators have pressed that a badly drafted Bad Samaritan law would be too costly from a moral and practical point of view. Practically, it would be very hard to prosecute someone for failing to rescue an imperilled individual: if I flee the scene of an accident, without anyone to see me, nobody will be any the wiser. If I fail to alert the police from the privacy of my home when I hear someone scream for help in the street, I can always pretend that I did not hear, or that the screams I heard seemed to come from the TV next door and not from the street. Or I can say that I didn't see very well, that the person in peril seemed all right, that the struggle I witnessed between assailant and victim was a lovers' quarrel, and so on.

As readers familiar with the literature on Good Samaritanism will have realized by now, I am alluding here to what is, possibly, the most notorious case of Bad Samaritanism in the US. On 13 March 1964, in the early hours of the morning, Kitty Genovese, a twenty-eight-year-old woman living in Queens (NYC) was attacked three times by the same individual (who first struck at 3:15 a.m., then came back and struck her on two occasions, at a few minutes' intervals to finish her off). Genovese cried for help, but the police were notified at 3:50 a.m. only, by which point she was dead. The police later established that thirty-eight of her neighbours, *none* of whom called the police before 3:50 a.m., had witnessed one moment or another of her ordeal. When asked later on by the police and disbelieving journalists why they had not done anything to help, some of those neighbours claimed that they thought what they had heard was a lovers' quarrel, or that they could not see very well, or that they felt too frightened to do anything. None of those thirty-eight neighbours was prosecuted for such failure. And, indeed, as the opponent of legal duties of Good Samaritanism would argue, how on earth could a court ever dispute their reasons for not doing anything to help Kitty Genovese?

This objection to Bad Samaritan laws does not strike me as convincing. For a start, although it may be very difficult in some cases to assess whether someone was in a position to help, it nevertheless is true that in other cases one will be able to make that assessment: some witness might see would-be rescuers driving away from the scene of an accident and might be quick enough to take down their plate number, thereby allowing the police to track them down. One may also be able to discern, under cross-examination, that the would-be rescuer did not have any good reason to be scared (he was safe at home), or that his plea to that effect in fact disguised an unwillingness to get involved.

Moreover, adverting to the difficulty of proving that someone culpably failed to act as a Good Samaritan cannot suffice to justify not enforcing duties to rescue. After all, it is usually not thought that the fact that rape (in particular marital rape) and racial and sexual discrimination are notoriously difficult to prove constitutes a good reason for not criminalizing them. It is unclear why failures to rescue should be treated differently.

Of course, other considerations, such as the moral costs attendant on enforcing duties of Good Samaritanism, may dictate against enforcement. A proponent of Bad Samaritan laws will find such considerations more difficult to deal with, but, as we shall now see, hardly decisive. The deepest critique of Bad Samaritan laws in that regard has been deployed by H. M. Malm.[9] According to Malm, such laws cannot lay down precise criteria for what counts as a reasonable cost for a would-be rescuer, in the precise circumstances in which he is called upon to rescue; nor can they lay down precise criteria for what counts as a reasonable risk. For there are too many possible scenarios for statutes to be able to foresee. Compare with taxation: it is not that difficult to legislate in such a way as to ensure that individuals contribute to welfare provision to the extent that they are in a position to do so—one can state, in the law, that taxes will be levied in proportion to income, with possibilities of rebate for, say, being a lone parent, having special medical needs, and so on. Whereas tax law can be relatively precise, Bad Samaritan laws cannot, with the effect that it will be up to the courts to decide, in every instance, whether a would-be rescuer would have incurred an unacceptable cost had he attempted the rescue, and whether his assessment of the risks attendant

---

[9] See H. M. Malm, 'Liberalism, Bad Samaritan, and Legal Paternalism', *Ethics* 106 (1995): 4–31; 'Bad Samaritan Laws: Harm, Help, or Hype?', *Law and Philosophy* 19 (2000): 707–50. The scenarios described in the next paragraph are taken from the latter and former pieces respectively. For the view that the legal right to being rescued should be narrowly defined, see D. Miller, 'But are they *My* Poor?', in J. Seglow (ed.), *The Ethics of Altruism* (London: Frank Cass, 2004).

on the rescue was plausible. In many cases, or so Malm argues, courts will end up penalizing individuals who were not, in fact, under a moral duty to rescue.

Malm makes her case by way of several examples, the following two of which are, in her view, particularly compelling. Suppose I nearly drowned ten years ago, and that I now find it extraordinarily difficult to get into the water; suppose further that I alone witness someone drowning, and that, paralysed by fear, I cannot bring myself to go to his rescue, even though rescuing him would be easy as the sea is very calm. As a result the imperilled swimmer dies. Should I be prosecuted? Should judges, or the jury, be lenient towards me? Suppose now that I have been attending weekly religious meditation meetings, without fail, for the last five years. It is crucially important to my understanding of the way in which I should lead my life, not only that I go to these meetings for the peace and comfort they bring me, but also that I unflinchingly commit myself to them. On my way to one such meeting, I drive past the scene of a car accident: I can see that the driver is slumped, motionless, over the wheel. There is no sign that emergency services are on the way. If I do stop and start helping, I will miss my meeting, so I speed along. In that scenario, there is no doubt that I would have incurred a high cost had I stopped. Again, what should the courts do? On what grounds can *they* decide that not missing one religious meeting is not important enough to justify my not helping?

In section 1.3.2, I noted that there are two kinds of claims one might invoke in order not to help someone in need. One might claim that, if one were to help, one would no longer have the all-purpose means necessary to lead a minimally flourishing life. One might also claim that, if one were to help, one would lose the means necessary to implement one's conception of the good, and that in turn would render one's life less than minimally flourishing. In the drowning and religious cases, I, as a potential rescuer, am not claiming that I need to have the full use of my body and person at all times, as an all-purpose means to implementing whatever conception of the good I have in mind. In fact, I can accept that I ought to lift a baby out of a small puddle, or that I should stop and help the car driver on my way *back* from my religious meeting. Rather, my claim is that being called upon to help *in those particular cases* would render my life less than minimally flourishing. Malm's point is that courts could not be expected to assess the validity of that claim.

Her pessimism is unwarranted. To be sure, in order to decide whether I should be exonerated from a duty to rescue in those two cases, we need to know more about the specifics of each. If I have become water-phobic as a result of nearly drowning ten years ago, it is likely that I should be able to claim, convincingly, that even if I simply could go into the water—by no means a given—I would experience such terror while attempting to rescue the swimmer that I could not really do a good job of it, indeed, that I would have run a serious risk of drowning myself. If I merely find it difficult, as opposed to quasi-impossible, to get into the water, I might not be able to make a convincing case for being exonerated from my duty to rescue. The courts might find, for example, that I was on some occasions able to swim, and might thus insist that my argument for not being able to do so on that particular occasion does not pass muster.

In the case where I do not rescue the imperilled because I want to attend a religious meeting, I simply could not say, without further ado, that my commitment to attending those meetings is so central to my life that it overrides the interest of the imperilled in being rescued. For, to reiterate a point made in section 1.3.2, individuals do not have a claim against others to be able to implement whatever conception of the good gives most meaning to their life; they have a claim to be given the freedoms and wherewithal we all need to implement a conception of the good which gives some meaning to it. Accordingly, in that particular case, I would have to show that my life would lose all meaning if I failed to attend those religious meetings, even if I do so on only *one* occasion, *and* that, having thought rationally, and with critical distance about alternatives, there is no other conception of the good which I would rather have. It is very unlikely that I would be able to make such a case, particularly if my religious beliefs, which I am so keen to live up to by going to those meetings, include a requirement to help those in need (as most religions, as far as I am aware, do).

I cannot, within the scope of this chapter, go through the multifarious excuses individuals might wish to deploy in order to be exonerated from a duty to rescue the imperilled. Let me simply make three points. First, in Chapter 4, I shall assess conscientious objections to the confiscation of cadaver organs, and my points there can be brought to bear on the issue at hand here. Second, I concede that the fact that there is risk involved in helping, which there is not in paying taxes, complicates the issue of enforcement. Third, I accept that it is not easy to establish whether or not the cost of rescuing was too high. However, the fact that drawing the line between acceptable and unacceptable risks and acceptable and unacceptable costs is a difficult task does not entail that one can *never* make such assessment. In other areas of the law, the standard of reasonableness is constantly used so as to assess, precisely, the risks and costs attendant on particular courses of action. I do not see why it cannot be used here as well.[10] Consider self-defence: if I am attacked, I must assess what risk I would incur by not shooting back and reasoning with the attacker; and, if I kill him, I will be called upon to explain why I thought killing was the only response to the attack. Consider also standards for convicting someone of a criminal offence: juries are asked to convict only if they find the defendant guilty beyond *reasonable* doubt. Consider, further, cost assessment in the context of paying taxes: someone who refuses to pay them on the grounds that the importance of providing others with the resources they need is outweighed by the importance for him of subsidizing a religious group is unlikely to be met with sympathy by judges. By contrast, judges might be inclined to be lenient (in fact, in the UK, have been lenient) towards needy individuals who

---

[10] For a similar argument, see J. Feinberg, *Harm to Others*, pp. 156–7.

refused to pay the poll tax on the grounds that they would not, as a result, be able to pay for heating in the winter.

Judges, then, do assess costs and risks on a regular basis, and therefore there does not seem to be any good reason not to ask them to do so when applying a Bad Samaritan law. Malm remains unmoved by such considerations, for the following reason: if judges make a mistake of judgment, and end up convicting someone who in fact was not under a moral duty to rescue (for the cost in her case was indeed too high), they will unfairly impose a penalty on her. The prospect of unfair convictions presents us with a dilemma. If we make the penalty light, i.e. a £100 fine, so as to alleviate the effects of unfair convictions, we send the wrong signal to genuinely Bad Samaritans, since we are, in effect, telling them that their failure to rescue is not that reprehensible—that it is less reprehensible, for example, than stealing a car, for which one can incur a jail sentence. If we do make failures to perform easy rescues punishable by a jail sentence (as is the case in France) in order to impress on them that their failure to rescue is very serious, we risk sending innocent people to jail.[11]

Again, one cannot but concede that such problems are serious, and may arise should duties of Good Samaritanism be enforced. But they also arise in other areas of criminal law, such as homicide. The risk of wrongfully convicting someone for murder is a good reason to oppose capital punishment; it clearly is not a good reason to oppose any kind of punishment whatsoever. Similarly, the risk of wrongfully convicting someone for failure to rescue may, indeed should, deter us from imposing harsh sentences, but it should not deter us from imposing any sentence at all. I cannot, in this chapter, offer guidelines as to which tariff would enable us to avoid being impaled on either horn of the dilemma. My aim, in any event, was more modest: it was merely to show that one has good reasons to confer on the state the moral power to enforce individuals' rights to be rescued.

2.4 CONCLUSION

To conclude, the imperilled have a right to being rescued against would-be rescuers provided that the latter would not run an unreasonable risk of incurring an unreasonable cost. Duties to rescue the imperilled, moreover, are not merely moral duties; they are duties of justice, owed to the imperilled themselves, protective of their fundamental interest in leading a minimally flourishing life. Or so should think liberal proponents of coercive taxation for the purpose of providing the needy with the material resources they need in order to lead such a life: for, as I have argued here, the use of our whole body, as deployed in rescue attempts, is a resource, and a scarce one at that, over which conflicts arise between those who need it and those who are in a position to offer it.

---

[11]   Malm, 'Bad Samaritan Laws', at 744.

3

A Civilian Service

3.1 INTRODUCTION

As discussed in Chapter 2, if one is committed to holding the comparatively wealthy under a duty to provide material resources to the needy, one is also committed to holding individuals under a duty of justice to provide a personal service of rescue to the imperilled. However, it seems that the very same considerations that dictate in favour of both duties also dictate, at least at first sight, in favour of a duty to provide more demanding services to those who need them. Imagine, for example, someone who would make a very good doctor, but would rather work as a poet. Should she not contribute to helping the needy by doing the former, rather than fulfil her own ambition? Conflicts between the requirements of distributive justice and freedom of occupational choice have exercised a number of philosophers, most notably radical egalitarians. On the whole, radical egalitarians believe that whilst one can demand of individuals that they help the needy by way of resource transfers, one cannot demand of them that they help them by entering a socially useful career, on pain of violating their freedom of occupational choice. In so arguing, they seem to assume that strictures on that particular freedom, other than those grounded in merit, are unacceptable.

In section 3.2, I argue that the theory of justice which I take as my starting point disallows the conscription of the talented into careers not of their own choosing, no matter how much they would thereby help the needy; but it does require that all able-bodied members of society perform, for a short time, some sort of civilian service—that is, work, for some time, as helpers in schools, hospitals, nursing homes, and so forth. Proposals for a short-term civilian service have elicited a number of objections, which I shall rebut in section 3.3.

3.2 JUSTICE AND THE IDEA OF A CIVILIAN SERVICE

As noted above, many radical egalitarians believe that one cannot force the talented to work for the sake of the worse off. Imagine the case of someone, call him Andrew, who could earn a very good living as a doctor, thereby contributing a substantial amount, by way of taxation, to collective wealth. As it happens, Andrew would much rather work as a gardener—a job he loves, but which pays little, and correspondingly contributes less to collective wealth. Is Andrew under a moral obligation, at the bar of justice, to work as a doctor?

One radical egalitarian, to wit, Joseph Carens, believes that justice requires of Andrew that he work as a doctor. According to Carens, a just society is one where individuals are given equal shares of material resources, and where they believe that they have a social duty to earn as much pre-tax net income as possible, so as to contribute to increasing the size of each share. On Carens's view, then, someone who could work either as a doctor, thereby contributing substantially to the tax yield, or as a gardener, thereby contributing hardly anything, would choose to do the former, rather than the latter: in such a society, the demands of equality are met without violating its members' freedom of occupational choice.[1] If Carens's argument is correct, it applies, *mutatis mutandis*, to justice understood not as requiring an equal distribution of material resources, but as requiring only that individuals have enough resources to have prospects for a minimally flourishing life. For, if the only way to meet the requirements of justice so understood is for Andrew to become a doctor, thereby yielding higher tax returns, then not only is Andrew under a moral duty to do so; if society is just, he himself believes that he is under such a duty.

Note that Carens assesses people's occupational choices relative to the tax returns which those choices yield; it is not clear whether, on his view, Andrew would have to work as a doctor, not so as to contribute to the maximum of his abilities to the collective wealth, but because his doctoring skills are needed. The overwhelming majority of liberals would argue that he is not under such a moral obligation, and a fortiori that he should not be *made* to work as a doctor. Indeed, some of them would point out that to make him do so would be tantamount to enslaving him.[2] Quite obviously, however, in so far as to be a slave means that one has no right over oneself, and in so far as Andrew would nevertheless retain some such rights even if forced to work as a doctor, he would not be enslaved. Still, to hold him under an obligation to work as a doctor, and a fortiori to make him do so, would amount to denying him freedom of occupational choice and would thereby place serious constraints on his ability to pursue his conception of the good life.

---

[1] See J. Carens, *Equality, Moral Incentives and the Market* (Chicago: Chicago University Press, 1987). Carens recognizes, of course, that trade-offs between doing one's social duty and maximizing one's leisure time and/or one's job satisfaction will occur. However, he believes that in an egalitarian society where individuals are socialized into believing that they are under an obligation to earn as much pre-tax income as they are capable of earning, the incentive to do one's social duty will be strong enough to lead individuals to take the relevant jobs, just as, in a private property-market society, the incentive to maximize one's income is strong enough to lead individuals to work in the relevant jobs.

[2] Judging by his treatment of the view that individuals' skills and labour should be auctionable, Dworkin is quite likely to regard making Andrew work as a doctor as an instance of slavery. See R. Dworkin, 'What is Equality? Part II: Equality of Resources', at 304–5. For a superb criticism of Dworkin's view, see M. Cohen-Christofidis, 'Talent, Slavery and Envy', in J. Burley (ed.), *Dworkin and His Critics* (Oxford: Blackwell, 2004).

Now, you recall that, on the theory of justice I defended in Chapter 1, individuals have a right against third parties to the material resources they need in
order to lead a minimally flourishing life, provided that the well off would not
jeopardize their own prospects for such a life by so helping. Once they have satisfied that requirement, however, the well off in turn have the right to use the
fruits of their labour as they see fit, most notably in order to implement their own
conception of the good. It should be clear that justice so understood disallows
conscripting the able-bodied into particular jobs for the sake of the needy. For, to
the extent that those whose talents are such that they could help by way of doing
certain jobs would hate having to do those jobs, and to the extent that there is
something soul-destroying about doing a job that one hates for forty-odd years,
justice cannot require of them that they do so. A sufficientist theory of justice
is in agreement with radical egalitarians, then, when insisting that freedom of
occupational choice should not be undermined. However, to ensure that it is not
undermined does not commit us to ensuring that it is not in any way curtailed.
As we shall now see, sufficiency requires that all able-bodied individuals perform
a civilian service.

The idea of a civilian service is not new. In countries such as the USA, for
example, it has a long and distinguished pedigree. Most famously, perhaps,
William James argues in his 1910 essay 'The Moral Equivalent of War' that many
of the virtues associated with military service, such as courage and a strong sense
of duty, could be fostered by a national civilian service.[3] More recently, a number of American academics and policy-makers have revived this idea. The best
known of such proposals by an academic has been advanced by Charles Moskos,
who advocates a national, voluntary service, whereby young people would give
one year of their time to work in, for example, schools, hospitals, prisons, and
day-care centres. In exchange they would receive a subsistence wage, and health
and life insurance while serving, and generous educational and job-training benefits on completion of their service.[4] In a similar vein, in 1989, Senator Nunn and
Congressman McCurdy introduced a bill with the support of the Democratic
Leadership Council, whereby young people would perform a civic service and, in
return, would receive a weekly stipend and health insurance for the duration of
their service, as well as substantial federal aid towards college fees, deposit for a
house, or job-training afterwards.[5]

Proposals for a civilian service such as those abound in the relevant literature,
and I shall not review all of them here.[6] Suffice it to say that they share, by and

[3] W. James, 'The Moral Equivalent of War', *International Conciliation* 27 (1910): 8–20.
[4] C. Moskos, *A Call to Civic Service—National Service for Country and Community* (New York:
Free Press, 1988).
[5] A watered down version of that bill, which severed the link between educational aid and civilian
service, was passed in 1990 under the title 'National and Community Service Act of 1990'.
[6] For an interesting review of those proposals as well as of existing service programmes in the
USA, see J. Perry and A. Thomson, *Civic Service: What Difference does it Make?* (New York: Armonk,

large, the following two features. First, they are proposals for a *voluntary* service, albeit with material incentives in the form of educational and housing grants, and, on some variants, political incentives such as the right to vote.[7] Second, with one or two exceptions, they defend the service by invoking the benefits accruing to those who serve, the necessity of fostering a sense of community in an era driven by self-interest and solipsism, and (relatedly) the desirability of instilling in each and every citizen a strong sense of civic duty.

My proposal for a civilian service differs from the aforementioned suggestions in both respects. At the bar of justice, or so I contend, the needy have a *right* that the able-bodied provide them with (some of) the personal services they need in order to have prospects for a minimally flourishing life, if their needs cannot be met otherwise. In such cases, performing such a service not only is morally mandatory but should be made legally so, on the grounds, not that it would foster a strong sense of community and civic duty amongst the servers, but that the needs of the badly off are pressing. To be sure, it may well be that civilian conscripts would benefit considerably from helping the needy. It may also be that a civilian service such as one defended here would foster amongst its actors a strong sense of civic duty. Indeed, as we shall see in section 3.3, such considerations will help defuse some of the objections raised against a mandatory civilian service. However, the justification I offer presently in its favour appeals to the needs of the badly off.

As we saw in section 1.3.2, at the bar of sufficiency, the badly off have rights against the comparatively well off to the resources they need in order to lead a minimally flourishing life. More specifically, to name but a few of the policies which would be required, a just society is one where the basic needs of very poor people are met by providing them with enough food, safe water, decent shelter, adequate transport, and minimum health care. It is also one where individuals all have enough resources to take up some of the available opportunities for a minimally flourishing life and to engage in forward-planning; and where the needy have access to social services such as health and family planning clinics.

Advocates of such policies standardly assume that the obligations under which the well off are to provide those goods and services can only be discharged via taxation, and that it is incumbent upon governments to use tax yields to pay for health-care professionals and equipment, social services staff, and so on. However, the returns from taxation are unlikely to suffice—indeed, we already know that they do not suffice. For, although governments may be willing to pay for the provision of certain services, vacancies in nursing, housing, and social care in general show that too few individuals are willing to work in those sectors, for reasons ranging from low pay to unattractive work conditions. Moreover, in

2004). For a similar review in the UK, Canada, and Germany, see Moskos, *A Call to Civic Service*, pp. 183–8.

[7] For the latter view, see R. Dagger, 'Republican Virtue, Liberal Freedom and the Problem of Civic Service', unpublished typescript.

many cases governments are unwilling to pay in the first instance: for example, they are unwilling to pay for extra staff to help the very elderly to live at home rather than in institutions, to read to the newly blind, to help children with behavioural difficulties adjust at school, to provide those who have to care full-time for a dependant with much-needed relief, and so on.

At this juncture, of course, some might be tempted to argue that, in a just society, taxation should be set high enough to allow governments to offer better pay and working conditions for social services and health-care staff. In such a society, however, it might nevertheless remain the case that, given the resources needed to pay for those services, taxes would have to be raised to such an extent as to deny the well off prospects for a minimally flourishing life. Moreover, even if it were possible to raise taxes to the levels required by the provision of the aforementioned services, levying personal services from the able-bodied might still provide a cheaper alternative, and enable us to use the extra taxes thus raised in better, more efficient, ways. Finally, it may well be that, no matter how high the (tax-financed) material incentives for people to embark on careers in, say, nursing and social care, there simply will not be enough takers for those jobs. It is against that background, then, that the question of the legitimacy of asking the able-bodied to provide personal services to the needy arises.

Now, as we saw in Chapter 2, it is appropriate to think of personal services in general as something which can, and does, fall within the remit of justice. In other words, the very same considerations which justify holding the well off under an obligation to help the needy by way of taxation, and the able-bodied under an obligation to help the imperilled, also justify holding the able-bodied under an obligation to help the needy by way of personal services. If the requirement that people have prospects for a minimally flourishing life is pressing enough to confer on them welfare rights to material resources and rights to emergency rescues, it is, at first sight at least, pressing enough to confer on them rights to personal services as well.

There are differences, of course, between providing emergency rescues and providing personal services of the kind I have in mind. As we shall see in section 3.3, however, those differences are not such as to undermine the view that the able-bodied are under an obligation to provide the latter, as well as the former. Pending argument to that effect, it is worth outlining in greater detail the kind of service which sufficiency requires. The model that comes the closest to my proposal is the German system for conscientious objectors.[8] Young German men who refuse to do their compulsory military service on conscientious grounds have to perform a nine-month-long civilian service (equal in length to its military counterpart), before which they receive basic training in care and nursing, and during which they are paid a subsistence wage and receive health insurance.

---

[8] I am very grateful to Alex Leveringhaus for providing me with extensive information about the German civilian service.

The jobs offered are typically in the social care and health sectors, and range from cleaning hospital beds and shopping for the housebound to working with severely autistic children. In a similar vein, on the view I defend here, every able-bodied eighteen-year-old (an age when people are unlikely to have demanding commitments such as raising children[9]) should, after appropriate training, serve for one year in one of the following areas: work in mental institutions, help with the care of long-term patients such as Alzheimer's and AIDS sufferers, care for the homeless and the elderly, help with the provision of adequate transport for the disabled and the aged, assist schoolchildren with their homework if their parents are unable or unwilling to do so, and so on. This list is not exhaustive, of course, but it gives an indication of the kind of work which civilian conscripts would be expected to do, and in return for which they would be paid a subsistence wage.

The foregoing thoughts invite some additional comments. First, it might seem as if my claim that the able-bodied are under an obligation to perform a civilian service along the lines sketched above is, in fact, a claim that they are under an obligation to society as a whole to support just institutions such as health-care services and care for the elderly. That is not so. For we are under a moral duty, at the bar of justice, to give some help to our bedridden neighbour, even if there is no such thing as institutionalized help for the elderly; and if there is such a thing, we are under such moral duty *to* our neighbour, not to welfare services. To be sure, we may well need welfare services in order to fulfil our duty to do the kind of jobs that a civilian service would provide. But the fact that just institutions are needed for the efficient implementation of the duty to perform a civilian service implies neither that we are under such a duty only if there are such institutions, nor that we are under such a duty to society as whole.

Second, civilian conscripts would not get the educational aid which many current proposals for a civilian service provide. Such aid is standardly meant as an incentive for young people to volunteer. But, on my view, in so far as all able-bodied individuals would have to serve, no such incentives are needed. Of course, one may wonder why a compulsory system is preferable to a voluntary system with incentives such that most people would, in fact, be willing to serve.

There are two reasons in support of compulsion—one moral, and the other practical. From a moral point of view, to make the provision of help voluntary with incentives attached would enable the very well off to opt out from contributing, and would place the burden of helping squarely on the shoulders of those who cannot afford not to take up those incentives. To be sure, the latter would

---

[9] Some eighteen-year-old individuals do have burdensome family commitments which would prevent them from discharging their obligation to provide personal services to the needy. Teenage single mothers come to mind, for example. In such cases, one could either allow them to defer their service until such time as they can do so without ill effect on their children, or enable them to discharge their obligation by, for example, serving one day a month over a much longer period of time. Quite obviously, which proposal to adopt would depend, in large part, on the availability of affordable child care.

benefit from, say, educational grants. It is unfair, though, to allocate such grants on the basis of willingness to serve as opposed to financial needs, and thereby to exonerate the well off from contributing. After all, taxes towards supporting the needy are to be paid by all: by the same token, personal services for the same purposes ought to be provided by all.[10] Moreover, from a practical point of view, it is easier to administer a compulsory service than a voluntary one, since in the former case, unlike in the latter, numbers of participants can be known in advance, and dealt with more efficiently.[11]

The foregoing needs qualifying in the following way. Although there is a strong case for making the civilian service compulsory, the following scenario suggests that, in some cases, some well-off individuals who are called upon to help might be able to avoid such service. Suppose that such an individual offers, instead, to pay for the cost of hiring someone to serve in his place. Should he be allowed to do so?[12] As is well known, a system of that sort—buying one's way out of military conscription—was in place in a number of countries, such as France and the USA, in the nineteenth century. As is also well known, it was opposed by many on the grounds that the rich were able to avoid running the risk of being killed at the expense of the poor. By the same token, many would object to my proposal on the ground that the well off can thus buy themselves out of having to provide personal services—an opportunity not afforded to the less well off. In fact, from the point of view of the needy, whether that well-off individual helps or pays someone to do it does not matter. And in so far as it is the plight of the needy which justifies holding the able-bodied under an obligation to provide personal services, then it seems that one can be allowed to help them by paying someone to serve in one's place. Note, though, that this does not undermine my case for a compulsory civilian service in the instance where there would not be enough individuals willing to work in the relevant areas (nursing, social care, etc.), even though they would be highly paid.

Third, it might also seem as if my proposal for a civilian service simply extends arguments for military conscription to civilians.[13] But, although both kinds of conscription are similar in one important respect, they are very dissimilar in another, no less important, way. They are similar in that they both hold *all* able-bodied individuals under a duty to provide personal services—in one

[10] In his *Spheres of Justice*, Walzer argues along similar lines for the view that society's dirty work (e.g. cleaning in hospitals) should be shared by all. See M. Walzer, *Spheres of Justice* (Oxford: Blackwell, 1983), ch. 6.

[11] E. Gorham, *National Service, Citizenship, and Political Education* (New York: State University of New York Press, 1992), p. 40.

[12] I am grateful to Richard Dagger for raising this issue.

[13] I will not examine which tensions may arise between a mandatory civilian service and military conscription. I shall simply note that *if* the latter is desirable (which, in many countries at least, is doubtful under current warfare conditions), one could offer conscripts the choice between serving in the army and serving in civilian institutions. Should the numbers of military conscripts become alarmingly low, one could provide greater incentives to serve in the army—and vice versa.

instance military; in the other civilian. They differ in that whereas the duty to serve in the army can most convincingly be justified on the grounds that national defence is a non-excludable public good (and to which we should therefore all contribute), the duty to provide personal services to the needy is best justified on the grounds of the latter's needs. For, although most of us do benefit to a greater degree from living in a society in which neediness is considerably reduced than we would benefit from living in one which abandons the needy to their plight, not all of us so benefit. Those who reside in exclusive mansions on London's Bishops Avenue or Manhattan's Upper East Side, and who can avail themselves of private health care, would be financially better off if they did not have to pay taxes towards a public, national health-care system for the benefit of the needy. To justify the duty to help by appealing to the fact that duty-holders benefit from so helping would imply, counter-intuitively, that the very well off, who are the least likely to benefit, ought not to have to help. It would also imply, no less counter-intuitively, that the very vulnerable, those from whose improving prospects we are least likely to benefit, have a much weaker claim to be helped.

Fourth, my argument for a civilian service rests on the claim, already deployed in Chapter 2, that personal services are relevantly analogous to material resources. In Chapters 4 and 5, I shall argue in a similar fashion for the view that, under conditions to be specified therein, the needy—in that instance the medically needy—have rights to the body parts of the able-bodied, dead or alive. At this stage, it is useful to bring out some similarities and differences between the provision of material resources via taxation, personal services, and body parts. Those in a position to help the needy by providing material resources, to wit, the well off, discharge their obligation to do so by contributing the same good, to wit, money, which is then 'converted' into whatever resources are required (income, housing, medical treatment, etc.); and they do so to different degrees, depending on their income. Moreover, in so far as they all do so, the burden of helping is shared by all, if not equally.

Compare the foregoing with the provision of rescue services and body parts. Those in a position so to help the needy, or the sick, to wit, the able-bodied, discharge their obligation by providing precisely that which is required, for example, swimming out to rescue a drowning person, or providing bone marrow. But although similar in that respect, the obligation to give blood on the one hand, and the obligation to provide rescue services or an organ on the other hand, differ in another, important, way. Whereas the former is discharged by all healthy individuals (as I shall argue in Chapter 5), the latter always falls upon a specific individual, to wit, not upon all good swimmers, but upon whichever good swimmer happens to be on the beach when the imperilled individual is in danger of drowning; not upon all healthy potential bone-marrow donors, but upon whichever healthy individual whose bone marrow is a match for a leukaemia sufferer.

As should be clear by now, the obligation to provide personal services by way of a civilian service is similar to the obligation to pay taxes or to give blood, in that just as the obligation to pay taxes befalls all the comparatively well off, the obligation to provide personal services, like the obligation to give blood, befalls all the able-bodied. In that respect, then, it differs from the obligation to provide a rescue service or an organ. It broadly resembles it, however, in that it too is discharged by way of providing whichever specific services are required (helping Alzheimer's sufferers, working with disabled children, etc.). I say 'broadly', for the following reason: in the case of Good Samaritanism, we know, from the fact that D is drowning and that S_w, a strong swimmer, happens to be on the beach, that D has a right against S_w. Similarly, we know, from the fact that P needs bone marrow and that Q is a match, that the former has a right against the latter that he help him (or so I shall argue in section 5.2). Contrastingly, in the case of personal services, all we know is that C will have to provide some specific personal services to some individual(s) who need(s) them. In so far as those services do not require specific skills, as the needs to be met are different, and as there is a vast number of civilian conscripts, we cannot, on principle, individuate the obligation to help. Thus, it does not follow from the fact that A has Alzheimer's disease and that C happens to be eighteen and is due to do her civilian service, that A has a right against C that she help him. A has that right only once a decision is made that C will help him.

The foregoing points raise the question of the way in which personal services ought to be distributed, as it were, amongst civilian conscripts. One can either ask each conscript to express a preference for a particular kind of job (as is the case in Germany), or one can allocate the jobs to be done randomly. Matching jobs with those who would like to do them is more likely to ensure that personal services will be provided adequately than random allocation would do; but it is less likely to ensure that the least popular slots would be filled. Whichever procedure is chosen, it would seem fair to offer some sort of compensation to those who, whether by choice or as a result of the lottery, would end up providing the most demanding and less rewarding personal services. Note, though, that the rationale for offering such compensation is not that it would provide an incentive for people to volunteer to offer such services, even though it might, as a matter of fact, do just that; rather, its rationale is roughly to equalize the burdens and benefits accruing to civilian conscripts.

3.3 OBJECTIONS TO A CIVILIAN SERVICE

Opponents of civilian service standardly deploy six criticisms (some of which, incidentally, apply to the idea of a voluntary service where the incentives to serve would be so high that vast numbers of people would volunteer):

(A) A mandatory service of the kind I have advocated would signal the end of volunteerism and altruism.

(B) In so far as it would consist in doing jobs which no one wants to do, it would bespeak a considerable lack of respect for the conscripts.

(C) It would constitute an unacceptable interference in young people's lives.

(D) It would have undesirable effects on the job market.

(E) Although it aims at meeting needs, as dictated by the sufficiency principle, it would in fact have undesirable effects on society's ability to meet the requirements set by that principle.

(F) It would be an organizational and budgetary nightmare.

In this section, I rebut each of those six objections and, in the course of doing so, somewhat qualify my proposal for a mandatory civilian service and flesh out in greater detail some of its practical features.

(A): Volunteerism, whereby individuals volunteer to perform socially useful tasks in exchange for money, and altruism, whereby they are willing to do those tasks without material rewards, are standardly thought to be highly desirable individual and social features.[14] As we shall see in section 6.3.1, they are often invoked to rebut the view that individuals should be allowed to sell their organs. But they are also used to reject the claim that they should be made to contribute to society's efforts by way of personal services, in exchange for a subsistence wage. The best argument to that effect holds that if the aim of a civilian service is to create, and foster, citizens' civic virtue, then a voluntary and altruistic service is more likely to do the job than a compulsory one.[15] That may be true. But if, as I have argued, the aim of such a service is to help the needy, and if the rationale for making it compulsory is the same as the reason why contributions in cash, via taxation, should be made compulsory, then the claim that making it compulsory would fail to instill civic virtues is irrelevant. In fact, it seems to prove too much, since it would imply, by the same token, that taxation should be voluntary. To be sure, one could argue (with libertarians) that personal contributions and contributions in cash should never be coercively taken. But to the extent that liberal opponents of a mandatory civilian service disagree with the libertarian position regarding taxation, they must explain why compulsory taxation poses little or no threat to altruism and volunteerism, and thereby to civic virtues, whereas a compulsory civilian service does. I cannot think of any convincing argument to that effect.

---

[14] Although volunteerism is standardly defined as the practice of volunteering to do socially useful tasks for free, it is important, in the context of this chapter, to distinguish that practice from that of volunteering to do socially useful tasks for which one may get material rewards (for example in the form of a wage). That latter practice I call 'volunteerism', whereas the former I call 'altruism'.

[15] See, e.g., Dagger, 'Republican Virtue, Liberal Freedom and the Problem of Civic Service'; B. Chapman, 'Politics and National Service: A Virus Attacks the Voluntary Sector', in W. M. Evers (ed.), *National Service: Pro and Con* (Stanford: Hoover Institution Press, 1990).

To be clear: I am not denying (and indeed no one denies) that it is more desirable that people should volunteer to do those jobs than be made to do so. The problem, of course, is that people are simply *not* volunteering to do them, let alone for free. To insist on the importance of volunteerism and altruism in the face of such apathy seems odd. Moreover, and most importantly, what is desirable about volunteerism and altruism need not be lost with the introduction of a compulsory civilian service. For to volunteer to work with an Alzheimer's sufferer is not, or at least not only, to do so even though one does not have to do it: it is to do so *irrespective of the fact* that one may have to do it. To work with an Alzheimer's sufferer in an altruistic spirit is not, or not only, to do so even though one does it for free: it is to do so *irrespective of the fact* that one does reap rewards—material or otherwise—from it. Accordingly, one can volunteer to perform a task, and do it altruistically, even though one is under a duty to do it. The claim that a legally mandatory civilian service would undermine altruism and volunteerism, thus, leaves untouched my argument that all able-bodied individuals are under a moral obligation to serve at the bar of justice.

(B): It is sometimes argued against the idea of a compulsory civilian service (or, indeed, a large-scale voluntary programme with strong incentives attached) that it is disrespectful of those who would serve, since they would have to do menial jobs which no one wants to do—jobs which neither governments nor markets want to do, or can fill, and thus which are 'not worth paying for'. This objection is particularly potent, at least at first sight, if it is stipulated that civilian conscripts can only take up positions which are not already filled, and if it is the case that conscripts would have to be allocated to meaningless tasks as there are more conscripts than jobs to be filled.[16] On closer inspection, however, the objections fails to distinguish between jobs which are not worth paying for (for example, paper-pushing), and jobs which are worth paying for but which can be funded via taxation only at the cost of more urgent needs, or which are so expensive to fund that those who need them simply cannot afford them via the market. In addition, if it turns out that there are fewer socially meaningful jobs than available conscripts in any one year, one can decide who will discharge their obligation to provide personal services to the needy through a lottery, with appropriate compensation given to those who end up being selected to do the least meaningful jobs.

(C): The third objection to compulsory civilian service, that it constitutes an unacceptable interference in conscripts' life, has two variants. On the most

[16] See, e.g., D. Bandow, 'National Service Initiatives', in Evers (ed.), *National Service*.

strongly worded variant, a compulsory civilian service is tantamount to holding the young in slavery. As one commentator puts it, '[in] effect, all adolescents become slaves for several years doing the dirty work of society'.[17] In addition, those who reject the idea of a compulsory service seem particularly worried about the kind of punishment which objectors to the service would incur: what makes the proposal particularly close to slavery, in their view, is that it could only be enforced effectively if objectors are imprisoned—just as army deserters are generally liable to custodial sentences.

Neither claim is convincing. To reiterate a point made in section 3.2, whether one is a slave is determined by the rights one enjoys, or lacks, over oneself. True, civilian conscripts would lack, for one year, the right to do only the kind of work they want (and for which they are qualified) as well as, obviously, the right not to work at all; they would also lack the right to get a market wage for doing the job they would be compelled to do. However, conscription into a civilian service cannot in any way be deemed slavery. For a start, as we also saw in section 3.2, to claim that individuals are under a duty to provide personal services to those who need them does not necessarily mean that they have no choice whatsoever in the kind of service they should provide. Moreover, whereas a slave works entirely at the behest of his master, conscripts are not under a duty to do whatever their employers wish them to do: in every respect, other than the fact that they have to work and are not entitled to receive market wages, conscripts have a right to be treated like any other employees. In addition, they still retain a considerable range of rights over themselves, such as freedom of expression, reproductive freedom, freedom of movement, and so on. To claim that compulsion alone is enough to turn a civilian service into the enslavement of the young is silly if meant literally, and singularly unhelpful if meant rhetorically.

The worry that those who refuse to serve might end up in jail is more understandable. Having said that, the claim that the able-bodied are under an obligation of justice to the needy to provide them with personal services in no way implies that they should be imprisoned should they fail to do so. One could, in fact, stipulate that defaulters should pay a heavy fine, and that jail sentences should be used as a very last resort—just as they are used as a very last resort against those who fail to pay taxes.

A more interesting objection to compulsory civilian service holds, not that it is tantamount to enslaving the young, but that it constitutes a very serious interference in their lives, in two ways. First, one might be tempted to argue, to actually provide a service to the ill, the elderly, or children in difficulty, can be very demanding physically and psychologically—much more demanding indeed than paying taxes. Second, one might also be tempted to argue, to hold the able-bodied under a duty to perform a civilian service amounts to unacceptably

---

[17] See, e.g., M. Anderson, 'Comment: The Dirty Work Philosophy of National Service', in Evers (ed.), *National Service*, p. 247.

denying them the right to choose how to spend their time for a year, as well as the right to earn what the market would enable them to earn.

The objection from interference, thus, highlights the burdens incurred by the able-bodied with respect to the process of providing services as well as the costs they incur as a result of providing services. It is more interesting than the objection from slavery, not only because it seems to undermine the analogy between material resources and personal services on which my case for a civilian service rests, but also because it appeals to one of the values which underpin my argument in this book, namely, that of individual autonomy. If it is correct, if, that is, holding the able-bodied under an obligation of justice to provide personal services to the needy constitutes a very serious interference with their life in the aforementioned two ways, then it might well be that the idea of a civilian service is inconsistent with the ideal of individual autonomy—and, in turn, with the requirement that individuals be treated with the respect they are owed as persons.

However, although there is no doubt that providing personal services can be quite demanding, and more so than filling out a tax return, that fact alone cannot justify opposing the idea of a civilian service; nor can the fact that they would be temporarily denied freedom of occupational choice do so either. Some may maintain, of course, that no one should ever be made to do anything remotely difficult for the sake of helping others. I rejected that claim in Chapter 1, and shall not return to it. What matters here, then, is the extent to which having to serve for one year would interfere with conscripts' life.

Now, as I argued in that first chapter, those in a position to help the needy are under an obligation to do so provided that their prospects for a minimally flourishing life would not be jeopardized. If that is correct, then the interference objection to a civilian service suffers from the following weaknesses: first, in so far as conscripts will receive a subsistence wage, they will not fall below the poverty threshold; and, second, as a reply to the claim that the *process* of providing personal services is too demanding, although conscripts will in all likelihood do difficult and demanding work, they will also learn considerably from it. Indeed, studies on the outcomes of various civic programmes in the USA report that the overwhelming majority of volunteers regard their experience in very positive terms.[18] Of course, it may well be that, had they been conscripted into those programmes, they would not have benefited from doing such work to the same degree; but it is unlikely that they would not have benefited at all. As I argued in section 3.2, that conscripts would benefit from performing such work is not the most pertinent justification for a civilian service; it does, however, undermine the charge that the civilian service constitutes too much of an interference in their lives.

Third, as a reply to the claim that the *loss* of their personal services for their own ends as incurred by conscripts would be too high, it is utterly implausible,

---

[18] For a review of such studies, see Perry and Thomson, *Civic Service*, ch. 5.

I submit, on the one hand to endorse coercive taxation, and on the other hand to hold that holding the able-bodied under a duty of justice to serve for one year renders their life less than minimally flourishing. For it is entirely unclear that having to pay taxes to the tune of 25 per cent to 50 per cent of one's income in the course of one's life constitutes less of an interference than having to provide personal services—for which one will be paid—for one year. To put the point differently, it is entirely implausible that the loss of time and resources a conscript would suffer for one year is more burdensome than the loss of resources taxpayers suffer, particularly if they provide less stressful forms of care than working with Alzheimer's patients and AIDS sufferers. At best, then, the objection from interference tells, not against holding the able-bodied under a duty to provide personal services, but against holding them under a duty to provide specific kinds of such services.

Finally, once one has taken on board the benefits accruing to the needy from constraining the able-bodied to provide them with personal services, the case against the interference objection seems unanswerable. To put it starkly, to hold that an eighteen-year-old ought not to be made to provide regular help to a bedridden patient on the grounds that it is more important that he get on with his studies or career than the latter be able to have a bath and eat properly, is to confer undue weight to the autonomy of the able-bodied, at the expense of the autonomy of the disabled. To reiterate a claim made in Chapter 1, in order to ensure that everybody has prospects for a minimally flourishing life, it is necessary to curtail, up to a point, the autonomy of those in a position to help them.

(D): Might it be the case, though, that although a compulsory civilian service would go a long way towards helping the needy, it would have highly detrimental effects on the economy? Some commentators believe that it would, in three ways: it would displace workers who would normally fill those jobs; it would depress their wages since conscripts would be paid below market rates; and it would deprive the economy of much-needed workers, since it would delay conscripts' entry into the workforce.[19] On the first count, it is essential to ensure that conscripts fill vacancies which would not otherwise be filled by either the public sector or the market. One way to do so is to stipulate (as most existing proposals for a large-scale civic service do) that the board or commission in charge of the service should include union representatives. On the second count, minimum wage legislation, properly drafted and implemented, would ensure that employers—private or public—could not invoke conscripts' low salaries as an argument to lower workers' wages. Finally, on the third count, it is unclear that the economic cost of delaying the young's entry into the workforce by one year would be

---

[19] W. Oi, 'National Service: Who Bears the Costs and Who Reaps the Gains?', in Evers (ed.), *National Service*.

so damaging as to outweigh the immense benefits accruing to the needy, all the more so as conscripts would, in the course of their service, acquire skills which might turn them into more productive, better, employees.

(E): Still, some critics would insist, even if a civilian service so designed would not suffer from the aforementioned weaknesses, it would nevertheless detract from the urgent goals of meeting more serious needs.[20] If that particular objection is correct, it is particularly damaging, since it invokes the principle of sufficiency to reject a proposal which, I argued, is mandated by that principle itself. Its proponents make the following three points: first, asking young people who would normally study towards socially useful careers such as medicine or social work to delay doing so by one year would create vacancies in those areas, as a result of which the needs of, say, patients and troubled children would not be met; second, the jobs which conscripts would be asked to do should be left to professionals, rather than to unskilled individuals who might jeopardize the health and welfare of those they are called upon to help; third, the resources used to fund the civilian service would be better spent training care professionals, financing housing for the homeless, raising the minimum income threshold, and so on.

Now, in reply to the first point, a properly structured civilian service could do either one of two things. It could either allow those conscripts who express a wish to, say, study medicine or social work, to discharge their obligation by doing jobs related to their course of study and by incorporating their service into the latter. Such is the case in Germany, where conscientious objectors who intend to go into medicine are assigned to work in hospitals, and can make their placement count towards their degree. Or those who wish to work in those sectors could be exonerated from spending a year as a civilian conscript before they embark on their chosen studies, but asked, once they are qualified as doctors, social workers, school teachers, and so on, to give some of their time against a small compensatory fee, on a regular basis, over the course of their career.

Assessing which of those two options would be best is beyond the scope of this chapter, so let me turn instead to the second strand of the objection under study, whereby professionals, rather than unskilled individuals, should perform the socially useful tasks I have in mind. By way of reply, it is not clear that highly developed skills are required to, for example, bathe a bedridden patient, help a housebound person with her meals and shopping, read to the blind, and help troubled children with their homework. It is true, however, that providing those services with the respect owed to the needy is quite difficult: bathing a bedridden patient is easy, doing so without offending her dignity is not.[21] But that is not

---

[20] Anderson, 'Comment: The Dirty Work Philosophy of National Service'.
[21] I am grateful for Alex Leveringhaus for pressing me on this point.

so much a matter of skill as a matter of attitude towards the kind of services one provides and the individuals to whom one provides it. It is likely, of course, that it would not do to entrust that enormously delicate task to a conscript who regards his service as a chore and bitterly resents having to do it. This, however, suggests, not that we should do away altogether with the view that the able-bodied are under a duty, at the bar of justice, to provide personal services to the needy; rather, it simply suggests that great care should be taken when deciding which kind of services should be provided to whom, and by whom.

Finally, in reply to the third strand of the objection, even if it is true that funding civilian conscripts would take resources away from, say, cancer treatments and social housing, this does not undermine the claim that the needy have a prima facie right that the able-bodied help them, any more than the claim that funding cancer treatments diminishes the resources available for housing, undermines the claim that cancer patients have a prima facie right to subsidized treatment—a right, that is, which ought to be respected, barring weighty considerations to the contrary such as the fact that other, needier individuals might have a more urgent claim to help.

(F): Last, but not least, let me examine the objection that implementing a mandatory civilian service would be an administrative nightmare and a budgetary folly: an administrative nightmare, because (or so it is claimed) it would be far too complicated for central government to summon every single young person in the country and allocate them to a socially useful job; and a budgetary folly (or so it is also claimed) because the costs of the service would vastly outstrip its benefits. Neither claim succeeds at undermining the idea of a mandatory civilian service. For a start, no one is suggesting that central government should get into the nitty-gritty business of matching conscripts and jobs. Here, again, the German example is useful: conscientious objectors apply for positions with hospitals, schools, day-care centres, and nursing homes (to name but a few of the participating institutions) and, if successful, inform the governmental authority that is in charge of civilian alternatives to the military service. In a similar vein, American advocates of a civilian service suggest that the task of matching volunteers with jobs should be entrusted to local institutions, such as city councils, charities, churches, and so on. In other words, central government should ensure that able-bodied eighteen-year-old individuals get 'called up', draft general guidelines for host institutions and services, fund conscripts, and act as an appeal forum in case of conflicts between the former and the latter; but it should leave the administrative specifics to already existing local institutions and organizations.

Not only would this greatly simplify the implementation of the service, but it would also save considerable amounts of money—which would go some way towards addressing the second of the aforementioned two claims, to the effect that a civilian service would be far too costly on collective resources. To alleviate such concerns further it is worth noting that studies on volunteer programmes in the USA suggest that their benefits outweigh their costs.[22]

3.4 CONCLUSION

In this chapter, we saw that, if one is committed to coercive taxation for the purpose of helping the needy, *and* to the view that the able-bodied are under a duty, at the bar of justice, to help the imperilled, one is also committed to holding them under a duty to provide personal services on a longer-term basis to those who need them. Personal services, on that view, are to be given not only in emergency situations, but also as a complement to material resources. None of the objections to a civilian service which we considered succeed in undermining the proposal, although they do drive home the point that not all the jobs which could potentially be done by conscripts ought to be allocated to them.

At this juncture, the following question arises, which for many, I am sure, would constitute an unanswerable claim against the proposal: if the able-bodied are under a duty to provide personal services in the ways suggested here and in the previous chapter, why not go even further, and hold them under a duty to divest themselves of their body parts for the sake of those who need them? Surely, many would think, my arguments so far commit me to that view; and in so far as that view simply cannot be correct (for does it not render individual autonomy nugatory?), it seems to follow that the needy and the imperilled do not have rights to personal services against the able-bodied. As I shall argue in the next two chapters, it is indeed the case that the very same considerations which support the rights of the needy and the imperilled to the material resources of the (comparatively) well off and the personal services of the able-bodied also support the rights of the sick to the body parts of the able-bodied. However, it is not the case that this particular implication of my arguments so far is so outlandish as to give us a reason to jettison them: as I shall show, one can confer on the needy and the imperilled rights to personal services and body parts against the able-bodied without thereby jeopardizing the value of individual autonomy.

[22] See Perry and Thomson, *Civic Service*, ch. 6.

4

Confiscating Cadaveric Organs

4.1 INTRODUCTION

Consider the following three scenarios:

1. Ann suffers from MS. If she does not get medical treatment, she will lead a less than minimally flourishing life.
2. Bob has been taken ill to hospital. If he does not get a blood transfusion, he will lead a less than minimally flourishing life.
3. Charles has been taken ill to hospital with liver failure. If he does not get a liver transplant, he will die.

Cases such as Ann's are discussed in great detail in the literature on distributive justice: cases such as Bob's and Charles's, hardly ever. Now, as we have seen, many theorists of distributive justice hold that the needy have a right, as a matter of justice, that well-off individuals give them the material resources they need in order to lead a minimally flourishing life, and in particular to be autonomous. Such a right, crucially for our purposes here, is standardly thought to include a right to health care. Accordingly, those theorists would claim that Ann has a prima facie right to the medicine she needs. However, the overwhelming majority of them would deny that Bob and Charles have a right, as a matter of justice, that the able-bodied give them the body parts they need in order to live a minimally flourishing life, or in order to survive. They would not deny, of course, that donating is morally commendable; in fact, they might even allow that not donating is morally wrong, when the sacrifice incurred by the donor is small and the benefits enjoyed by the recipients considerable. But even in such cases, they would maintain, the recipients do not have a *right* against potential donors that they donate. Yet, body parts are scarce, with devastating consequences for thousands of people, whose quality of life, indeed whose life *tout court*, depends on getting blood, bone marrow, or an organ.[1] To be sure, cloning, xenotransplantation, and the elaboration of sophisticated prostheses give us some reason

---

[1] For the latest statistics in the UK, see <http://www.uktransplants.org.uk>. For relevant statistics in the USA on organ transplants and blood donations, see <http://www.unos.org>, <http://www.rhsa.org>, and <http://www.census.org>. All the numerical data in this chapter and the next come from, or are calculated on the basis of, those sources.

to think that, in the not too distant future, patients who need new organs will not be dependent on the willingness of suppliers and (in the case of cadaveric organs) of their relatives. However, the technical and ethical problems posed by those various procedures are far from being solved: in the meantime, thousands of people throughout the world die every year, and many more lead a less than minimally flourishing life, whilst waiting for a transplant. Yet theorists of distributive justice are remarkably silent on this important and complicated issue. As to bioethicists, when discussing how organs should be obtained for donation purposes, they argue either that someone's expressed wishes with respect to the disposal of her organs should be respected, even posthumously, or that the wishes of her next-of-kin, in posthumous cases, should prevail, should the wishes of the deceased not be known, or even irrespective of her wishes.[2] Hardly anyone, however, argues that patients who need an organ should have a say. By contrast, and to reiterate, one of the central questions in discussions of distributive justice is that of the interest of the badly off in the financial assets of the well off.

Let us return to Bob and Charles: the former needs blood, which he can get from a live donor only; the latter needs a liver, which he can get from a dead or live donor. In this chapter, I focus on the confiscation of cadaveric organs: I aim to show that if one thinks that the poor's interest in leading a minimally flourishing life, and a fortiori in remaining alive, is important enough to confer on them a right to some of the material resources of the well off, by way of taxation and, in particular, by way of restrictions on bequests and inheritance, one must think that very same interest is important enough to confer on the sick a right to the organs of the now-dead able-bodied.[3] I make a case to that effect in section 4.2 and rebut two objections to it in section 4.3.

Before I start, let me delineate the scope of this chapter. The debate on *post-mortem* organ transplants revolves around three questions: when we can declare that someone is dead; how we should procure much-needed organs; who should get those organs. Here, I focus on the second question. To be sure, a *full* treatment of *post-mortem* organ transplants should address the first and, most importantly, the third. But we do not need to decide who, of the young and the old, of those with a good chance of recovery and those with a not so good chance, should get available organs, in order to decide how organs should be procured. Accordingly, I use the phrase 'the sick' as shorthand for 'whoever is eligible for transplants', assuming agreement on eligibility criteria. Focusing on

---

[2] For useful reviews of those arguments, see, e.g., P. Boddington, 'Organ Donation after Death—Should I decide, or Should My Family?', *Journal of Applied Philosophy* 15 (1998): 69–81; J. Muyskens, 'An Alternative Policy for Obtaining Cadaver Organs for Transplantation', *Philosophy and Public Affairs* 8 (1978): 88–99.

[3] By body parts, I shall mean internal organs such as kidneys, corneas, liver lobes, and pancreas, tissues such as bone marrow, and blood. I shall not consider limb transplants, which do not (yet) restore relevant bodily functions as well as prostheses do (see D. Dickensen and G. Widdershoven, 'Ethical Issues in Limb Transplants', *Bioethics* 15 (2001): 110–24).

the question of procurement and ignoring the issue of allocation should not prove too controversial: by the same token, whilst a fully developed theory of distributive justice, when applied to income and wealth, needs to decide how to allocate those resources amongst those in need, an argument for the view that those who are eligible for help have a right against the well off to such help does not hinge on the way we answer allocative questions.

Moreover, recall that my argument to the effect that the sick have a right to these organs of the dead is located in ideal theory. By implication, this gives rise to the following two, important, assumptions: first, individuals fulfil their obligations to one another, and, accordingly, the needy actually have access to the material resources they need in order to lead a minimally flourishing life; and, second, doctors neither actively try to hasten someone's death nor withhold treatment from a very ill patient for the sake of procuring organs. Concerns that they might be tempted to do so should organs be routinely taken from dead bodies are real, and would have to be addressed if a proposal such as defended here were to be implemented. My aim, however, is not to offer a detailed policy blueprint; it is to lay down principles of justice for the procurement of organs. Whether we should forgo implementing justice in the face of professionals' failure to respect potential organ procurers' rights not to be killed and to be given medical treatment is a question that I do not address here.

Two final remarks. First, as we saw in section 1.2.2D, there is no such thing as a posthumous right. As it happens, my argument for confiscation does not presuppose the truth of that claim. In fact, it is entirely compatible with the view that we can have such rights. One may wonder, then, why I do not argue for the confiscation of cadaveric organs on the assumption that individuals do not have posthumous rights to the disposal of their body. I choose a slightly less straightforward route because, in so far as the overwhelming majority of people assume that we have such rights, my argument for confiscation is all the more powerful for allowing that assumption to be made.

Not only is my argument for confiscation compatible with the view that we can have posthumous rights: it is also compatible with the view that we cannot have them. On that view, however, it does not straightforwardly follow that the needy have a right to decide what to do with our estate or body, since other parties, in particular the next-of-kin of the deceased, may well have an interest in making that decision. Accordingly, throughout section 4.2, I shall argue not merely for restricting individuals' (putative) right to dispose of their body posthumously as they wish: I shall also argue for restricting their right to dispose of their deceased relative's body as they wish. In sum, I shall argue that, whether or not individuals can have posthumous rights, and in particular the posthumous right to dispose of their body as they wish, those who need organs have a right to those of the now-dead able-bodied.

The point needs qualifying, however, and this is my second remark: whereas, as we saw in Chapter 2, one ought not to invoke the no-responsibility condition when deciding whether to rescue someone in peril, one may sometimes do so when deciding whether someone has a right to someone else's organs (whether the organ provider is dead or alive). For it may sometimes be possible, in those cases, to assess whether someone is responsible for needing an organ, either because the cause of their predicament is rather obvious (as when a very drunk driver, who not otherwise an alcoholic—and thus not in the grip of an addiction—is brought to the hospital for emergency medical treatment), or because it can be known thanks to third parties' testimonies (as when a badly injured skier is brought to the hospital by emergency services who know that he was skiing off-piste), or because it can be known thanks to tests (as when someone is tested for genetic conditions). In those cases, we can hold on to the no-responsibility condition, as those individuals cannot demand to be treated with respect unless they are prepared to take responsibility for their choices.

4.2 THE CASE FOR CONFISCATION

4.2.1 Who Should Decide?

In neither the USA nor the UK are doctors allowed to remove organs from someone's dead body without their consent; in practice, the wishes of the next-of-kin are given overriding importance, even if the deceased made it clear that she wanted to donate her organs. By contrast, in Continental Europe, individuals have to opt out of being a *post-mortem* donor, but, in practice, there too the wishes of their family tend to be given overriding importance.

In keeping with those various legal provisions, most people think that whilst choosing to make one's or one's relative's organs available after death may be morally commendable, it is certainly not owed to the sick as a matter of right. And yet, or so I shall now argue, the very considerations which lead proponents of coercive taxation to confer on the poor a right to the material resources of the well off, and in particular of the dead, should lead them to confer on the sick a right to the organs of the latter.

As we saw in 2.3.1, X has a right that others provide him with a particular good, G, if G is a kind of good of which it makes sense to say that one can have a right to it. More specifically, G must be such that to be under a duty to transfer it to someone else does not change its nature, and that transferring it from one individual to another does not violate the former's personhood. Cadaveric organs meet both conditions. They meet the first condition, for unlike love, whose nature is such that it can only be given voluntarily, they remain organs whether they are transferred voluntarily or not. They also meet the second condition, in that one can be held under a duty to give one of one's organs posthumously without ceasing to be a person, for the obvious reason that, once dead, one is no longer a person.

Of course, to think of organs as goods, as resources, might sound odd. After all, to point out the obvious, we—or at least most of us—feel more intimately connected to the parts that make up our body than to the objects we use or to the wealth we have. As Sartre puts it, 'I am not in relation to my hand in the same utilizing attitude as I am in relation to my pen.'[4] Generally, it is true that we do not stand in relation to the things we use as we do to the parts of our body we use. And the reason why that is so is twofold. First, once our body ceases to exist, we too cease to exist; by contrast, our continued existence is not dependent on that of our wealth. Second, on the conception of personhood I outlined in Chapter 1, self-consciousness and the capacity for rational and moral agency are necessary, but not sufficient, conditions for personhood: one must also have, and continually perceive oneself as having, a body. And this in turn is partly because that body acts as a filter between oneself and the external world: it is thanks to that body that we are a subject of experiences—experiences on the basis of which we can act as rational and moral agents. The same cannot be said of the things we use.

However, the foregoing points do not invalidate the view that cadaveric organs can be thought of as resources. For, if that conception of personhood is correct, it follows that once we are dead, once, that is, we no longer have the capacity for rational agency, our organs no longer make up the body of a person since there is no longer a person to speak of. However intimate a connection we may have with our body when we are alive, it is false that we have that connection once we are dead. Accordingly, as a would-be organ supplier, I can envision my body being divested of its essential organs without my person being under threat.

For that reason, cadaveric organs are the kind of goods of which it makes sense to say that the sick can have a right to them. I now have to show that they do indeed have such a right. As we saw in Chapter 1, an advocate of coercive taxation for distributive purposes who believes in the moral importance of ensuring that people lead a minimally flourishing life is claiming the following: 'some people do not lead a minimally flourishing life, for they lack material resources. In cases where they lack such resources through no fault of their own, for example because they were born in a certain family or social class, they have a prima facie right to the material resources of which the well off have a surplus; more specifically, they have prima facie rights to a minimally flourishing income, housing, and health care, by way of taxes on that surplus.' That argument rests on three considerations: the fact that some resources are needed to render a life minimally flourishing, the provision of which ought to be protected by a right; how one came not to lead a minimally flourishing life; how to fund the help the needy should receive. In what follows, I argue that all three considerations can justify conferring on the sick a right to the organs of the now-dead able-bodied, on the assumption (which the overwhelming majority of people endorse) that

---

[4] J. P. Sartre, *Being and Nothingness* (London: Methuen and Co., 1957), p. 373.

individuals can have posthumous rights regarding the disposal of their wealth and body once they are dead.

To start with the first consideration, it seems obvious that unless one has access to housing and income, as well as access to health care when one is ill, one will not be minimally autonomous, as a result of which one will not lead a minimally flourishing life. Now, someone whose kidneys are failing and who needs to undergo a dialysis several times a week does not lead a minimally flourishing life any more than someone who has hardly any money and whose whole existence is geared towards satisfying his most basic needs does. Someone whose heart and lungs, or liver, are failing and who will die unless he gets a transplant has equally bleak prospects as someone who will die of starvation unless he gets food. Someone who is totally blind lacks a fundamental resource and consequently can take up far fewer opportunities than someone who is not.

Notice that I am not saying that we always need all our organs in order to be autonomous. Indeed, some blind people, or some patients on kidney dialysis, would argue that they are pursuing a conception of the good life with which they can identify. Analogously, some individuals actually do not need the material resources most of us do in order to lead a minimally flourishing life. However, just as we should regard as reasonable a very poor person's claim that her life is not minimally flourishing as a result of her extreme poverty, we should regard as reasonable a blind or kidney-less person's claim that her life is less than minimally flourishing as a result of her condition. The fact that some disabled people are used to their disability does not undermine the point that it is reasonable for people who suffer from that condition to regard it as a disability, rather than as an inconvenience. It merely suggests that those who do not wish to avail themselves of organs ought to be given the right to refuse treatment.

To be sure, it does not follow from the fact that someone has a disability that he has a prima facie right to get treated for it, since, as we saw in section 1.3.2, those who can clearly be shown to be responsible for their neediness do not have a claim to help at the bar of justice. By contrast, however, those who are not responsible for not leading a minimally flourishing life have a prima facie right to be helped. Now, whether or not one has healthy organs is largely a matter of brute luck: indeed, people are often not responsible for developing lung cancer, for kidney or liver failure, for being blind, for suffering from a very weak heart, in short, for needing organs.

Finally, to advert to the third element of the theories of distributive justice under study here, it is claimed that the needy's right to material resources is a right held against the well off that the latter divest themselves of part of their own surplus of resources, by way of taxation. When unpacking more precisely what 'taxation' means, in that context, advocates of distributive justice do not regard income tax as the only way for the needy to have access to the well off's resources. Taxes on inheritance have an important role to play here. Note, incidentally, that there are two conceptions of such taxes in the relevant literature. The majority of advocates of distributive justice argue that inheritance should be subject to a special tax. Others, by contrast, reject estate duties, and claim (a) that inheritance should be included in the tax base of the heir, and (b) that bequests should not give rise to tax deduction, pre-death, for the donor. Both conceptions hold that there is no reason to exempt inheritance from taxation, on the twofold grounds that to leave donors free to bequeath their wealth as they wish has a negative impact on the prospects of the needy, and that there is something unfair in granting the heir full, unrestricted access to wealth simply in virtue of his connection to the deceased.[5]

Whichever conception of financial restrictions on inheritance is the correct one (and I need not take a stand on this), the important point here is that many advocates of distributive justice deem it just that the needy should have access to some of the material resources left by the dead, by way of financial strictures on inheritance. But, by the same token, they must deem it just that the sick—who are needy in some crucially important respect—should have access to the organs left by the dead. For consider: just as to leave individuals free to bequeath their wealth to their friends and relatives contributes to preventing the needy from getting the material resources they lack, to leave individuals free to ask their next-of-kin to have their body buried or cremated intact amounts to denying the sick access to the personal resources (in that instance, body parts) they need. Just as to allow individuals to inherit wealth without restrictions amounts to subjecting the needy to the bad brute luck of not being related to the deceased, to allow individuals to withhold the organs of their next-of-kin from the sick amounts to subjecting the latter to the bad brute luck of not being related to him.

To recapitulate, I posit the following: we all have an interest in having a minimally flourishing life; that interest is important enough to be protected by a right to the surplus of material resources left by the well off and which we need in order to lead such a life, by way of taxation in general and of financial restrictions on inheritance in particular; we also need body parts to lead such a life and, in many

---

[5] For the claim that inheritance should be subject to a specific tax, see, e.g., B. Ackerman and A. Alstott, *The Stakeholder Society* (New Haven, Conn.: Yale University Press, 1999); D. Haslett, 'Is Inheritance Justified?', *Philosophy and Public Affairs* 15 (1986): 122–55; M. L. Ascher, 'Curtailing Inherited Wealth', *Michigan Law Review* 86 (1990): 69–151; J. Le Grand, 'Markets, Welfare and Equality', in J. Le Grand and S. Estrin (eds.), *Market Socialism* (Oxford: Oxford University Press, 1989); J. Le Grand and D. Nissan, *A Capital Idea: Start-Up Grants for Young People* (London: Fabian Society, 2000); M. B. Levy, 'Liberal Equality and Inherited Wealth', *Political Theory* 11 (1983): 545–64. For the view that inheritance should not be subject to a specific tax but should be included in the tax base of the heir, see L. Murphy and T. Nagel, *The Myth of Ownership: Taxes and Justice* (Oxford: Oxford University Press, 2002), ch. 7. In the remainder of this chapter, I use the phrase 'having a right to inherit' to mean that someone has a right to inherit an estate, or, so to speak, the care of a dead body, irrespective of the wishes of the deceased. The right to inherit so defined is thus different from the right to receive bequests, which is conferred on the heir by virtue of the wishes of the deceased. I use the word 'inheritance' to denote both ways of transferring rights over estates and bodies. Note, finally, that I am committed neither to the claim that taxing inheritance is the only way in which we can bring about economic justice nor to the claim that taxing inheritance should only serve to achieve that end.

cases, lack them through no fault of our own. If these points are correct, they constitute good grounds to confer on the 'medically poor' a right to the organs of the 'medically rich', to wit, of those who, being dead, no longer need their organs. This, note, is *not* an argument for the view that the state has a right to appropriate the organs of the deceased for the greater good of society. This cannot be stressed strongly enough. Opponents of the confiscation of cadaveric organs usually assume that one can only defend it by invoking the rights of the community and the state over individuals and their body, and often remind us that such was the attitude of totalitarian regimes.[6] As should be clear by now, it is possible to mount an individualistic defence of the confiscation of cadaveric organs—one which claims that an individual in need of an organ has a right against an eligible donor that the latter relinquish that organ posthumously, and that the state, in mandating medical staff to take that organ and transplant it, would act on behalf of that sick individual.

4.2.2 Questioning the Analogy

My defence of the confiscation of cadaveric body parts rests on an analogy between the posthumous transfers of rights over an estate and the posthumous transfer of rights over a dead body. However, someone might be tempted to question the analogy as follows. Arguments for restricting inheritance are usually driven by a concern for the plight of those who happen to be born in a poor family. Individuals who happen to be born in a rich family do not have a right to inherit the whole of their parents' estate, or so it is often argued, precisely so as to ensure that those who were not so lucky do not fall below the poverty threshold through no fault of their own: financial restrictions on inheritance, thus, are meant to compensate those individuals for their parents' failure to provide for them, whatever the reasons for such failure. *If* that is so, however (or so might some people be tempted to object), my assimilation of the transfer of material wealth with the transfer of organs rests on four *non sequitur*. First, financial restrictions on inheritance are meant to restrict *inter*generational transfers from the preceding generation to the succeeding one which would otherwise result in unacceptable *intra*generational inequality of prospects for a minimally flourishing life between members of the second generation. The confiscation of organs, by contrast, would operate in a rather different way: in so far as eligible dead suppliers of organs tend to be younger than recipients, it could not be meant always to regulate an intergenerational transfer from parent to child, and thereby to ensure that members of the second generation have prospects for a minimally flourishing life.

[6] See, e.g., R. M. Veatch, *Transplantation Ethics* (Washington, DC: Georgetown University Press, 2000), pp. 144–6. For the view that the organs of the dead should be considered as state property, see J. Harris, *Clones, Genes, and Immortality* (Oxford: Oxford University Press, 1992), p. 125; and H. Steiner, *An Essay on Rights* (Oxford: Blackwell, 1994), p. 273.

Second, even when the deceased is older than the average eligible supplier and when her next-of-kin *is* her child, it seems odd to claim that her dead body is *transferred* to her child in the same way her estate is since her child cannot really be said to acquire the right to use her body *as a resource*, whereas she would acquire such a right over her estate.

Third, advocates of restricted inheritance do not usually take a firm stand on whether we should defer to the wishes of someone who states in his will that his money be withdrawn from the bank and, literally, buried or burnt after he dies, or that his land or house be left intact but vacant; nor do they take a firm stand on whether we should defer to similar wishes as expressed by the heir of the deceased. But *if* they think that we should defer to those wishes, they should argue that the wishes of someone who wills that his body be buried or cremated intact, or similar wishes as expressed by her next-of-kin, should not be thwarted.

Fourth, restrictions on bequests and inheritance apply to all testators and all heirs. By contrast, restrictions on the ways in which individuals or their relatives can dispose of their body once they are dead only apply to those whose blood type, tissue type, and organs match patients' demands: the burden of not being able to bequeath and inherit wealth falls on all testators and heirs, but the burden of not being able to dispose of one's or one's relative's body falls on some people only, and for reasons which are outside their control.

Now, my argument for the confiscation of cadaveric organs is not guilty of the first *non sequitur*. For, although most philosophical works on inheritance conceive of it exclusively as a transfer of property from parent to child, such transfers may and do in fact occur between spouses and friends, or from child to parents—in short, outside family relationships, between members of the same generation, and from the younger to the older generation. Moreover, when wealth is passed on from someone to her child, this may not only create inequalities between her child and her child's contemporaries: it may also create *inter*generational inequalities between her child and *her* own contemporaries. On that more complex view of inheritance, the proceeds of financial restrictions on the posthumous transfer of wealth should be distributed to all those who do not have enough resources to lead a minimally flourishing life. Accordingly, the posthumous transfer of rights over dead bodies from the deceased to their next-of-kin is analogous, in that particular respect, to the posthumous transfer of rights over estates from the deceased to their heir.

Nor, furthermore, is my argument guilty of the second and third of those *non sequitur*. To be sure, it is true (as per the second *non sequitur* claim) that allowing the next-of-kin to dispose of his parent's body cannot really be couched as permitting a transfer of resources to take place; it is also true (as per the third *non sequitur* claim) that a wish to be buried or cremated intact, or to have one's relative buried or cremated intact, is analogous to a wish to have one's or one's relative's estate not used by anyone. Yet, my argument for the partial confiscation of dead bodies, as modelled on arguments for the partial confiscation of estates, does go through.

For consider: regarding the second *non sequitur* claim, the salient issue, in discussions of inheritance, is not so much transfers of resources; rather, it is the issue of *rights of access* to resources. Critics of unrestricted inheritance argue that the heirs of the well off are not morally entitled to have privileged access to their parents' wealth, given that others, who are not lucky enough to be born and raised in a rich family, need extra resources to meet their needs. By the same token, they are committed to the view that the next-of-kin of the deceased are not morally entitled to have privileged access to their parent's body, given that others, who are not lucky enough to be related to an eligible supplier, need the organs of the deceased in order to lead a minimally flourishing life, let alone to survive.

As for the third *non sequitur* claim, some authors actually wonder whether we should accede to the wishes of someone who requests that her estate not be used by anyone after her death;[7] others do not explicitly claim that we should. In any case, their commitment to restricting inheritance should lead them to deny that we should, and to treat similar wishes as expressed by heirs and next-of-kin in an identical way. Clearly, strictly speaking, if advocates of restricted inheritance justify their position by appealing to the injustice inherent in some people having no prospects for a minimally flourishing life through the bad brute luck of being born in a poor family whilst others have such prospects through the good brute luck of being born in a rich family, they do not have a reason to oppose the wish of the deceased or that of her relatives, since her children, *ex hypothesi*, will not receive any inheritance.

However, advocates of restricted inheritance are not solely concerned with inequalities of prospects resulting from the unequal transmission of wealth. They are also concerned with the fact that, irrespective of how others are doing, some people are needy through bad brute luck, period. And, most often, it is their concern with neediness per se which leads them to condemn inequalities of prospects.[8] Accordingly, they are committed to refusing to defer to the wishes of the deceased, or of her relatives, that her wealth be burnt or buried, for, if they defer to those wishes, they are placing themselves in the following situation. On the one hand, when advocating financial restrictions on inheritance, they invoke the neediness of the poor in order to block the wish of the deceased that her wealth be transferred to her children in its entirety, and they thereby imply that it overrides the harm she may incur posthumously if her children do not get the whole of her estate; or, when examining the right to inherit as opposed to the

---

[7] See, e.g., J. Callahan, 'On Harming the Dead', *Ethics* 97 (1987): 341–52, at 350.

[8] Thus, while Ackerman and Alstott claim, in *The Stakeholder Society*, that inheritance taxes should serve to bring about equality of opportunity, in fact they are mostly concerned with ensuring that every single American be able to implement a meaningful conception of the good, irrespective of his or her social and familial background.

right to receive bequests, they invoke the neediness of the poor in order to block her children's interest in getting the estate in full, and they thereby imply that it overrides whatever grievance the children of the deceased may have as a result of losing part of the estate. On the other hand, they refuse to invoke the neediness of the poor to block her wish, or her children's, that her estate be burnt; and, in respecting those wishes, they deny that the neediness of the poor overrides her and her children's grievances at the prospect of not controlling what happens to the estate. Given that advocates of restricted inheritance are concerned with relieving poverty, it would be odd indeed to make the strength of the poor's claim to the estate depend on the attitude of the deceased and of her relatives vis-à-vis the wealth of the former. Advocates of restricted inheritance, then, are committed to refusing to endorse someone's wishes that her estate, or that of her deceased next-of-kin, be wholly destroyed, or left unused; by the same token, they are committed to refusing to endorse someone's wishes that her body, or that of her deceased next-of-kin, be buried or cremated intact.

Finally, my argument is not vulnerable to the fourth *non sequitur* claim. That claim, you may recall, holds that the burden of not being able to bequeath and inherit wealth entirely as one wishes falls on all testators and heirs, whereas the burden of not being able to dispose of one's or one's relative's body only falls on eligible suppliers or on their relatives, and for reasons based on biological factors which are outside their control. It is unfair, or so the objection goes, to hold the eligible suppliers under a duty to relinquish their organs, simply because they suffer the misfortune of being compatible with a patient. (The same point, obviously, could be raised in relation to the next-of-kin's duty to release the organs of the deceased.) By contrast, it is said, such considerations of fairness do not arise in relation to financial restrictions on inheritance.

I do not think that this constitutes a strong enough objection against my claim that holding individuals under a duty to help the poor by way of financial restrictions on inheritance entails a commitment to holding individuals under a duty to help the sick by way of relinquishing their cadaveric organs. I also think that the problem of fairness identified above can, at least in part, be solved.

Indeed, I pointed out three paragraphs ago that advocates of restricted inheritance are concerned with neediness per se, and not simply with inequalities which result from differential transfers of wealth. This non-comparative understanding of the poor's claim to the proceeds of financial restrictions on inheritance opens the door to a non-comparative understanding of testators' and heirs' duties to help. A good reason why a tax should be levied on part of their estates, as a contribution to helping the needy, is not merely that they all happen to have an excess of resources which the needy lack; it is also that they *each* find themselves in a better position to help the needy, independently of the fact that all of them are in such a position. Furthermore, generally, the fact that we may find ourselves in a position to help someone for reasons beyond our control whilst others cannot help at all, or cannot help as much, does not exempt us from a moral duty to help. As we saw in Chapter 2, if S—a very strong swimmer—can, at little cost to himself, save D, who is drowning, then S is under a stringent moral duty to do so, indeed, he is under a duty of justice to do so. If S were to refuse to help D on the grounds that he should not incur a cost simply because, for entirely arbitrary reasons, he is the only one in a position to help, he would be guilty of a very serious wrongdoing. Accordingly, it would not be wrong, at least prima facie, to hold a potential organ supplier under a duty to relinquish his organs posthumously even though he would thereby incur a cost, for reasons entirely beyond his control, which other individuals would not incur: to each according to his needs, from each according to his abilities, irrespective of other people's abilities.

I say 'at least prima facie', because there is a difference between holding someone under a duty to relinquish a part of his or his relative's estate, and holding him under a duty to relinquish his or his relative's organs. In the former case, he is not asked to do anything which other individuals in possession of a similar good (to wit, wealth) do not also have to do. In the latter case, he is asked to help, even though other individuals are also in possession of a similar good (to wit, an organ, but one which is not needed as it is not a match). This is where a problem of fairness does indeed arise. And yet I believe that this problem can be solved, at least in part. For consider: as a matter of fairness, as we saw in section 2.3.1, Good Samaritans ought to receive compensation from the community. Similarly, organ suppliers ought to be compensated for having to transfer their or their relatives' organs posthumously, out of a scheme funded by all taxpayers.[9] Granted, it would not solve the problem entirely since for some people, one can plausibly surmise, receiving compensation would not make up for the fact that they had to relinquish their control over their, or their relative's, dead body. However, and to reiterate a point I made in that section, similar considerations arise in relation to compensation for expropriation: just as those considerations are not *always* strong enough to warrant not expropriating property owners from their estate, they are not always strong enough to warrant exempting individuals from a duty to make their, or their relatives', cadaveric organs available to the sick. I shall provide an account of cases where those considerations are relevant in section 4.3.2.

In short, then, just as the well off lack a right posthumously to dispose of their wealth entirely as they wish, and just as their heirs lack a right to inherit their estate in full, the able-bodied lack a right to dispose of their dead body, posthumously, as they wish, and so do their next-of-kin lack that right. However, absent further qualification, this *in itself* does not entail that the sick have a right to the

---

[9] There are various ways of setting up the scheme: the state could, for example, relax financial restrictions on the testator and/or heir if the former does not turn out to be an eligible donor; if he turns out to be eligible, one could deduct the compensation from taxes on inheritance, etc. I need not go into details here.

cadaveric organs of the able-bodied. Consider, once again, standard arguments for financial restrictions on inheritance. The fact that the well off cannot dispose of their estate as they wish, and that their heirs cannot inherit it in its entirety, does not entail that the poor have a right to the specific parts that make up the estate; they do not, for example, have a right to the house of the deceased, or to whatever paintings, jewels, and company shares he may have owned. They only have a right to the monetary equivalent of a share of the estate. By the same token, could one not allow the relatives of the deceased to keep her body in its full integrity provided they pay body duties on it? On that proposal, just as the heirs of a rich person are entitled to keep her estate provided they can pay taxes on it, the relatives of the dead should be entitled to dispose of the latter's body as they wish provided they can pay body duties.

However, the proposal is highly problematic, since it does not take sufficient account of the possibility that the only eligible donor for a given patient might be a dead person—call her Mary—whose relatives are unwilling to renounce their rights over the body in exchange for not paying taxes on it.[10] If, then, Mary happens to be the only eligible supplier for a patient who has been on the transplant waiting lists for a while and who is extremely unlikely to find a compatible supplier before his condition starts deteriorating, her relatives should not be allowed to decide what should be done with her body, nor should her pre-humously expressed wish to be buried or cremated intact carry weight (unless, as I shall argue in section 4.3.2, for her not to be buried or cremated intact would render her or her next-of-kin's life less than minimally flourishing).

To recapitulate, none of the aforementioned *non sequitur* claims undermines my case for the confiscation of cadaveric organs. This is not meant to imply, of course, that the fact that one is in a position to contribute suffices to be held under a duty to do so. Considerations such as the cost of contributing have to be taken on board: to these I now turn.

4.3 TWO OBJECTIONS AGAINST THE CONFISCATION OF CADAVERIC ORGANS

My argument for the claim that, just as the poor have a right to decide what to do with the wealth of the wealthy, the sick have a right to decide what to do with the organs of the dead, presupposes that organs and material assets are not relevantly disanalogous and that they can be transferred in relevantly similar ways. In the last section, I dispelled some worries about assimilating the posthumous

---

[10] A similar problem bedevils another proposal for the procurement of organs, to wit, the proposal that individuals who express the wish to be buried or cremated intact will not have their organs taken away from them posthumously, but thereby forgo any claim to receiving an organ transplant should they need one. On that proposal, a patient in need of an organ will not receive a transplant if the only eligible donor has indicated that he wanted to be buried or cremated intact.

transfer of rights over wealth and the posthumous transfer of rights over organs. In this section, I assess arguments grounded in non-conscientious (section 4.3.1) and conscientious (section 4.3.2) reasons to the effect that organs, unlike wealth, are such that they simply cannot be taken away from individuals without their, or their next-of-kin's, consent.

By conscientious reasons, I mean reasons informed by views such that for their holders not to be able to live by them would render their life less than minimally flourishing. In section 1.3.2, I argued that justice cannot require that people help others at the cost of their own prospects for a minimally flourishing life. Here, I shall bring that claim to bear on the issue at hand, and argue that non-conscientious objections cannot, but that conscientious objections can, justify exempting individuals from a duty to make their organs posthumously available to the sick. Note that I shall only deal with arguments against the confiscation of cadaveric organs which do *not* assume that the status of the dead is comparable to that of the living (that the dead, for example, have feelings, influence our life, are influenced by us, and so forth). I could not hope to do justice, within the scope of this chapter, to the complicated question of how to solve conflicts between competing conceptions of the ontological status of the dead.[11]

One final point before I start. I argued in section 1.2.2D that there can be no such thing as a posthumous right. If that claim is correct, it implies that one cannot object to the confiscation of cadaveric organs on the grounds that individuals have a posthumous right to personal integrity. However, as I indicated at the outset of this chapter, in so far as the view that there is no such thing as a posthumous right is highly controversial, I shall assume for the sake of argument that it is false, and argue that, even if individuals can have posthumous rights, they lack the posthumous right that their body be left intact once they are dead.

Of course, from the claim that there can be no such thing as a posthumous right, it does not follow that the living have the right to behave however they wish towards the dead, for the fact that the living do not have obligations to the dead is entirely compatible with the view—which I believe to be correct—that they have obligations with respect to them. Could it not be the case, then, that although the dead cannot have any rights, the living are under an obligation to respect their personal integrity, and have that obligation to some third parties, and in particular the next-of-kin? However, my argument against the view that individuals' presumed posthumous interest in personal integrity is important enough to be protected by a right will also apply to the next-of-kin's interest in his deceased relative's personal integrity. By the same token, my argument in favour of (limited) conscientious objections to the confiscation of

[11] For an excellent account of the challenges posed to liberalism by the view that the dead have the same status as the living, see T. Mulgan, 'The Place of the Dead in Liberal Political Philosophy', *Journal of Political Philosophy* 7 (1999): 52–70.

cadaveric organs applies not merely to such objections as deployed, whilst alive, by prospective organ suppliers, but also, when they are dead, by their next-of-kin.

4.3.1 Non-conscientious Objections

The most important objection against the compulsory *post-mortem* taking of organs invokes the commonly held view that individuals have interests which, unlike their interests in, say, experiencing the intellectual joys of literature, the sensual delights of great food, and the relief of mindless TV, are crucial to the way their life is going, and can, and must, be respected posthumously unless they indicate otherwise. Interests in autonomy and personal integrity, the objection goes, are such interests: if we are committed to respecting people's autonomy, we have to respect their personal integrity, even posthumously; accordingly, we have to confer on them a posthumous right *not* to grant others access to their body, however much the latter might need organs.[12]

Now, let us assume, for the sake of argument, that we can have posthumous interests, and that we therefore can have posthumous rights. Let us also assume that, unless we indicate otherwise, we do have posthumous interests in personal integrity and autonomy. Can one argue that we have a *right* that those interests be protected against people who need organs? I do not think so. After all, we do not always have a right that our wishes concerning the care of our dead body be respected. Consider the following scenario: John states in his will that he wishes not to be buried in a coffin but, rather, directly in the soil on the bank of his favourite stream. However, he dies of a very contagious illness, so that if he were buried there, his body would contaminate the stream, which in turn would seriously harm the farmer who lives nearby and who relies on its water for drinking, washing, and cooking purposes: under the circumstances, cremation would be the most appropriate way to dispose of his body. In the face of the harm which would be incurred by the farmer, I cannot think of any plausible argument to the effect that John's wish to be buried there should be honoured. Similarly, in the face of the harm which the medically needy would incur if we decided to withhold our organs from them, one cannot, I think, plausibly defend the view that we have a right that our personal integrity be preserved if we so wish, *on non-conscientious grounds*.

Many might be tempted to object to the foregoing point as follows:[13] in John's case, his wish to be buried by the stream, if deferred to, would *harm* the farmer; by contrast, someone's decision to withhold their organs from transplant patients does not harm them, but only *allows* harm to happen to them. Whereas the farmer has a negative right against John not to be harmed by him, transplant patients only have a positive right against a potential organ supplier to be helped

---

[12] See, e. g., Veatch, *Transplantation Ethics*, ch. 9, esp. p. 160.
[13] This objection was put to me at a philosophy seminar at Bristol University.

by him. In so far as positive rights are weaker than negative rights, the correlative obligations they impose on others are weaker. In the present context, those positive obligations to give help are overridden by potential suppliers' interests in personal integrity and autonomy.

The thesis that there are conceptual and moral differences between harming someone and allowing harm to happen to them is a familiar one; so too is the thesis, which is thought to derive from it, that negative rights not to be harmed are stronger than positive rights to be helped. In the present context, however, neither thesis is relevant. For my case in favour of the confiscation of cadaveric organs is targeted at the advocate of coercive taxation for distributive purposes who believes, *ex hypothesi*, that the fact that the well off, in withholding material resources, only allow harm to happen to the needy does not constitute a strong enough reason not to hold them under a positive obligation to help. In order to confer on the needy a right to the material resources of the well off, block John's request to be buried by the stream, *and* deny the sick a right to the organs of the dead, one would have to point to some morally relevant difference between helping someone with material resources and helping someone with organs. *That* is the salient issue.

I can think of two non-conscientious arguments which someone might want to deploy here. First, she might point out that many people do experience understandable feelings of disgust and repugnance at the idea that their body will be cut up and dismembered or that their organs will be used by other people. ('I find the idea of my heart beating in someone else's chest difficult to accept!', or 'I do not like the idea of someone else breathing through my lungs!', or 'The very idea that my kidneys will clean up someone else's body is disgusting!', etc.) By contrast, or so one might claim, people do not feel disgust at the idea that their wealth will be posthumously transferred to the poor.

Now, I concede that those feelings of disgust may be very strong indeed; still, they do not constitute a good reason for acceding to someone's demand that his body be buried or cremated intact. For to claim that they do amounts to asserting that potential suppliers' interest in not experiencing strong disgust overrides the interest of the sick in living a minimally flourishing life, indeed in remaining alive. I simply do not see how one could justify putting so high a premium on living a squeamishness-free life in the face of such urgent needs. As we saw in sections 1.3.2 and 2.3.2, one cannot be exonerated from a duty to help the needy or the imperilled on the sole grounds that if one is required to help, one's life will become difficult. Rather, one must show that being required to help would render one's life as it is less than *minimally* flourishing. To that effect, one must in turn show either that one would thereby be deprived of the all-purpose means necessary to implement any conception of the good, or that one would be prevented from implementing one's current conception of the good, which, upon close, rational, and critical reflection, is the only one that gives meaning to one's life. On any conception of what a minimally flourishing life is, it is wholly implausible to claim that feeling squeamish about what happens to our body after death passes either test.

Second, the advocate of coercive taxation for distributive purposes who opposes the confiscation of cadaveric organs might be tempted to argue that one must treat the body of the dead with respect on pain of not treating the dead themselves with the respect they are owed as persons. After all, she might go on, the overwhelming majority of people feel very strongly about, for example, thugs who desecrate graves and exhume interred bodies, about soldiers and militia men who mutilate their dead enemies' bodies, or about murderers who disfigure their victims knowing that they are already dead. To be sure, she would concede, there is a crucial difference between mutilating someone's dead body as a sign of contempt, and taking their liver or kidneys to save someone else's life. Yet the fact remains that there is a strong connection between respecting someone's dead body and treating them with respect.[14]

This objection to the confiscation of cadaveric body parts is obviously more powerful than the squeamishness claim. For, if taking organs from persons without their consent once they are dead does involve a failure to treat them with the respect they are owed as persons, it constitutes a blatant violation of justice. However, although the mandatory taking of organs from the dead evokes, to many people, grave desecrations and posthumous mutilations, the fact that the former is motivated by a wish to save other people's lives whilst the latter are motivated by contempt for them is absolutely crucial. To stress the obvious, to take someone's liver from their body does not in any way amount to a desecration when done for transplant purposes. Indeed, transplant teams often speak of their tremendous respect for the individuals whose organs they are using. To put the point more generally, even if it is true that respecting someone posthumously requires respecting their body posthumously, it is false that to take away body parts from the body of the deceased, against their wishes, always amounts to disrespecting the body itself, and thereby the deceased: intentions and aims *do* matter.

At this juncture, it has been objected to me that non-conscientious objections may carry more weight than I give them here, even though they are neither moral nor religious. For, after all, there are non-moral or non-religious things the loss of which would make our life go badly. However, it strikes me that, when it comes to the *posthumous* disposal of their body, most opponents of confiscation press the kind of reasons which I have considered so far. These reasons, I maintain, are not strong enough in the face of the needs of transplant patients.[15]

---

[14] Many parents whose dead children's organs were taken away by doctors in a British hospital for medical purposes, unbeknownst to them, did say, precisely, that their children themselves had been violated. I owe this objection to David Miller. (For accounts of the Alder Hey Hospital scandal, to which I am referring here, see the *Guardian*, 30 January 2001.)

[15] I am grateful to Sue Mendus for pressing me on that point and (to anticipate the next section) for insisting that I take conscientious objections to my proposal much more seriously than I was inclined to do.

The foregoing points are unlikely to succeed against those who believe that the body is sacrosanct, and that its parts should never be used without one's consent for the sake of helping someone else. Against that view, though, there is very little that can be said, except that it is unclear why personal integrity should be given such overriding importance, posthumously, in the face of other people's needs.

4.3.2 Conscientious Objections

We shall have an opportunity to revisit the view that the body is sacrosanct in section 5.3, when we assess some objections to the confiscation of live body parts. Meanwhile, it is time to examine the claim that conscientious objectors to the confiscation of cadaveric organs should be exempt from the duty to help the sick. Although I shall focus on such objections as raised by the organ supplier, everything I say below applies, *mutatis mutandis*, to their next-of-kin.[16]

The conscientious objector to the confiscation of his organs is not claiming that the reason he should be exonerated from donating is that his interests in personal integrity would be compromised to an unacceptable degree; nor is he merely expressing disgust at the idea that his kidneys, say, or his heart, would be placed in someone else's body. His claim, rather, is that he holds beliefs such that, if he were held under a duty to make his organs available after death, his moral identity would be destroyed.

Conscientious objections are most often deployed against military service, but they can, with some degree of intelligibility, be deployed against a duty to make one's organs available to the sick posthumously. In that context, they raise the following two questions: under what conditions, if any, can someone raise a conscientious objection to making his organs available after death? In the light of my claim that endorsing the confiscation of material resources commits one to endorsing the confiscation of cadaveric organs, can conscientious objections as deployed against the latter also work as against the former?[17]

In what follows, I shall argue that one may sometimes raise a conscientious objection to having to donate one's organs after death and to paying taxes. Before

---

[16] Note that what I say here can be brought to bear on my treatment, in section 2.3.2, of the woman who fails to rescue someone in peril on the grounds that it would prevent her from attending an important religious meeting.

[17] It is worth noting for the record that a conscientious objection to doing x can take one of two forms. On the one hand, the conscientious objector may believe that doing x is always morally wrong; on the other hand, he may believe that although doing x is permissible in some cases, it is morally wrong in other cases, and, accordingly, he may object to the latter, not the former. For example, there is a difference between claiming that one ought not to be made to donate one's organs, or to pay taxes, because the loss of such goods would be too great, and claiming that one ought not to be made to donate one's organs, or to pay taxes, because the purposes for which one is made to do so are unjust. A full treatment of conscientious objections should be sensitive to the issues raised by both kinds of claim. A sketchy treatment such as the one offered here need not be so, however, for my points in favour of conscientious objections apply to either claim.

building my case, however, let me say a few words on the conditions an objection must meet in order to have the status of a *conscientious* objection. As I have claimed on more than one occasion, and most notably in section 1.3.1, a just society is one where persons respect one another as persons, that is, where they give one another opportunities to live as self-respecting persons. This imposes constraints on the way they should behave towards one another, and dictates, more specifically, that they confer on one another some fundamental freedoms as well as the resources they need to lead a minimally flourishing life. But the requirement of respect also imposes constraints on the way in which they justify using the full power of the law to deny those freedoms to, and withhold those resources from, one another. Not only, in fact, must they give reasons for their decision so to act; they must give appropriate reasons.

Articulating which kind of reasons counts as appropriate is the task which so-called justificatory liberalism sets itself. Without entering into the nuances and details of each strand of justificatory liberalism, the following will capture well enough, for my purposes here, the central tenets of that ideal. A citizen who seeks to impose on others a coercive law, as well as to deny them the resources they need to live a minimally flourishing life, must, if she is to accord them the respect they are owed as persons, pursue a high degree of rational justification for her decision and desist from so deciding if she cannot do so. Moreover, she must be willing to have her reasons for so deciding subject to critical scrutiny by others who do not share her point of view. In addition, not only must her justification be highly rational, it must also be public. That is, it must be on principle intelligible to others, from their own parochial point of view. Finally, her justification cannot invoke the denial of the claim that all individuals are owed equal respect as persons.[18]

In the light of the foregoing points, the task of the conscientious objector to the confiscation of cadaveric organs consists in providing just such reasons for being exonerated from a duty to make his organs available after death. Furthermore, he must provide these reasons not merely to those would not receive his organs, and whose prospects for a minimally flourishing life would, as a result, be jeopardized; he must provide them to those who will not be exempt from that duty. This last point is particularly important, since the gist of his plea is not that *no one* should have to perform that duty; rather, it is that *he* should not have to do what others have to do. To be sure, as a matter of fact, some conscientious objectors regard as unjust, regardless of one's religious and moral convictions, the principle which they request not to have to obey. But a conscientious objector

---

[18] I borrow this very short summary from C. Eberle, *Religious Convictions in Liberal Politics* (Cambridge: Cambridge University Press, 2002), pp. 104–5. The best-known defences of justificatory liberalism are B. Barry, *Justice as Impartiality* (Oxford: Oxford University Press, 1995); G. Gaus, *Justificatory Liberalism* (Cambridge: Cambridge University Press, 1996); C. Larmore, *Patterns of Moral Complexity* (Cambridge: Cambridge University Press, 1987); J. Rawls, *Political Liberalism* (New York: Columbia University Press, 1993).

need not call into question that principle itself: all he asks is that, in the light of his own convictions, he should be able not to submit to it without being liable to punishment. His justificatory burden is heavier, therefore, than that shouldered by the person who objects to the principle per se, since he must show that he has special reasons, which others may lack, to be exonerated from obeying it. More specifically in the present context, the conscientious objector to the confiscation of cadaveric organs need not affirm that one's whole body is an all-purpose means necessary to the pursuit of any (posthumous) conception of the good; in fact, he may well believe that some (posthumous) conceptions of the good do not require that one's body be kept intact at death. What he must show, though, is that, were *he* called upon to donate, he would be unable to implement his own conception of the good—a conception such that it is the only one that coheres with his moral identity.

Now, it is a central tenet of the conception of justice which I articulated in Chapter 1 that individuals are not under a duty to help others if doing so would jeopardize their own prospects for a minimally flourishing life. At its most abstract, one leads such a life if one respects oneself as a rational and moral agent—more specifically, as someone who has the capacity to frame, revise, and implement a conception of the good with which he can identify, and which is shaped by strong commitments of a moral nature, whether secular or not. The stronger those commitments, the harder it is for their bearer to be able to violate them *and* retain his self-respect, and the more tenuous, then, his prospects for a minimally flourishing life. Thus, at a minimum, a conscientious objector must show that, if he had to give his organs at death, he would violate that kind of commitment. Usually, conscientious objectors' commitments are of a religious nature. For example, some people think that the body must be preserved in its integrity so as to be prepared for the day when the righteous will be, literally, resurrected; for them to be deprived of the possibility of being resurrected would truly, I think, blight their life. Others believe that the human body belongs to God, and that it should not, therefore, be dismembered by other human beings. For them to violate God's command would also blight their life. Note, though, that conscientious objections need not be informed by religious beliefs in order to count as such: non-religious persons may very well wish to have their body preserved after their death, and their wish may very well be absolutely central to their life, so that not fulfilling it would compromise their moral identity.

Thus, it is necessary for a conscientious objector to show that his moral identity would be compromised if he were made to divest himself of his organs at death: for then he can invoke, against patients, the fact that his life *would be blighted* as a result of donating, and against other duty-bearers, the fact that *his life, unlike theirs,* would be so blighted. However, assuming that he can make that case, he will not have done enough. For his objection, as we saw, must meet a high standard of rationality; it must also be capable of resisting others' critical views of it, and be on principle intelligible both to those who will not get his organs and to those who are under a duty to provide theirs, from their own parochial point of view.[19] Accordingly, a claim, expressed nowadays, such as 'I cannot lose some of my organs, such as my heart, after I am dead, because I am Jesus Christ, and must be in a condition such as to be resurrected' does not pass the test; for it rests on an irrational belief, held by a mentally unbalanced individual, which is not genuinely religious but which merely takes a religious shape. To be clear: I am not suggesting that we can take organs from such a person once he is dead. Indeed, the knowledge that he will not die in a condition such as to be resurrected might aggravate his mental illness, and this is a good reason for exempting him from a duty to donate. Rather, I am claiming that his would not be a conscientious objection to the confiscation of cadaveric organs.

Moreover, religious beliefs cannot be advanced in support of a refusal to supply organs posthumously if they rest on highly questionable interpretative grounds. Suppose, for example, that someone refuses to supply his organs because, or so he claims, God explicitly says in the Bible that we cannot 'eat someone else's flesh'. Not only would that person have to show that for her to violate this particular command of God's would render her life less than minimally flourishing; she would also have to rebut the objection that eating someone else's organs is not the same as receiving them in a transplant, and thus that a prohibition on cannibalism does not entail a prohibition on organ transplants.[20] Should she not succeed in doing so, her objection simply would not be robust enough in the face of critical scrutiny.

Furthermore, in so far as respect for others requires that we not ground our objection to being held under a particular duty to them in what we believe is their inherent unworthiness, this rules out, for example, arguments along the lines: 'It is a central principle of my ethical life that black people are impure, I simply cannot stand the thought that organs might be transferred to a black person. Thus

---

[19] Generally, then, the mere fact that doing something for someone else (or indeed refraining from doing something to someone else) may render one's life less than minimally flourishing is not *always* enough to justify, as a matter of justice, not providing help. In the remainder of this book, statements of the form 'P is not under a duty to help Q because doing so would jeopardize his prospects for a minimally flourishing life' should be taken to imply, unless otherwise stated, that, in the case at hand, the loss of such prospects is a sufficient condition for P not to have to help Q.

[20] The religious objection to organ transplants I am imagining here mirrors the justification which Jehovah's Witnesses offer in defence of their prohibition of blood transfusions. They point to a number of passages in the Bible where God forbids human beings to drink blood (e.g. Deuteronomy 12: 23–5, Leviticus 17: 10, 11, 13, Acts 15: 20 and 29), argue that receiving a blood transfusion is the same as drinking it, and conclude that blood transfusions are illegitimate. Oddly enough, Jehovah's Witnesses allow organ transplants *provided* that they are bloodless (that is, provided that the patient does not receive a blood transfusion during the operation). I say 'oddly enough', because their argument against blood transfusions commits them to rejecting organ transplants: in so far as God considers cannibalism to be a grievous sin (Micah 3: 2–4), and in so far as, *ex hypothesi*, receiving blood is the same as drinking it, then receiving an organ surely must be the same as eating it. For the Witnesses' position on this issue, see their official web site at <http://www.watchtower.org/>.

I refuse to have my organs confiscated posthumously, lest they should end up in a black person's body.' (Incidentally, current practice, at least in the UK, rules out making the gift of an organ conditional upon its potential recipient's race.) The reason why those beliefs, which may indeed be absolutely central to their holder's life, should be ruled out, is that they violate the idea of fundamental equality.

Thus, we have ruled out from the kinds of reasons some objectors might be tempted to deploy those which rest on dubious scriptural interpretation, irrational beliefs, and denial of others' status as moral equals. In addition, the ideal of public justification requires that we also rule out reasons which merely invoke God's authority on the matter. This is not because to believe in God's existence is irrational: indeed, it does not seem more irrational to believe in it than not to believe in it. Rather, this is because whether God exists or not is not amenable to proof. In fact, just as one could not say 'God exists; He tells me not to give my organs; therefore I should not give them,' one could not argue, in reply, 'God does *not* exist; therefore your objection fails.' Patients and other duty-bearers can say, though, that in so far as they do not believe in God, they cannot accept the objector's view that they should either be deprived of prospects for a minimally flourishing life or shoulder a burden that he thinks he should not shoulder. If the view that God exists is entirely non-intelligible to me, a claim to the effect that God commands one not to donate one's organs and that this is enough to justify not having to donate, will strike me as non-intelligible, and will fall foul of the requirements of public justification.[21] By contrast, a conscientious objection to the confiscation of organs which presupposes the existence of God and adverts to the latter's commands will be intelligible to me if it can also show that one can reject confiscation on other grounds. Thus, although many conscientious objectors to military service object on religious grounds, others do so on other, secular, grounds, but they all hold that killing another human being is abhorrent, and they can easily understand one another's position.

Thus, if a moral commitment, religious or not, is such that not abiding by it would violate its holder's moral identity, if it neither rests on false claims nor violates fundamental equality, if it is robust in the face of criticisms, and if it exhibits both a high degree of rationality and publicness, it can ground a conscientious objection to being exonerated from a (legal or moral) duty to transfer one's organs posthumously. Those points dovetail with the account of interests which I offered in section 1.2.2A. There, you recall, I argued that something, G, is in X's interest if either of the following two propositions is true: either (a) G contributes to X's pursuit of some goal or project of his, consistent with his good

---

[21] Which is to say, in line with most justificatory liberals, that religious beliefs alone cannot ground imposing a coercive law on others, withholding help from them, and being exonerated from a duty to do what others have to do. For an argument to the contrary, see C. Eberle, *Religious Convictions in Liberal Politics*, esp. chs. 5 and 9.

as a person, and there is no other goal that X would rather have if he thought rationally about alternatives; or (b) G contributes to X's acquiring that other goal. Accordingly, to hold on (so to speak!) to his organs posthumously is in X's interest if doing so contributes to his pursuit of some goal or project (for example, his commitment to some moral or religious world view), consistent with his good as a person, and if there is no other such world view that X would rather have if he thought rationally about alternatives (that is, once he has subjected his present world view to rational and critical scrutiny).

To recapitulate, I have shown that it is possible, in principle, to raise such an objection to making one's organs available posthumously. I have not yet shown, however, that one can also conscientiously object to paying inheritance taxes. And one might think that it is an impossible task. Indeed, whereas most people would argue that one ought to be exonerated, on conscientious grounds, from a duty to donate one's organs posthumously, they would claim that one ought not to be exonerated from inheritance taxes on conscientious grounds. For it is simply implausible, they might press, to say that being under such a duty would compromise one's moral identity in the way being under a duty to give one's organs might.

If the objection succeeds, it will have shown, by implication, that material resources crucially differ from organs; and that in turn might considerably weaken my argument that they are analogous in such a way that confiscating the former commits us to confiscating the latter. However, if the claim that one's moral identity would be destroyed by a requirement to donate one's organs posthumously can succeed under the justificatory conditions outlined above, so can a claim that one's moral identity, and thereby one's prospects for a minimally flourishing life, would be destroyed by a requirement to pay inheritance taxes, under similar justificatory conditions. True, it is hard to imagine what kind of belief one might hold to make that claim plausible. And it is correspondingly easy to imagine what kind of belief one might hold to make it highly implausible: the eighteenth Earl of Toffshire could not expect his heir to be exonerated from paying inheritance taxes on the conscientious grounds that the only way for him to pay such taxes would be to sell a number of Old Masters' paintings which, or so it has been drummed into each Earl-to-be since childhood, it is incumbent upon him to keep in the family. For, however important the preservation of his family's heritage might be to his conception of the good, it is hard to believe that, were he to have to divest himself of those paintings, his *moral* identity would be destroyed and his prospects for a minimally flourishing life thereby undermined. Likewise, one could not expect to be exonerated from paying inheritance taxes on the grounds that not to accept God's existence is such a grievous offence to God himself that God forbids one to lend financial support to a secular state. For, however central such belief in God's existence is to one's conception of the good, such an objection rests on the view, asserted as fundamental truth which we all ought to accept, that God exists. As we saw, though, such a view cannot suffice to exonerate its holders from doing what others are under a duty to do.[22]

Having said that, it would be unwise to rule out, from the outset, the possibility that someone might succeed in showing that financial restrictions on his right to bequeath his whole estate would destroy his moral identity. For, whereas the mere possession of money itself might not be the kind of good which can plausibly be said to be central to anyone's moral identity, estates more widely understood may sometimes be; and so may some conceptions of the good for which money is necessary. Such would be the case, for example, of someone's deeply held belief, backed up by relevant textual support, that God *requires* that all Muslims go to Mecca once in their life, as a condition for acceding to heaven. Were that believer to have to pay inheritance taxes on his parents' estate, at the cost of going to Mecca, he might well be able to mount a successful conscientious objection to so doing.

To many, my sketchy argument in favour of conscientious objections to paying inheritance taxes will sound wildly implausible. It is important to bear in mind, however, that conscientious objectors both to posthumous organ donations and restrictions on wealth transfer should be expected to make up for being exonerated from a duty to donate. At the end of section 4.2.2, I rejected the view that individuals should be allowed to pay body duties so as to buy themselves or their deceased relatives out of a duty posthumously to transfer their organs to the sick, in all cases where the deceased is the only eligible donor for a transplant patient. I undertook there to qualify my rejection here. To recapitulate, then: if, and only if, for someone to be buried or cremated intact is necessary to the preservation of his moral identity and thus to his prospects for a minimally flourishing life, she should be exempt from the duty to transfer her organs posthumously, on conscientious grounds. By the same token, if, and only if, for someone to bury or have his next-of-kin's body cremated intact is necessary to the preservation of his moral identity and thus to his prospects for a flourishing life, they should be allowed to bury or cremate the deceased intact. In both cases, they ought to either pay body duties, or perform some sort of civic service in addition to the service they would have had to do upon reaching the age of eighteen; by the same token, so should objectors to financial restrictions on the posthumous transfer of wealth. To be sure, as I pointed out above, cases might arise where the *only* eligible supplier for patient P is a conscientious objector, with the effect that P

[22] However, one might be able to object to paying taxes on the grounds that taxation is instrumental to the survival of a government guilty of grievous wrongdoing such as the enslavement of black people, and that in contributing to that government's survival, one is complicitous in slavery. Such was H. Thoreau's view in his famous essay on civil disobedience (with some qualifications, which need not detain us here). Note, though, that Thoreau's argument is not so much that *he* should not pay taxes irrespective of what his fellow citizens ought or ought not to do; rather, his claim is that all American citizens ought to desist from paying taxes. See H. D. Thoreau, 'Civil Disobedience', in H. A. Bedeau (ed.), *Civil Disobedience* (Indianapolis: Pegasus, 1969).

would die or lead a less than minimally flourishing life. But to reiterate: justice, requiring as it does that we treat one another with the respect owed to persons as such, could not insist that this particular donor have his moral identity destroyed, and his prospects for a minimally flourishing life thereby jeopardized, in order to help P.

Let me note, before concluding, that the proposal I have just outlined does not merely justify opt-out systems that prevail in Continental Europe. For, in such systems, one need not give any reason to justify one's wish not to have one's organs removed posthumously in order to be exempt from having to donate. Under my proposal, one cannot give just any reason for being exempt, on conscientious grounds, from having to donate: it must be the case that to donate would destroy one's moral identity, and thereby one's prospects for a minimally flourishing life.

4.4 CONCLUSION

To conclude, I have argued that if the interest of the needy in leading a minimally flourishing life is important enough to be protected by a right to material resources, by way of taxation in general and financial restrictions on inheritance in particular, then the sick have a right to the organs of the dead if they need them in order to lead such a life. To put it differently, the living cannot, and do not, have a right to dispose of their body as they wish posthumously; nor do their relatives have that right.

The foregoing, of course, raises the question of *ante-mortem* cases: if my argument works after death, does it not work during life too? Not necessarily: it clearly does not follow from the fact that we have a duty to make our organs available posthumously that we have a duty to do so prehumously. For obvious reasons, in most cases,[23] having parts of one's body taken away when alive is more burdensome than having them taken away after death. Accordingly, objections to the former may well arise that do not apply in the case of the latter. Having said that, I do think—and will argue in the next chapter—that those objections can be dealt with. Even if I am wrong, in so far as those objections do not apply to the confiscation of cadaveric organs, and barring rebuttal of my arguments against the objections that do apply to it, my defence of the view that the sick have a

---

[23] Not in *all* cases, though. Suppose that you very strongly believe that you must be buried intact in order to be resurrected by God, and that such belief is central to your life. If a liver lobe is taken from you while you are alive, your liver will have (in all likelihood) regenerated itself before you die. But if a liver lobe is taken from you once you are dead, your liver will not regenerate itself. In the light of your religious beliefs, having to donate a liver lobe once you are dead will indeed blight your life, whereas having to do so while you are alive will not.

right to the organs of the dead survives. To be sure, as we saw, some individuals will be exempted from a duty to donate. However, the overwhelming majority will not; the qualifications introduced at the close of this chapter should not blind us to that insight. Nor, more generally, should they blind us to the far-reaching implications of our commitment to the coercively directed distribution of material resources.

5

Confiscating Live Body Parts

5.1 INTRODUCTION

We have just seen that justice requires that those who need organs in order to lead a minimally flourishing life have a right that the able-bodied make their organs available to them posthumously. Does it require that they have that right against the able-bodied whilst the latter are alive? To be sure, it may be that were we to take organs from dead bodies as a matter of course, patients' needs for livers, kidneys, corneas, and so on would be met. However, blood and bone marrow must be transplanted live, and, in some cases, the only eligible suppliers of, say, kidneys and livers might well be live individuals. For all these reasons, the question of the confiscation of live body parts must be addressed.

Interestingly enough, although it has not exercised theorists of distributive justice, it has exercised some moral philosophers. Thus, J. Harris argues that it would be permissible, from a utilitarian point of view, to take a live person's organs, thereby killing her, in order to save the life of two persons; J. J. Thomson, for her part, claims that it is not permissible to do so, except in one case: if someone maims some other individuals in the hope that they will die, and is thereby responsible for the fact that they need organs as a matter of life and death, it is not unjust to take his organs so as to save his victims' lives, thereby killing him. In this book, I reject the kind of utilitarianism posited by Harris; and I focus on issues of distributive, as opposed to retributive, justice. I therefore do not discuss either view.[1]

Rather, my aim is to defend the following two claims: (1) if one thinks that the badly off have a moral right, as a matter of justice, to the material resources they need in order to lead a minimally flourishing life, then, in some cases to be described below, one must be committed to conferring on the sick a moral right that the able-bodied supply them the body parts they need in order to lead such a life; (2) one can confer such a right on the sick without compromising the autonomy of the able-bodied to an unacceptable extent. I make an argument to that effect in section 5.2. In section 5.3, I rebut two objections to it, to wit: to confer on the sick a right to the live body parts of the able-bodied (a) violates the

---

[1] See J. Harris, 'The Survival Lottery', *Philosophy* 50 (1975): 81–7; J. J. Thomson, *Rights, Restitution, and Risk*, ch. 6.

bodily integrity of the latter, and (b) constitutes too much of an interference in their life. Finally, in section 5.4, I consider an unpalatable, and possible, implication of my arguments in favour of the duties to provide personal services and body parts, namely, the coercively directed provision of sexual and reproductive services.

Before I start, I should make it clear that I shall not consider whether it is ethically acceptable to take body parts from under-age children, animals, individuals in a persistent vegetative state, aborted foetuses, and mentally disabled individuals. As indicated in Chapter 1, my concern is with what *persons* owe one another. Nor shall I deal with the difficult question of how to allocate body parts amongst the sick.[2] My main concern, in sum, is to show that, assuming agreement on eligibility criteria for medical treatment, the sick have a right, as a matter of justice, to (some of) the body parts of healthy adults.

5.2 ARGUING FOR THE CONFISCATION OF LIVE BODY PARTS

I pointed out at the outset of this book that very few philosophers address the question of the demands of justice with respect to our body. Eric Rakowski is one of those who do. In his view, justice requires that people have equal amounts of mental, material, and physical resources and be compensated for unchosen addictions. It sanctions voluntary arrangements whereby adults enter pools of suppliers and receivers of organs, as well as the compulsory taking of organs from minors—who are not capable of making the decision to enter such a pool. Rakowski claims that enough people would enter such schemes to meet the need for organs.[3] It is unclear to me whether he is correct, for the likelihood of ever needing an organ is very small, and it is therefore entirely conceivable that someone may decide to take a calculated risk, and not to enter a pool of donors/receivers. As Rakowski himself concedes, a situation may well arise, then, where the only eligible supplier for a given patient turns out to be someone who has elected not to enter such a pool and who is therefore under no obligation

---

[2] In particular, I do not take a stand on the following questions. Is someone eligible for a transplant simply in virtue of needing an organ at time *t*? Is someone eligible for a transplant if she will have had a minimally flourishing life *overall*, even though she will not have led one from the moment she needs the transplant? Those questions also arise when the allocation of material resources is at issue: it also matters there whether the decisive factor, when determining someone's eligibility for help, is the overall quality of her life over time or the mere existence of her need at time *t*. Advocates of coercive taxation for the purpose of helping the needy do not pay much attention to this issue, and tend to assume that someone has a right to receive help at *t* if she is needy at *t* (and provided that no one else is needier than she is, that there are enough resources to help her, etc.).

[3] E. Rakowski, *Equal Justice* (Oxford: Oxford University Press, 1991), ch. 8. For a similar view, see R. Audi, 'The Morality and Utility of Organ Transplantation', *Utilitas* 8 (1996): 140–58, at 148–9.

to make his organs available. In such a situation, equality of (physical resources) would not obtain.

Rakowski's proposal is rather modest, since individuals must consent to be considered as suppliers in order to be held under a duty to supply. By contrast, in arguing for the compulsory taking of live body parts, I am arguing that it is unjust to deny one's organs to those who need them, even if one does not consent to be considered as a supplier, where what is at stake is the possibility for them to lead a minimally flourishing life, and a fortiori to survive. To put it differently: the sick, or so I argue, have a moral right against the able-bodied that the latter give them (some of) their body parts whilst alive.

Now, we saw in Chapter 4 that body parts are the kind of goods of which it makes sense to say that one can have a right to them. At this juncture, however, it is worth revisiting that claim. There I argued that the provision of a good can be protected by a right if the good is such that to be under a duty to transfer it to someone else does not undermine our personhood. I then pointed out that to be under a posthumous duty to transfer our body parts meets that condition, since we no longer have an intimate connection with our body once we are dead. However, whilst we are alive, and in those cases where transferring a body part to someone else would cause us to die, being under such a duty will destroy us as a person (since we cease to be a person when we die). Accordingly, justice cannot require of us that we divest ourselves of our brain, our heart, our lungs, and the whole of our liver. Of course, that it cannot do so is contingent on the state of medical technology, for the simple reason that the fact that losing our heart, lungs, or liver would destroy us as a person is so contingent. Suppose someone needs a heart, that I am a compatible donor, and that my heart (unlike the patient's) could be replaced by a machine. If I had to transfer my heart to that patient, under such conditions, I would not cease to be a person. One can imagine similar scenarios involving the lungs and the whole liver (but not the brain). In any event, as long as we have not developed the relevant technologies, justice cannot require of us that we divest ourselves of the aforementioned body parts. However, it *can*—which is not to say (yet) that it does—require of us that we transfer our kidneys, corneas, blood, bone marrow, and *part* of our liver, since we would still be a person even if we were under a duty to transfer them to the sick.

As I conceded in Chapter 4, the claim that body parts can be regarded as resources to be redistributed will sound odd to many. But, as I noted there, if the conception of personhood I sketched in section 1.2.1 is correct, whereby one must have, and continually perceive oneself as having, a body in order to be a person, then, as a would-be organ supplier, I can envision my dead body being divested of its essential organs without my person being under threat. And I can, in turn, quite easily conceive of my organs as resources for someone else. Here, however, I claim that they ought to be conceived of as resources to be distributed even when the suppliers are alive. And that may seem deeply wrong. For, if having a body is necessary to being a person, surely, one might be tempted to insist, we cannot really think of it as a set of resources. Remember Sartre's words: 'I am not in relation to my hand in the same utilizing attitude as I am in relation to [my] pen.'[4] Recall Dworkin's argument to the effect that body parts should not be regarded as social resources, on the grounds that they belong not to someone's circumstances, but rather are part of his person.[5] And consider Fried's claim, to the effect that 'certain attributes—for instance one's bodily organs . . . are so closely related to a conception of oneself that to make them available for trading-off in a scheme of morality would be, as it were, to gain the world and lose one's soul'.[6]

However, there are three related points to be made which support the view that live body parts are resources in the sense in which things are resources. First, we need them both in order to implement our conception of the good; lacking either of them, let alone both, may constitute a serious handicap; and they can be taken away from us without our ceasing to exist as a person. I do not mean to imply that we ought to relate to our kidneys, corneas, blood, and bone marrow exactly as we relate to other resources which we are in a position to transfer to those who need them, such as wealth: indeed nothing I have said so far implies that we ought to be able to detach ourselves from our body parts just as we ought to be able to detach ourselves from the money which we have deposited at the bank and on which we have to pay taxes, or from a plot of land which we have bought and from which we are expropriated. Rather, I only mean to suggest that we ought not to be so attached to them as to consider them essential to being a person *tout court*. Indeed, that we do not have the same utilizing attitude to our hand as to our pen does nevertheless allow for the fact that we can and do regard our hand as an instrument, with the qualification that we do not *only* regard it as such.

Second, as we saw in section 1.2.1, although we cease to exist when our body and brain cease to exist, we are more than the sum total of our body. Accordingly, we can distance ourselves from its parts, and talk about them, as if they were not parts of ourselves. Although Sartre is right to note that we do not relate to our hand as we relate to our pen, he goes too far when claiming that he uses his pen in order to form letters but not his hands in order to hold the pen. As he puts it, '*I am* my hand.'[7] However, we *do* use our hand in order to hold the pen and our fingers in order to hit the computer's keys. We are aware that they can perform tasks that our feet cannot. We are also aware that in other respects, they will not do: we use a screwdriver precisely because we know that our fingers are

---

[4] Sartre, *Being and Nothingness*, p. 373. [5] Dworkin, 'Comment on Narveson', at 39.
[6] C. Fried, *An Anatomy of Values* (Cambridge, Mass.: Harvard University Press, 1970), p. 205. For a devastating rebuttal of Fried's and Dworkin's objections to the mandatory taking of organs, see Rakowski, *Equal Justice*, pp. 183–8.
[7] Sartre, *Being and Nothingness*, p. 373.

not strong enough for the task of screwing a shelf on to the wall. We simply *are not* our hands. It is *I* who write, and not my hand; it is *I* who smile, and not my mouth; it is *I* who experience humour, and not that part of my brain which does. And so on.

Third, Sartre's claim that his attitude to his hand is different from his attitude to his pen derives whatever strength it has from being a claim about the hand; it would be equally strong, or almost as strong, I think, if it distinguished the foot from the shoe, and the eyes from the glasses. But it would be considerably less powerful as a claim about kidneys, pancreas, the liver, blood, and tissues. For consider: if being embodied is necessary to being a person, it is because we need a body as a filter between ourselves and the world, through which we experience the latter. Moreover, we literally see ourselves as embodied beings: as I type this sentence, I see my fingers move on the keyboard, I am aware of my eyes looking at the screen, and so on. Finally, we are aware that others' perception of us is in large part perception of the body we happen to have. It is natural, then (if misguided), that we should think of those parts of our body which enable us to experience the world, and which others can see—limbs, eyes—as instruments perhaps, but as parts of ourselves for sure.

In contrast, although our internal organs and tissues enable our body to function as a filter between us and the world, they are not the means through which we are a subject of experience. Accordingly, even if it were correct to claim that body parts which are such means ought not to be conceived of as resources on those very grounds, it would not be correct to rule out from distributable resources those body parts which are not such means. Nor would it be correct to rule out from distributable resources those body parts which, for being internal, cannot be seen by us and others, and thus do not constitute that part of us which we present to the world and the loss of (part of) which could conceivably change our perception of ourselves.

In short, apart from the brain, the heart, the lungs, and the liver as a whole (the loss of which would undermine our personhood), all body parts are the kind of goods of which it makes sense to say that the sick *can* have a right to them against the living. Of course, this is not enough to establish that they actually do have that right. However, in Chapter 4, I argued that the considerations which support the view that the needy have welfare rights to some of the resources of the now-dead well off also support the view that the sick have a right to the organs of the now-dead able-bodied. Similarly, the considerations which support the view that the needy have welfare rights to some of the resources of the live well off also support the view that the sick have a right to some of the body parts of the live able-bodied. The argument made there in favour of the confiscation of cadaveric organs applies, *mutatis mutandis*, to the case of live body parts, and I shall not restate it here. Suffice it to stress, at this stage, that someone who suffers from leukaemia may very well die if she does not receive a bone-marrow transplant. Likewise, someone who badly needs a hip replacement and whose operation is postponed because of a shortage of blood supplies will lack the mobility necessary for her to get on with her life; and a haemophiliac who needs a blood transfusion when he has to undergo even minor operations such as a tooth extraction, on pain of facing very serious medical complications, will see his autonomy impaired if he does not get the blood. And so on.

That individuals all need body parts in order to lead a minimally flourishing life does not entail that those who lack them have a right to whatever body part they need. As I posited in section 1.3.2, justice requires that the needy get the *all-purposes* material resources required to live a minimally flourishing life: it does not require that they get whatever resources they need in order to implement their particular conception of the good. By the same token, it does not require that they get the body part they need in order to implement their particular conception of the good. Accordingly, whereas someone without kidneys might have a claim for one kidney against a healthy individual (within limits set below), a person with only *one* kidney does not have a claim for the second kidney he needs in order to be a world-class athlete.

In order to decide how much help they can legitimately ask from the able-bodied, one must assess the magnitude of the burden the latter would have to shoulder if called upon to help. As I argued in section 1.3.2, in cases where having to help those in need would render the life of the able-bodied less than minimally flourishing, they should not be held under a duty to do so; in cases where it does not, they should be held under a duty to do so. Our task, then—and a very difficult one at that—is to identify cases where potential suppliers would not lead a less than minimally flourishing life were they called upon to help.

Now, on the one hand, it is trivially obvious that for the able-bodied to lose their kidneys or corneas may very plausibly render their life less than minimally flourishing, as they would be deprived of some all-purpose means necessary to implement a conception of the good that would give some meaning to their life. In those cases, the sick do not have a right that the able-bodied transfer (some of) their body parts to them. On the other hand, it seems clear that to donate one pint of blood, to give some bone marrow, or to lose a liver lobe does not jeopardize one's prospects for a minimally flourishing life, for those body parts are regenerative.[8] In fact, I submit that losing those particular body parts consti-tutes much less of a restriction on the projects the able-bodied want to pursue than losing, say, between 25 per cent and 40 per cent of their income through

---

[8] I am assessing here whether the *loss* of a body part constitutes too much of a sacrifice and undermines our bodily integrity to an unacceptable extent. I am not assessing whether its *coerced removal* constitutes too much of a risk. The loss of a liver lobe does not fall foul of the objection from sacrifice, but its removal, performed as it is under general anaesthetic, might still fall foul of the objection from risk, which I assess in section 5.3.2. (There is ample evidence that, in patients who have had a liver lobe removed, the liver fully resumes its functions four to six weeks after the operation. See A. L. Caplan, 'Living Dangerously: The Morality of Using Living Persons as Suppliers of Liver Lobes for Transplantation', *Cambridge Journal of Medical Ethics* 1 (1992): 311–17.)

taxes. Accordingly, they can be held under a moral duty to make them available to the sick, provided that they are not called upon to give so often that they would be unable to make any plans, or that it would endanger their health. The British National Blood Service recommends that healthy adults between the ages of eighteen and sixty not donate more than three times a year, and one could take that as a benchmark. With respect to bone marrow and liver lobes, one could, similarly, follow guidelines from health authorities.

The hardest question, though, is whether one can hold the able-bodied under a duty to give a kidney or a cornea to someone who lacks one. Whereas losing both kidneys or corneas would deprive the able-bodied of an all-purpose means, losing one such organ would not do so. Accordingly, the able-bodied could mount a successful challenge to being held under a duty to donate only if they could show that, by losing one such organ, they would be unable to implement their current, preferred conception of the good, *and* that, upon close, rational, and critical scrutiny, there is no alternative conception of the good, compatible with losing those organs, which would render their life minimally flourishing.

Clearly, losing a kidney or a cornea in adulthood not only restricts the range of conceptions of the good one can frame and pursue; it may also necessitate revising one's existing conception of the good—something which, as one grows older, is increasingly difficult to do. This, incidentally, is even more true with respect to corneas, since one has, on the whole, a greater need for full vision than for two functioning kidneys. However, whether losing a kidney or a cornea would prevent the able-bodied from leading a minimally flourishing life in the way described in the last paragraph in part depends on (a) the medical complications arising from the loss of those body parts, (b) the kind of life the able-bodied are living, and (c) how easy it would be for them to find an alternative, meaningful conception of the good, were they to lose one of those organs. On the first count, available data suggest that the side-effect of a nephrectomy are minimal.[9] To be sure, someone who has transferred one of his kidneys to the kidney-less would incur some risk of disability and impairment if his one remaining kidney fails. But, assuming that his condition could only be treated by a kidney transplant, he himself would be eligible for such an operation and would have a right against third parties. Still, were the probability of suffering from total kidney failure be so high as to constitute a higher risk than the risks the able-bodied standardly incur, and would therefore impose on others in their everyday life, then they ought not to be held under a duty to donate. If that were the case, however, that would not undermine my case for the claim that the sick have a right against the able-bodied that the latter give them blood and bone marrow.

On the second and third counts, whereas having to give a cornea might have catastrophic consequences for a fifty-year-old professional painter or

[9] See A. Garwood-Gowers, *Living Donor Organ Transplantation* (Aldershot: Ashgate, 1999), pp. 41–5.

photographer, it may be bearable for a piano-tuner. Similarly, whereas having to give a kidney might blight the life of a world-class athlete, it may have very little effect on the life of a sedentary academic. Moreover, it might blight the athlete's life only temporarily, but not for ever: after all, many athletes who suffer a career-ending injury retrain and do something else. I cannot fully deal with such comparisons here. I shall simply note that, in the light of the immense difficulties encountered by the kidney-less and the blind, we cannot afford not to take seriously the suggestion that the able-bodied might be able to help them by giving them the relevant organ without incurring the costs we tend to think they would.

And, indeed, determining how much individuals owe to one another on the basis of their conception of the good and engaging in the kind of calculations described above is not a novel idea. Theorists of justice who hold the tenets of standard morality to be true and who argue that justice requires that everyone have prospects for a minimally flourishing life believe that no one can be held under a duty to help the needy at the cost of his freedom of occupational choice, but that one can be held under such duty at a lesser cost. Imagine a badly paid musician who could work as a highly paid lawyer but who loves his job. It would be wrong, or so these theorists believe, to tax him in proportion to the earnings he could make as a lawyer, since one would thereby force him to give up on his preferred conception of the good and to spend his working life doing a job he hates. But it would not be wrong, or so many of them would argue, to increase his tax rate to the extent that, although he could still work as a musician, he would have to do less photography—an expensive hobby he loves—than he currently does. If such considerations can be brought to bear, albeit in a rough and ready way, on the legitimacy of taking material resources from those who can afford to help the poor, they can also be brought to bear, in as rough and ready a way, on the legitimacy of taking body parts from those who can afford to help the sick. (How such calculations could be made in practice is another matter.)

So far I have argued that able-bodied individuals are under a duty to transfer some of their body parts if other people need them in order to survive or to lead a minimally flourishing life. But that in itself does not tell us who should fulfil that duty in cases where there are more eligible suppliers than needy recipients. In cases involving blood and bone marrow, where the needed body part is divisible and can be supplied by several individuals, there are two ways of selecting who should fulfil the duty to transfer. One can either ask all eligible suppliers to do it, or one can select at random amongst eligible suppliers. In the former scenario eligible suppliers all bear the burden of contributing, whereas in the latter scenario eligible suppliers all have an equal chance not to bear the burden, but some suppliers will shoulder a greater burden than others. It is fair, I think, that all eligible suppliers contribute. Compare this with taxation: its advocates are not claiming that one should select at random amongst all potential taxpayers those who will have to pay a tax; instead, they are claiming that all taxpayers should pay. Having said that, should the costs of using all eligible suppliers prove too high, one could devise a rotation system whereby each supplier would be called upon to transfer some of their blood or bone marrow once every *n* years.

Cases where the needed body part is indivisible (for example, kidneys and liver lobes) are trickier, since the burden of having to transfer them cannot fall equally on all eligible suppliers. My argument for conferring on the sick a right to the body parts of the able-bodied implies that, in such cases, all eligible suppliers *equally* are under a correlative duty to transfer the relevant body part to the sick. This, together with the fact that only one of them must actually fulfil their duty, in turn implies that they all have an equal claim not to have to shoulder the burden of fulfilling the duty. In such cases, it seems right to select the supplier at random, since randomness ensures that people have an equal chance of having to bear the burden of giving body parts, and that no one is selected who has a stronger claim than others not to shoulder that burden.[10]

Note, however, that if it is indeed the case that selling one's body parts is legitimate (as I shall argue in Chapter 6 that it is), then, just as a well-off individual could, in principle, buy himself out of having to perform a civilian service (as we saw in section 3.2), a well-off individual who is called upon to provide one of his body parts to help a patient could, in principle, buy himself out of performing that duty by paying a willing third party to donate instead.

In the case of blood, this suggests that someone who is called upon to donate, like everyone else, every year, might be able to pay another donor to stand in for him. That other donor, then, would contribute more than his fair share, but would do so against payment. In the case of non-divisible body parts, the qualification I have just introduced supposes that there is more than one eligible supplier for the needed organs (let us say, for simplicity's sake, that there are two of them), that a wealthy individual has been selected at random to help the sick, and that he wishes to pay the other eligible supplier to stand in for him. To reiterate here a point made in section 3.2, if the grounds for the obligation to help is the neediness of the sick, then there is no reason to rule out the possibility that the wealthy might be able to transfer, so to speak, the performance of their duty on willing individuals. Note, though, that in both cases, as the well-off person is, in fact, trying to get out of doing what he is called upon to do, he may have to pay whatever price asked by the potential seller. (This is another way of saying that he would lack a claim to being protected from exploitation—a claim which, as we shall see in section 6.3.2, sellers and buyers in all other cases do have.) Neither case undercuts my case for the confiscation of body parts, since there might be instances where the able-bodied, and wealthy, individual who is called upon to help cannot find an alternative donor, or cannot, or is unwilling, to meet the alternative

---

[10] The foregoing considerations apply, obviously, to cases where two dead individuals turn out to be eligible donors for one transplant patient.

donor's financial requirements. In those instances, then, he or she *is* under an obligation to contribute.

Before I review objections against the view that the sick have a right against the able-bodied that they give them some of their body parts, two loose ends need tying. I have argued that the able-bodied are under a duty to transfer some of their body parts to the sick, but—and this is the first loose end—I have not said anything here about compensating them. Yet, as I argued in Chapter 4, in cases where the burden of donating falls on a small number of individuals, suppliers of body parts should be compensated. This is not merely because whether or not someone is endowed with tissues and organs which are in demand is a matter of bad brute luck, but also (and relevantly to our concern in this chapter) because an eligible supplier who has had to relinquish a body part whilst alive may incur higher life-insurance premiums or lose income whilst in hospital, and so on. A properly designed compensation scheme would cover such costs.

The second loose end is this: I have argued that the able-bodied are under a duty to transfer (some of) their body parts to the sick; but I have not distinguished between cases where potential suppliers of body parts are materially quite well off from cases where they are not. Nor have I distinguished between cases where those who need organs are also materially needy, and cases where they are not. We may be faced, then, with a situation where the patient (P) is relatively well off but where the only eligible supplier (S_u) is not. Some might think that, in that case, S_u ought not to be held under a duty to provide P with a body part, on the grounds that it would be unfair to confiscate, against his wishes, some of the body parts of a poor individual, so as to help a wealthier transplant patient. For the former, after all, is worse off than the latter. Were his organs to be confiscated, not only would he be materially worse off than the transplant patient, which is unjust; he would also suffer the additional injury of not having his wishes concerning his body respected.[11]

I do not think that whether or not one is under a duty to make one's body parts available to the sick depends on one's share of material resources. For a start, I assume at the outset of this book that justice does not require that material equality obtain. Accordingly, the fact that S_u is materially worse off than P is not unjust, provided that he has the resources he needs, and to which he is entitled, to lead a minimally flourishing life. Thus, the objection under study cannot allege the putative injustice of this inequality as a reason to exempt S_u from helping P.

Moreover, and more importantly, the objection seems to prove too much. Suppose that a drowning but relatively well-off person (D) can only be rescued by a swimmer (S_w), who happens to be materially worse off than D, although not

---

[11] That objection was put to me in the context of the confiscation of cadaveric organs. I actually think that it is stronger, although, as we shall see, not decisive, when applied to the confiscation of live body parts.

needy in ways forbidden by justice. It would seem odd to allow S_w not to rescue D on the grounds that the latter is materially better off than he is. The fact that S_w knows how to swim is what matters, not S_w's material situation relative to D's. By the same token, the fact that S_u has something—a body part—which P needs so as to lead a minimally flourishing life is what matters, not S_u's material situation relative to P's.

Finally, that someone may be sick—and undergoing medical treatment—does not disqualify him from a duty to help the materially needy by way of taxation. Suppose that P, who needs a body part but can hold down a job, earns enough to be able to give some material resources to H, who is able-bodied but homeless. Were P to say that he will henceforth stop helping H, on the grounds that it would be unfair, because of his poor health, to diminish his total holdings of resources, we would accuse him, rightly, of failing to fulfil his obligation of justice. If P is in a position to help N by way of taxation, without having so little by way of material resources that he cannot lead a minimally flourishing life, there is no reason why he should not do so. By the same token, if S_u is in a position to help P, by way of a body-part transfer, without jeopardizing his health to such an extent as to jeopardize his prospects for a minimally flourishing life, there is no reason why he should not do so.

I have assumed so far that S_u is worse off than P but not materially needy. Let us assume that he is, though, in that he does not have the resources he needs to lead a minimally flourishing life. In so far as we are working in ideal theory, S_u's situation is acceptable at the bar of justice: it may be, for example, that S_u chose not to avail himself of the resources to which he had a right; or it may be that S_u can be clearly shown to be responsible for his plight and therefore does not have such a right in the first instance. Can we, in that case, hold him under a duty to help P? My hunch is that there is no reason why we should not. *Ex hypothesi*, P does not owe it to S_u to improve his material situation; and S_u has something which P desperately needs. Let us return to the drowning case. D is in serious peril; S_w can help him, but, it turns out, is a homeless person who has consistently refused perfectly acceptable, publicly funded, housing. Why should S_w be exonerated from any obligation to rescue D, simply because he happens to be very needy, and need not be? Things would look different if S_w were entitled, as a matter of justice, to housing which, for whatever reason, he cannot get (an all too familiar situation, even in welfare state countries such as ours). In that case, S_w might have enough of a grievance not to be held under a duty to help D. I say 'might', note, because I am not entirely sure that he does. Still, in a situation where he is responsible for his neediness, he does not have such a grievance, and correspondingly does not have a claim not to help D. By the same token, S_u does not have a claim not to help P (provided that we can apply the non-responsibility condition, that is, provided that we can assess that S_u is responsible for his plight without getting him to make shameful revelations about himself).

5.3 TWO OBJECTIONS AGAINST THE CONFISCATION
OF LIVE BODY PARTS

I have argued so far that if one thinks that the needy have a right to material resources against the well off, one is committed to the view that individuals who need body parts in order to survive or lead a minimally flourishing life have a right that the able-bodied give them those parts (except for the brain, the whole liver, both kidneys, corneas, the heart, and the lungs). Now, one could obviously object that my argument does not take sufficient account of the fact that those resources—material or bodily—are of a different nature. The following words, from the pen of one Judge John P. Flaherty, vividly capture what most people think of the mandatory taking of body parts: 'Forcible extraction of living body tissue causes revulsion in the judicial mind ... You can picture the man being strapped to the table and then the extraction.'[12]

The confiscation of live body parts standardly elicit two objections: (a) to confer on the sick a right to the body parts of the able-bodied violates the bodily integrity of the latter; (b) it constitutes too much of an interference in their lives, in a way that conferring on the needy a right to the material resources of the well off does not. Note that the objection from bodily integrity, which I address in section 5.3.1, differs from the objection from interference, which I address in section 5.3.2, since one can undermine someone's bodily integrity without in any way interfering with their life. If I come into your room at night knowing that you are asleep and very heavily sedated, and if I take blood from you, I am not interfering with your life, since I am not preventing you from doing anything. Yet, by taking that blood, I take something from your body and thereby might be thought to diminish its integrity. Conversely, if, as you walk down to the beach, I stand in your way but do not touch you, I am interfering with your life, but not violating your bodily integrity. However, although it is conceivable to object to the confiscation of body parts on the grounds that it undermines the suppliers' bodily integrity without making reference to their interest in not being interfered with, I shall argue at the close of section 5.3.1 that the objection from bodily integrity derives much of its force from the view that in violating people's bodily integrity, one *is* interfering with their life to an unacceptable extent.

5.3.1 Bodily Integrity

To argue, as I do, that, under some circumstances, the sick have a right against the able-bodied that they give them body parts amounts to claiming that the latter do not have a right to full bodily integrity. Quite obviously, someone might object that they do, in fact, have such a right, which, if correct, would disprove my case.

---

[12] *McFall* v. *Shimp*, Allegheny Court, USA, 1978.

Now, there are two ways in which one might construct that objection. As we saw in Chapter 4, one might argue that bodily integrity—to wit, having control over one's body—is important in its own right, just as leading a minimally flourishing life is, and that we have an absolute right that nothing be done to our body, or with it, without our consent (provided that we do not use it to harm others without good reasons). Against that variant of the objection, which directly entails the opposite of my claim that the able-bodied do not have a right to full bodily integrity, there is very little that can be said. It bears reiterating, though, that it is unclear why our interest in bodily integrity should be given importance in its own right, *alongside* our interest in leading a minimally flourishing life.

And, indeed, someone might be tempted to argue, more convincingly, that bodily integrity serves other, fundamental values, and that it is therefore important enough to be protected by an absolute right. For example, someone might argue, very plausibly, that individuals need to have control over their body in order to lead a minimally flourishing life.[13] On that view, the body is an all-purpose means necessary to implement any conception of the good, which suggests, if true, that individuals cannot lead a minimally flourishing life if its integrity is undermined.

However, so to object to the compulsory taking of live body parts is also problematic, for two reasons. First, individuals clearly need not have control over the *whole* of their body in order to lead such a life. Second, in conferring on the able-bodied the absolute right to control what is done to their body, we would allow for a world where a number of people are left without the body parts they need in order to lead a minimally flourishing life: we would, in fact, undermine the very value from which bodily integrity gets its appeal. To promote the value of a minimally flourishing life, thus, might require undermining the bodily integrity of some individuals.

Others still might be tempted to point out that in denying the able-bodied the absolute right to control what happens to their body, one fails to give them the respect they are due as persons. This objection, in turn, has three variants.[14] The first variant claims that in losing her body parts, a person would stop being a person (or at any rate would not remain the same person), then asserts that it is up to each person to decide whether to remain a person (or at any rate whether to remain the person that she is), from which it concludes that the mandatory taking of body parts is morally wrong.

---

[13] For an objection along those lines, see D. Lamb, *Organ Transplants and Ethics* (London: Routledge, 1990), p. 106. For a good account of the view that bodily integrity is a condition for autonomy, see Feinberg, *Harm to Self*, p. 54.

[14] The first and third variant were put to me at an Oxford seminar in May 2000 (the first one can also be found in Fried, *An Anatomy of Values*, pp. 205ff.), the second one by C. Mackenzie. There are similarities between the second and the third variant (namely, their insistence that the confiscation of live body parts is incompatible with the requirement that we should respect one another's personhood), but it pays to address them separately.

The second claim is correct for there can be fewer more fundamental interests of persons than their interest in remaining a person. On that basis, one can either argue that persons therefore should decide whether to remain such, or one can aver that they are not even at liberty to jeopardize their interest in remaining such. I defended the latter view in section 1.2.3. In any event, whichever of those two views one adopts, they both rule out the mandatory confiscation of body parts, *provided* the first claim is correct.[15] Unfortunately for the proponent of the objection under study, however, it is not correct. To reiterate some of the points made earlier, persons are more than the sum total of their body, and so can distance themselves from its parts and remain persons; indeed they can remain the same person even if they lose some of its parts. To the extent that I am not advocating, in this chapter, complete body transplants, indeed to the extent that I am advocating limited losses of organs (such that the individual who would lose them would remain the same person), this variant of the bodily integrity objection fails.

The second variant of the objection holds that to interfere with an individual's body in the way defended here is to inflict the same kind of psychological trauma as inflicted through torture and rape—trauma so serious that it can contribute to undermining his or her personhood. Now, it is true that torture and rape can and do have that effect. It is no less true, though, that the coercive taking of some blood, some bone marrow, a liver lobe, and a kidney ought not to do so. I shall address the supposed analogy between non-consensual sex and the confiscation of body parts in section 5.4, so let me here focus on the case of torture. Torturers cause enormous physical pain to their victims, and moreover intend to do so, either as a means to, for example, obtaining important information, or as an end in itself. And it is those two factors—the experience of the unimaginable pain and the awareness that they simply do not count as persons—which often lead to the disintegration of their victims as persons. But neither factor is usually present in the confiscation of live body parts, first, because the removal procedure is done under anaesthetic and causes suppliers little pain afterwards (if at all), and, second, because the aim of neither the sick nor the medical staff is to destroy suppliers. Having said that, some people who suffer from needle phobia would experience such terror, were they to have to undergo the removal procedure, that their personhood might be destroyed. It seems to me that this would constitute a strong enough reason to exempt them from donation, just as (as we saw in section 2.3.2) my being water-phobic would constitute a reason to exonerate me from a duty to rescue a swimmer in difficulty.[16]

---

[15] Note that if it is correct that a person stops being a person if she loses her body parts, the second view also rules out *giving* and *selling* one's organs. More on the latter in Chapter 6.

[16] I am grateful to M. Kramer for drawing my attention to the case of the needle-phobic, which is relevantly similar to that of the individual who does not want to give his organs posthumously because he believes that he is Jesus Christ and that Christ's body must remain intact (see section 4.3.2). Both suffer from a serious medical condition which is characterized by, respectively, irrational fears and irrational beliefs.

It is simply not true, then, that confiscating body parts from individuals is akin to torturing them; in those very few instances where the effect of the removal procedure on suppliers is similar to the trauma incurred by torture victims, my argument to the effect that there are limits to the sacrifices we can expect individuals to make for the sake of the needy would apply. This is not the end of the bodily integrity objection, though. For it has a third variant, which goes like this: to be a person is amongst other things to have the capacity for moral and rational agency, and more specifically to have the capacity for framing, revising, and pursuing a conception of the good which is not subsumed under someone else's ends but rather is one's own. It is crucial, in order to exercise the capacity for moral and rational agency, and more specifically to pursue their conception of the good, that individuals each have separate bodies, are therefore separate *loci* for pain and pleasure and are aware of themselves as being different persons. In the light of these facts about what being a person consists of, individuals should treat one another as separate persons, which, as vague a requirement as it is, is usually taken to mean that, following Kant, they should treat one another not merely as means but also as ends. But—the objection continues—the compulsory taking of body parts undermines that requirement. For, after all, *my* blood would run through *your* veins, *my* bone marrow would produce *your* cells, *my* kidney or my liver would purify *your* body, *my* eye would be *your* window to the world, and so on. Although I am at liberty to choose to give you those body parts, in requiring that I give them to you, you are treating my body, and therefore me, merely as a set of resources to be used for your own purposes, and not as a separate person with her own ends. In so acting, you fail to give me the recognition respect I am owed as a person.

At first sight, this variant of the objection from bodily integrity has a lot of intuitive appeal. From Rawls's well-known complaint that utilitarianism does not treat persons as separate to Nozick's assertion that granting them self-ownership rights is the only way so to treat them, the idea of the separateness of persons is central to liberal thought. Moreover, unlike the variant we examined a few paragraphs ago, this variant need not deny that someone whose bodily integrity would be compromised by the mandatory transfer of body parts would still be a person (and, indeed, this particular individual would retain her capacity for moral and rational agency, still have self-consciousness, and still be sentient). All it says, in effect, is that in *requiring* of someone that she transfer parts of her body to someone else, one fails to recognize that being a person is not all that matters: being able to live as one is crucial too. To prevent them from so doing is to fail to give them the recognition respect they are due as persons.

In reply, let me concede that being able to live as a person does, of course, matter very much. By way of an extreme example, recall the case, mentioned in section 1.2.1, of a dicephalic being, that is, a being which has one body but two heads. Such a being in fact consists of two distinct persons, each with her own thought processes, desires, memories, intentions, and so on. If being a person were all that mattered, these persons would have no claim for help. However, in so far as they share the same body, they are each entirely dependent on the other's agreement for every single act of their life. Although they are persons, they cannot live as such, and they do, therefore, have a (prima facie) claim for help.

Yet this objection to the confiscation of live body parts fails, because it presses into service an erroneous interpretation of the Kantian requirement that we treat one another as separate persons with our own ends. The requirement as articulated by Kant states that we should not treat one another as means only, but also as ends. This in turn implies that we can treat one another as means provided we also treat one another as ends. The objection works, therefore, only if violating the bodily integrity of the able-bodied amounts to treating them solely as means. However, violating someone's bodily integrity does not, in and of itself, imply that one is not regarding them as having their own projects and attachments. Suppose that I slip and fall off the ice-covered pavement, and that you could do me considerable good simply by helping me to get back on my feet, which would take you about ten seconds. As we saw in Chapter 2, to claim that you are under a duty to help me amounts to denying that you have the right to control what happens to your body, since you would have to use your arms, hands, and legs to haul me off the ground. And yet you could not plausibly object that in requiring that you help me, I am treating you solely as a means to my end, and not as a person with her own projects to pursue: for, after all, you would, in fact, have more than enough time and energy to do whatever it was you wanted to do before I fell. Similarly, when assessing whether requiring that the able-bodied transfer some of their body parts to the sick infringes the Kantian requirement that people be treated as ends and not only as means, one must gauge whether the removal and loss of their body parts would prevent them from pursuing their own projects. One must, in short, decide the extent to which so violating their bodily integrity would interfere with their life.

5.3.2 Freedom from Interference

More convincingly, then, someone might be tempted to object to the claim that the sick have a right to some of the body parts of the able-bodied on the grounds that to hold the latter under the corresponding duty interferes in their lives to a much higher degree than holding the well off under a duty to give material resources to the needy. In support of her claim, she might conceivably go on to make the following three points:[17]

(A) If the able-bodied are liable to be called upon at any time to give some of their body parts, they always have to factor that in decisions they make to

---

[17] For the general claim that the confiscation of body parts constitutes an unacceptable interference in our lives, see, e.g., Cohen, *Self-Ownership, Freedom and Equality*, pp. 243–4. Points

take a trip, go for job interviews, spend time with their children, and so on and, as a result, it is hard for them to introduce some sort of routine in their lives.

(B) If their body parts are not theirs to control but can be used by someone else, and if they are under a duty to make them available to the needy, the able-bodied are under a duty, by implication, to maintain them well, and not to engage in practices which might damage them or render them unusable, and which might thereby render them ineligible as suppliers (such as unsafe sex, smoking, dangerous sports, etc.).

(C) Moreover, simply to *risk* incurring the serious, sometimes life-threatening consequences of a surgical operation would also prevent the able-bodied from making mid- and long-term plans.

In short, being held under a duty to transfer body parts to the sick would place unacceptable constraints on our autonomy. None of those three kinds of cost—unpredictability, constraints on our occupational choices, risk of disability and death—are incurred by the well off when they are called upon to help the needy by way of material resources. Accordingly, holding them under a duty to do so does not commit one to holding the able-bodied under a duty to transfer their body parts to the sick.

Neither of those three points denies what I sought to show in section 5.2, namely, that the *loss* of some body parts need not render our life less than minimally autonomous and thereby less than minimally flourishing. Rather, to advert to the distinction between the burdens attendant on the transfer of a resource and the burdens attendant on the loss itself of that resource which we encountered in section 2.3.1, each of those three points focuses on a particular feature of the moral duty to *transfer* a body part to the sick. To reiterate, however, imposing an absolute prohibition on the confiscation of body parts on the grounds that the suppliers' interest in leading a minimally flourishing life would thereby be harmed does undermine the value of promoting that interest in general, since it would leave a number of people without the body parts they need in order to lead a minimally flourishing life. Our task, then, is to assess the conditions under which, if any, the able-bodied can legitimately withhold their body parts from the sick and thereby deny them prospects for a minimally flourishing life. So let us address each strand of the objection under study.

(A)–(C) were put to me at seminars in London and Bristol in October 2000. The opponent of the confiscation of live body parts might also make another point, namely, that to have to give, say, blood, or one of her liver lobes, violates some of her most deeply held religious beliefs; such an interference with her religious life, she might then argue, would be unacceptable to her. To reiterate, my argument in section 4.3.2. about conscientious objections to the confiscation of cadaveric organs applies here, and I need not restate it.

(A): The first strand holds that being under a duty to transfer a body part, unlike being under a duty to transfer some material resources, is unacceptably disruptive, since suppliers cannot know when they will be called upon to contribute. However, although not knowing whether one will have to transfer body parts does, to some extent, disrupt our lives, it does not seem difficult, as a matter of policy, to minimize such disruption. Concerning blood, if suppliers know that they are due to give blood once a year, at a given date, they can plan around that. Concerning body parts, patients waiting for a transplant do not need to undergo the operation at a few days' notice. One could therefore warn eligible suppliers several weeks in advance that they will have to spend some time at the hospital, and give them, for instance, a two-week bracket within which they could choose when to have the operation. One could also make it statutorily mandatory on employers to accommodate their employees' requests for leave of absence if called upon to donate. To be sure, someone who is called upon to donate may have to postpone some of the plans he will have made (just as he will have to do so, incidentally, if he is called upon to serve on a jury). But, given that patients themselves have to give up on major life plans, and not simply postpone them, it does not seem too much of a price to pay.

(B): Consider now the claim that, under my proposal, the able-bodied are under a duty to remain healthy, which, or so some would argue, constitutes too much of an interference in their lives. This claim assumes that individuals, on my view, hold their body parts in trust for the benefit of the sick. Strictly speaking, however, to claim that the able-bodied are under a moral duty to help the sick does not imply that they are under a duty to remain able-bodied in case some people, in the future, fall sick and need their organs. As we saw in Chapter 3, to claim that the well off are under a duty to give a share of their wealth to the poor does not imply that they have to work to the best of their productive abilities in case more people come to need their resources in the future, or in case those who are already poor come to need more resources than they are currently given. It only means that, on the assumption that the well off already own x, they must give the existing poor a share of x; it also means that they should not defraud the poor and pretend that they do not own x. Analogously, all I am claiming here is this: in cases where the needed body part is one which one ought to supply only once, the able-bodied, once selected for a donation *and only then*, must ensure that they will remain eligible on the day the transplant is to take place. Moreover, they should not try to defraud the sick by pretending that they are not healthy enough to go through the removal procedure. In the case of blood collection, where the able-bodied are called upon to donate at regular intervals, they are not under a duty to make sure that they are eligible to donate, but they are under a duty not to try and commit a fraud. I believe that for the able-bodied to be under such a duty does

not constitute such an interference in their life as to make it less than minimally flourishing.[18]

(C): Let us assume, then, that the foregoing points are correct, and let us suppose that someone is selected for a donation. If the donation necessitates an operation under general anaesthetic, she incurs a risk of suffering serious complications during and after the procedure; in fact she risks death. Surely, some would object, she cannot be under a duty to incur such risks for the sake of a transplant patient? Clearly, in that respect, the duty to provide material help is relevantly disanalogous to the duty to provide body parts—disanalogous in such a way, that is, as to undermine support for the latter.

We encountered that point in section 2.3.1. There we saw that the claim that the able-bodied cannot be held under a duty to die for someone else's sake does not entail that they cannot be held under a duty to run the risk—however small—of dying for their sake. Generally, you recall, individuals can be held under a duty to incur a reasonable risk for the sake of helping someone in peril, whereby a reasonable risk is one possibly as great as, but no greater than, the risks they standardly incur, and impose on others, in their everyday life, such as when driving or cycling. And so, if it is indeed the case, as I showed in that section, that the able-bodied are under a moral duty to help out of the water someone who is drowning, or to drive to the hospital, ambulance services failing, someone who is in serious pain, and if the risk of dying during or after the operation is as acceptably low as the risks one incurs whilst driving or rescuing a drowning person from quiet seas, one must accept a moral duty to transfer body parts under general anaesthetic. As it happens, the risk of dying incurred by individuals on the operating table is considerably higher than the similar risk they incur when taking an average car trip.[19] Be that as it may, my point here is that if rescuers are under a duty to incur a risk, when the probability of actually incurring the harm is sufficiently low, then we must hold the medically well off under a duty to incur a similar risk of a similarly low harm.

---

[18] By the same token, to be under a duty to make one's organs available posthumously does not imply that one should live in such a way that one's organs will be good enough for transplant purposes once one is dead.

[19] According to UK statistics, the risk of dying from an operation under general anaesthetic is about 1 in 1,000 year on year. By contrast, in the period 1999–2001, the risk of dying from a average car trip was roughly 1.3 in 1,000,000. The latter figure was calculated as follows: in that period, roughly 3,400 people died in a car accident. At the same time, a UK resident took, on average, 639 car trips a year, for an average total of 8,800 kms (which gives an average car-trip length of 14 kms). In that same period, the population of the UK was 57 million inhabitants, so we can put the number of person-trips at 57million × 639 = 36,423,000,000. Correspondingly, the risk of dying in an average car trip was 3,400/36,423,000,000 = 1/10,712,647. The risk of suffering a serious injury in a car accident was 1/78,329 (on the basis of 465,000 persons a year suffering from such an injury). Sources: <www.dh.gov.uk> and <www.dft.gov.uk>. I am grateful to François Fabre for his help with calculating those probabilities.

At this juncture, the opponent of the confiscation of live body parts might be tempted to counterclaim that people in need do *not* have a right against us that we help them when the help they need is our time, our energy, indeed the use of our body, as described in the previous paragraph, if there is the *slightest* risk that we may be harmed as a result. But her counterclaim would be vulnerable to the objection that, every time we drive or every time we cycle, we put, or contribute to putting, other people at risk to suit our purpose—people, in fact, who do not have much choice in the matter (after all, they *have* to go shopping, to take their children to school, and so on, and thereby expose themselves to risks). More to the point, we accept being put at risk by ambulance and fire-engine drivers, for the sake of ensuring that people whose prospects for a minimally flourishing life are at stake get to the hospital in time, or are helped out of their burning house in time. It is unclear, then, why people in need of body parts are not allowed to put others at risk by asking them to undergo an operation, all the more so as suppliers, to reiterate, would receive compensation. At this stage, of course, someone might object that individuals accept incurring that risk because they in turn might need to be taken to the hospital very quickly. But this will not do: for, by the same token, they should accept the risk attendant on general anaesthetics, knowing that they might one day need a transplant.

My opponent's counterclaim, therefore, seems to prove too much. To be sure, there is a difference between being put at risk by an ambulance driver for the sake of someone who needs to get to the hospital and being put at risk by a surgeon for the sake of a patient in need of an organ. In the ambulance case, the patient's end is not served by putting pedestrians at risk. In the transplant case, by contrast, putting the donor at risk is instrumental to the patient's end: the patient would not be able to stay alive, or to lead a minimally flourishing life, if the donor did not incur the risk. But unless one thinks that individuals should never be put at risk as a means to someone else's ends, one cannot point to that difference in order to block the compulsory taking of body parts. On what grounds, then, could one argue that individuals should never be put at risk as a means to someone else's ends? I suspect that many a proponent of that view would claim that by putting someone at risk as a means to achieve one's own or someone else's ends, one is requiring that they make a considerable sacrifice, without asking their consent, and one fails, thereby, to treat them as persons with their own projects, attachments, ends to pursue, and so on. Suppose that you are suffering from a very serious bout of influenza, and that you can get some relief only if I take a fifteen-minutes cycle ride, both ways, on a busy road, to the nearest pharmacy. I would undoubtedly incur a small, but real, risk of being run over by a car. If the claim under study is correct, it follows that to hold me under a duty to go to the pharmacy constitutes a failure to treat me as a person with my own ends to pursue, and therefore that I should not be held under that duty. I for one cannot think of many people who would hold that view: as we saw in section 2.3.1, it is hard to see how merely putting me at a *small* risk involves denying that I am such a person.

Let us nevertheless assume, for the sake of argument, that it does. Even then, the objection from risk could not be deployed against the claim that the able-bodied are under a duty to transfer body parts under *local* anaesthetics, since they would not incur any risk in doing so: more specifically, given the state of medical advances, this implies that they are under a duty to transfer their blood, bone marrow, and liver cells (once it becomes possible to extract them under local anaesthetic).[20]

5.4 JUSTICE, SEX, AND REPRODUCTION

The claim that those who need personal services and body parts have a right that those who are in a position to provide them do so might be thought by some to have the following unpalatable implications: if the imperilled and the needy have the right that those in a position to help provide them with personal services and body parts, on the ground that they would not, otherwise, lead a minimally flourishing life, does it not follow, then, that those who need sexual and repro-ductive services get them as a matter of right, in other words, that there ought to be a sexual and reproductive lottery?[21] Fortunately, I do not think that my case for a right to personal services and body parts has those implications. I say 'fortunately', for, if it did, then it would for many count as a reason—and a plausible one at that—to reject the view that those in need of personal services and body parts have a right to get them, even under the strict conditions spelled out so far.

Let us turn, first, to the view that I am committed to endorsing duties of, as it were, sexual Good Samaritanism. An argument to that effect might plausibly go like this: regular sexual intercourse is one of the things (most) human beings need in order to flourish. As it happens, many people suffer from severe sexual deprivation, as they cannot get sex by meeting potential partners in the usual ways (e.g. they are severely disabled, very ill, too old to attract sexual partners, or are male resident aliens who have not mastered the language of their country of refuge and whose fellow nationals are overwhelmingly male, etc.). In most of those cases, they (or, at least, the men amongst them) can resort to prostitution. Now, I have argued so far that would-be rescuers are under a duty to provide personal services to the imperilled on the grounds that the imperilled need those services in order to lead a minimally flourishing life; I have also argued that the

---

[20] It is already possible to transplant liver cells on to patients under local anaesthetics: it is hoped that this technique, which is still on trial, can be used to relieve the plight of diabetes sufferers. See J. Meikle, 'Tests Hold out the Hope of Cure for Diabetics', *Guardian*, 27 January 2001.

[21] I am grateful to N. Humphrey, A. Leveringhaus, D. McDermott, and C. Mackenzie for pressing me rather hard on this question.

able-bodied are under a duty, in some cases at least, to provide body parts to those who need them. Duties to help, then, do not stop at material resources: they involve the body. In addition, they do not stop at the surface, as it were, of the body: they involve the body in invasive ways. If all those points are true, then, by the same token, it seems that individuals are under a duty to make themselves available to the sexually deprived—and, conversely, that the latter have a right to sexual services against the former.

However, there are a number of reasons as to why my argument in favour of duties of Good Samaritanism and the confiscation of body parts is compatible with the claim—which the overwhelming majority of people would endorse—that the sexually deprived lack that right. In section 2.3.1, you recall, I argued that the provision of a good G can be protected by a right if G is such that to be under a duty to transfer it to someone else does not change its nature. Sex, undeniably, is a good which has great value for most people, whether they partake of it or not. No less undeniably, it is also a good whose value resides in the fact that it is given, and exchanged, freely (although not necessarily, as we shall see in Chapter 7, for free). I do not mean by this that no one, as a matter of fact, can enjoy sex *as sex* unless it is given freely: some rapists are indifferent to the fact that their victim does not consent to sex; others, in fact, derive pleasure precisely from the fact that their victim does not consent. All I mean is that most people value sex precisely to the extent that it is given freely. And that, in fact, is also true of many rapists, who rape because they lack the opportunity to have sex with willing partners, and of many individuals who visit prostitutes and then spend a good deal of time, during the prostitutional encounter, pretending that the prostitute is having sex with them out of desire rather than for financial gain.[22]

That most people value sex in that way suggests that, if sexual services were provided as a matter of right, the act of transfer would change the nature of sex, and the sexually deprived, or at any rate most of them, would not get what they most value about it. From the point of view of those individuals, then, justice could not coherently require the provision of sexual services. As I conceded in the last paragraph, however, some people might be indifferent to the fact that their partner does not consent to sex; in fact, might positively welcome the fact that he or she does not consent. From *their* point of view, it would be entirely coherent for justice to require such provision. The good of sex, then, lies somewhere between love, which logically cannot be transferred as a matter of justice, and personal resources such as a kidney, blood, or the use of my arm, which, like material resources, can always be so transferred without change to their nature.

Be that as it may, although justice can coherently, from the point of view of those indifferent to, or welcoming of, partners' lack of consent to sex, mandate

---

[22] For an interesting account of the psychology of rapists which supports my claim in this sentence, see A. Wertheimer, *Consent to Sexual Relations* (Cambridge: Cambridge University Press, 2003), ch. 4.

the provision of sexual services, it ought not to do so. In fact, my case in favour of Good Samaritanism and the confiscation of body parts implies that there is no such thing as a right to sexual services. As I have argued throughout this book, those in a position to help others are not under a duty to do so if they would lose their own prospects for a flourishing life by so helping. Now, as is well known, non-consensual sex is extremely harmful to the victim. Not only is the act itself harmful, both physically (even when the perpetrator does not need to physically overcome his victim, he will, if intent on penetrating her, hurt her) and psychologically; its consequences are harmful, most particularly psychologic-ally: the overwhelming majority of rape victims report long-lasting loss of normal (not merely sexual) functioning in everyday life.[23] Moreover, sex itself is dan-gerous, carrying as it does risks of disease and, for women, unwanted pregnancy and its attendant physical risks (to name a few, infertility if they miscarry, last-ing problems resulting from abortion, severe back and urinary problems, death in childbirth, etc.). As I argued in Chapter 2, and earlier in this chapter, potential rescuers and healthy individuals are not under an obligation of justice to provide personal services and body parts at such costs to themselves. By the same token, individuals ought not to be held under an obligation of justice to provide sexual services to the sexually deprived.

There is another, crucial, consideration against the right to sexual services, which does not apply to other rights to personal resources. The act of rescuing someone from choppy seas, or of hauling him on the pavement after he has fallen off his bike, does indeed consist in making our body available to the imper-illed; the act of providing blood does indeed consist in making it, or one of its constituents, available to the sick in an invasive way. But they usually do not require that we subject ourselves to having an *intimate* interaction with those who need us. In contrast, sexual intercourse, by definition, does consist in mak-ing one's body itself available to someone else and in interacting, in the most intimate way possible (physically, if not emotionally), with that person. Invas-iveness is problematic, then, to the extent that it is accompanied by forced intimacy.

To be sure, there are kinds of sexual acts, such as manual sex, which individu-als can perform on their partners with minimal physical intimacy; there are also kinds of sexual act, such as phone sex, which they can perform without mak-ing their body available to their partners. Contrastingly, there is also one kind of rescue act which is physically intimate, to wit, mouth-to-mouth resuscitation.[24] Those concessions, however, do not undermine my claim that being under a duty to provide rescue services and body parts does not imply that we are also under duties of sexual Good Samaritanism. For, when performing physically intimate rescue acts on the imperilled, Good Samaritans do not subject themselves to

---

[23] See Wertheimer, *Consent to Sexual Relations*, p. 104, for a list of studies of rape victims.

[24] I am grateful to S. Uniacke for bringing that point to my attention.

their partner's intimate thoughts, desires, fantasies, and so on. However, when performing non-physical sexual acts, individuals do so subject themselves. To require of them that they engage in such intimate relationships without their consent would constitute too much of a violation. It would also place them in a position where they would have to have sex with someone who would not desire them for the person that they are, but who would merely want to have sex with someone—anyone—with desirable (to them) physical characteristics. The problem, of course, is that sex, for most people, is a rather complicated affair; it does not merely consist in the mutual use of bodies, but is tightly bound up with our sense of ourselves, our self-esteem, and our perception of others. Although sex is not the main determinant of our identity as sexed beings, it is *a* central component of it, whether or not we decide to have it, and however we decide to have it. And so it is entirely reasonable for anyone to decide that they will only have sex with individuals who do desire them, and who do not treat them merely as sexual partners but as whole individuals with aspirations, desires, and ends. In fact, it is entirely reasonable for them to decide, on any given sexual encounter, that they want to be so treated, even if they have consented to purely instrumental sex on many past occasions.[25] To require of them that they let themselves be treated, without their consent, only, or primarily, as a means to someone else's sexual satisfaction, would deny them an opportunity for self-respect.

To the foregoing, someone might be tempted to press the following objection: 'Look, I don't particularly want to be made to have sex with someone I don't desire—in fact I don't particularly want to be made to have sex, period. But I would certainly rather do that than be made to give one of my kidneys. That surely goes to show that I attach more value to my bodily integrity in general than to my *sexual* integrity in particular.' Indeed it does. As we saw in section 5.3, though, we are not under a duty to give a kidney (or a cornea) to someone else, in so far as the removal procedure does carry a risk of dying (through general anaesthetic), and as the loss of the organ itself might blight our life. I suspect that it is precisely for those reasons that some of us might prefer going through non-consensual sex to having to part with one of their kidneys. I also suspect that, by the same token, they would well prefer parting with some of their blood rather than going through non-consensual sex.

I might be wrong, of course: there might be some people for whom non-consensual sex is *always* preferable to the imposed loss of a body part, however minimal the costs of the latter. Be that as it may, that fact alone does not support the view that *those* individuals, who can be held under a duty to give blood, can

---

[25] Accordingly, raping a prostitute is as morally wrong as raping someone who is in a committed and loving sexual relationship. Note, by the way, that my points against a duty to provide sex apply not merely to sex between strangers, but also to sex within an established relationship. For an argument to the contrary, see Wertheimer, *Consent to Sexual Relations*, ch. 11.

also be held under a duty to give that against which they have far fewer objections, namely, sexual services. For, in order to decide who might be held under that duty, in the light of their views concerning the relative importance of sex versus other things, one would have to get all potential 'providers' to make intimate revelations about themselves, and potentially shameful ones at that: we could not, after all, take at face value someone's claim to the effect that she does mind very much being made to have sex, much more so than to give blood. One would have to inquire into her reasons for so thinking, and that might compel her to bring into the open facts about her past relationship history, sexuality, and so on. In so doing, one would, in fact, demean her, and, as I argued in section 1.3.1, one would thereby deny her an opportunity for self-respect. For that reason too, one ought not to hold individuals under a duty to provide sexual services to the sexually deprived.

So much, then, for sexual Good Samaritanism. What about reproductive goods and services? The former—gametes—are needed by those whose eggs or sperm are lacking. The latter are needed either by women whose uterus cannot bear a child to term, or by men who do not have a female partner who can do so (for example, single heterosexual males and gay males). If for some reason they cannot, or are unwilling to, adopt, the only way for them to have a child is to have recourse to a surrogate mother. Does my argument in favour of duties of Good Samaritanism commit me to set up a surrogacy lottery, as it were, whereby women of childbearing age would be called upon to bear children for infertile women and gay and single men? Clearly not. For a start, and to reiterate, under the conception of justice I take as my starting point, individuals are under an obligation to provide the sick with all-purpose personal resources (within limits), but are not under an obligation to provide others with the resources to further their specific conception of the good; accordingly, they are not under an obligation to help them become parents.[26] In addition, as we saw above, both the costs and risks attendant on pregnancy are quite high—higher and more numerous than the risks we impose on one another in our everyday life[27]—indeed too high for them to be held under a moral duty to help the fertile. Moreover, to hold a woman under a duty to become a surrogate mother would impose on her an enormous, emotionally destructive cost, which neither Good Samaritans nor organ providers have to face, namely, that of having to relinquish, perhaps against her wishes, the child she is carrying. If any sacrifice short of giving one's life away is deemed too high, that one surely is. And to

---

[26] This implies, incidentally, that justice as I define it in this book allows, but does not require, that the infertile receive free medical treatment for their condition.

[27] The risk of dying in pregnancy or childbirth is 1 in 200,000, compared with the 1/10,712,647 of dying in the course of an average drive. I do not know what is the risk of dying in the course of a twelve-hour drive (twelve hours being the average length of labour). Even if the former is equal to, or lower than, the latter, it still is not enough to establish that we can hold women to bear children for the sake of the infertile, for reasons adduced in the text above.

claim, by way of reply, that a surrogate mother ought not to be made to do so, and thus that she is only under a duty to give prospective parents a *chance* of parenthood (so that she can change her mind and decide not to relinquish the child) will not do; for, even though she would avoid paying the aforementioned cost, she might nevertheless find herself in the position of having to pay the lesser, but nevertheless extremely high, cost of unplanned parenthood.

Some of the foregoing points, note, apply against the view that my argument in favour of the confiscation of body parts supports the confiscation of gametes. Just as women are not under an obligation to provide their womb so as to ensure that the infertile can implement their conception of the good—to wit, parenthood—neither men nor women ought to be made to provide their gametes to that effect. Moreover, to the extent that there are good reasons to allow children born from gamete donations to know their genetic parents, to hold the fertile under an obligation to donate would impose on them the cost of unwanted parenthood. Finally, even if their identity is protected, one would impose on them the emotional cost, which for some of them might be unreasonably high, of knowing that a child of theirs exists, out there, with whom they have nothing to do, but for whose welfare they might feel desperately concerned. It would be entirely reasonable for those individuals to claim that, having thought about the issue critically and with a high degree of scrutiny, the knowledge that they are a parent, albeit only biologically, would blight their life. Accordingly, they should not be made to donate their gametes.

To conclude, then, on the one hand one can hold the view that the imperilled and the sick have a right, at the bar of justice, to personal services in the form of emergency rescue and body parts, and on the other hand deny that the sexually deprived and the infertile have a right, at the bar of justice, to sexual services, reproductive services, and gametes. Thus, my case for the former right does not fall foul of the view that it has those unacceptable implications.

5.5 CONCLUSION

In this chapter, I argued the following: if one holds that the badly off have a right that the comparatively well off give them the material resources they need in order to lead a minimally flourishing life, then one must hold the view that the sick have a right against the able-bodied that the latter give them some of their body parts. To put the point differently, the able-bodied have a qualified right to personal integrity: a right to personal integrity, in so far they are not under a duty to make all parts of their body available, but a qualified one, in so far as they are under a duty to make some of those parts available. By that token, the sick have a qualified right to the person of the able-bodied: a right to the latter, in so far as the able-bodied are under a duty to make some of their body parts available, but a qualified one, in so far as the able-bodied retain the right to decide what to do with those body parts which they are not under a duty to transfer.

More precisely, then, the sick have a right to the blood and bone marrow of the able-bodied, as well as to those body parts the removal of which, under general anaesthetic, would not cause the able-bodied to die, and would pose a minimal risk. To many, drawing a distinction between body parts which can, and body parts which cannot, be taken from the living might simply be impossible. Yet, although in many cases such judgements will be hard to make, in other cases, or so I have sought to show, they are not. Moreover, it is no more difficult to decide when we can take body parts from the living than to decide how much money we can take away from taxpayers. Those who do not regard this difficulty as a good enough reason to reject the claim that the needy have a right to some of the material resources of the well off should not regard it as a good enough reason to reject the claim that the sick have a right to some of the body parts of the able-bodied.

To be sure, someone faced with the argument deployed in this chapter might decide, against liberals committed to coercive taxation for distributive purposes, not to endorse the coercive transfer of material resources to the needy, on the grounds that its implications for personal integrity—to wit, the loss of individual autonomy—are unacceptable. But in so doing, she would concede one of my central claims—which the overwhelming majority of liberals have resisted—namely, that, at the bar of justice, material resources and body parts are relevantly analogous. In addition, she would fail to take on board the following, crucial, point: if one thinks that the badly off do *not* have a right to help against the well off if the latter would end up leading a less than minimally flourishing life as a result, one is committed to the view that the sick do *not* have a right to the body parts of the able-bodied if the latter would end up leading a less than minimally flourishing life as a result. In so far as, under my proposal, the able-bodied, leading a minimally flourishing life as they would, would retain some degree of individual autonomy, my opponent would fail to realize that holding the able-bodied under a duty to transfer some of their body parts to the sick does not undermine their autonomy.

That the confiscation of body parts is subject to the aforementioned restrictions is one of two reasons why it does not undermine the autonomy of the able-bodied. The fact that the confiscation of body parts is compatible with their commercialization is the second reason. As I averred in the Introduction, the view that the able-bodied are under a duty of justice to provide the imperilled and the needy with personal resources is compatible, under certain conditions, with the view—called for by the autonomy principle—that they also have the right to sell body parts, as well as hire their body out for sexual and reproductive services. Moreover, the confiscation of body parts is also compatible with the view that, under certain conditions, those who need body parts and personal services but cannot get them for free have the right to buy them. Thus, someone who on one occasion has had to perform an emergency rescue can on some other occasion avail himself of the body part or service he might need or want, but which justice does not guarantee him. To confer on that person the right to enter such transactions is one way to protect his interest in autonomy, notwithstanding the fact that he once had to discharge his obligation to help the needy. To the issue of commercialization, then, I now turn.

6

Organ Sales

6.1 INTRODUCTION

Recall that I take as my starting point two principles of justice, to wit, the principle of sufficiency and the principle of autonomy. According to the principle of sufficiency, individuals have a right to the material resources they need in order to lead a minimally flourishing life, provided that those who are in a position to help them would not lose their own prospects for such a life by so doing. As I argued in Chapters 2–5, sufficiency does not merely require that the needy get the material resources they need; under some circumstances, it also requires that they get the *personal* resources they need, namely, personal services and body parts, from those who are in a position to help them. However, according to the principle of autonomy, individuals should be allowed to enjoy the fruits of their labour in pursuit of their conception of the good once sufficiency obtains. Against that background, the following questions arise: once the able-bodied have fulfilled their obligation to help the needy or the imperilled by providing them with personal services, can they raise income, at the bar of autonomy, so as to pursue their conception of the good, by selling parts of their body? Can those who need (or want) an organ but do not have a right to it at the bar of justice nevertheless buy it?

Let me be more specific. In Chapter 1, you recall, I distinguished a claim-right to do A, which imposes on others a duty not to interfere, and a power-right to do A, which is an ability under some rule to change one's relation to someone else, for example, by transferring to him one's rights, powers, and liabilities over some resource. Selling and buying are paradigmatic instances of a power: to say that X has the power to sell something, G, to Y is to say that X and Y can change their relation over G, in that Y acquires X's rights, powers, and liabilities over G, whilst X acquires Y's rights, powers, and liabilities over Y's money. Moreover, X's and Y's powers are protected by two claim-rights against third parties, to wit, a claim-right that they not interfere with the transaction and a claim-right that they acknowledge it as valid. By implication, their powers to buy and sell are protected by a right that the state not make the transaction unlawful and that it acknowledge it as valid. The question, then, is whether individuals have the moral power to buy and sell organs to and from one another, and, should they have it, whether that power is protected by claim-rights against the state—that is, not merely that the state not interfere with such transactions, but also that it recognize them as legally valid.

In section 6.2, I argue that individuals lack the power to sell their body parts in the following two cases only: (1) the sick have a claim to those body parts as a matter of justice; (2) the seller sells a body part the loss of which would be so catastrophic that his decision to sell would amount to consenting to being treated as purely instrumental to the buyer's end, and thus as less than a person. However, although in those cases the seller lacks the power to sell, and, correspondingly, although the buyer lacks the power to buy, there are good reasons as to why the state ought not to make such transactions unlawful. In all other instances, or so I argue, individuals have the power to buy and sell body parts, and such power is protected by the aforementioned two claim-rights to non-interference and legal recognition. These are controversial claims, of course, against which two reasons, which I examine in section 6.3, are standardly advanced, namely, that they are exploitative of sellers, and that they bespeak a troublesome relationship between persons and their body. I sketch out a regulatory framework for organ sales in section 6.4.

Before I begin, a point about terminology, which I made in section 1.2.2, but which bears restating here, and a point about the scope of this chapter. It is standard usage to talk of the *right* to sell to mean the power to do so as well as the claim-rights which protect it. From now on, I shall follow standard usage, unless otherwise specified. Finally, I shall restrict my enquiry in this chapter to the sale of non-reproductive body parts, and address the sale of gametes in Chapter 8 when dealing with the issue of surrogacy contracts.

6.2 A CASE FOR THE RIGHT TO SELL AND BUY BODY PARTS

As we saw in Chapter 5, the able-bodied are, under certain circumstances, under a moral duty to make some of their body parts available to those who need them, as a matter of justice, and should receive compensation for so doing. One might think that holding the able-bodied under a duty to make their body parts available and compensating them for shouldering that burden amounts, for all intents and purposes, to conferring on them the right to sell those body parts. On that view, the able-bodied have two rights, namely, the right to make a part of their body available and the right to do so for a financial reward; but they would also be under a duty to do the former. That view would be coherent, for generally one can have the right to do something which one is under a duty to do. However, to be entitled to compensation for giving something which you are under a duty to give is not the same as having the right to sell that thing. For when A sells something to B—be it goods or services—A is thought to be entitled to make a profit from the transaction, and thus to improve his financial situation. In contrast, when A receives compensation from B, B restores A to the *status quo ante*, that is, to the state of affairs that obtained before A incurred the harm which warranted compensation. Moreover, discussions of the right to sell in general standardly pertain not merely to the right to divest oneself of a property for a profit, but also to the right to decide *whether* to sell. In contrast, to say that A has a right to receive compensation for a good—in that instance, a body part—which he is under a duty to provide anyway is to say, precisely, that he cannot decide whether to make his body part available to the sick.

One might also think that, once it has been established that the able-bodied must give some of their body parts, one need not assess whether they can sell them, since, if they have to give, they will not be in a position to sell anyway. However, that justice mandates confiscation in some cases does not render the question of the legitimacy of commercialization moot, for two reasons. First, as I made clear in Chapter 5, there are a number of body parts which healthy individuals are not under a duty to make available as a matter of justice, to wit, those body parts the loss or removal of which would jeopardize their prospects for a minimally flourishing life. It does make sense to ask whether they have the right to divest themselves of those body parts, not merely for free, but for a financial reward.

Second, justice, or so I averred at the outset of this book, requires that the needy have a right to the material resources necessary to lead a minimally flour-ishing life. I argued there that although demanding to be treated with respect implies that one should pay for the cost of one's choices, the no-responsibility condition (whereby individuals who are responsible for their predicament lack a claim for help at the bar of justice) still should not be used when allocating material resources. However, as I pointed out in Chapters 4 and 5, it might be possible in some cases to assess the extent to which the medically needy are responsible for their predicament without getting them to disclose shameful facts about themselves—thus, without failing to respect them. In those cases where they are so responsible, the able-bodied cannot be held under a moral duty to help. Moreover, justice requires that the needy get the resources necessary to lead a minimally flourishing life: by implication, it does not require that they get the resources necessary to maximize their autonomy. Consider, for example, individuals who undergo an operation, during which they will need a blood transfusion, for a condition which does not render their life less than minimally flourishing; or consider individuals who have one fully functioning kidney and nevertheless would like to have a second one, in order, for example, to practise sports at competitive level. In neither of those cases, which involve the satisfac-tion of the needs of those responsible for their plight and the satisfaction of the wants of, as it were, the unfulfilled, do individuals have a claim for help against the able-bodied at the bar of justice. In those cases, it is also worth asking whether potential providers of body parts have the right to sell.

And indeed, there are good reasons, or so I now argue, as to why organ selling and buying should be protected by rights, *in those cases*. As we have just seen, in many instances individuals who desperately need, or simply want, body parts will not be able to get them unless the able-bodied are willing to relinquish them. Allowing the latter to sell, and not merely to give, would increase the quantity of available organs and enable those needy patients to have prospects for a minimally flourishing life even though they have no claim to body parts at the bar of sufficiency; it would also enable individuals to implement their conception of the good above and beyond that threshold. Why not give them that opportunity? After all, to deny the able-bodied the right to sell amounts to denying the sick or the unfulfilled the right to buy. It is one thing to deny them the right to get body parts without the consent of the able-bodied; it is quite another to deny them the right to buy body parts which the able-bodied are willing to relinquish for a profit. To do so would be analogous to denying needy individuals who are ineligible for housing benefits (on the grounds, for example, that they have turned down three perfectly acceptable council houses for spurious reasons) the right to rent a flat from those who are willing to lease accommodation at a profit; it would also be analogous to denying those who want goods or services they cannot get for free the opportunity to buy them from willing suppliers. If one thinks that the needy, in those cases, have the moral right to pay for housing, and if one thinks that individuals in general have the right to buy non-essential goods and services (a claim which no one could plausibly dispute), then, pending argument to the contrary, there is every reason to think that the sick and the unfulfilled have the moral right to pay for body parts.

Moreover, and crucially for our purposes here, to outlaw the sale of body parts does not merely affect buyers; it also affects sellers, and that is problematic. For the principle of autonomy stipulates that, provided everybody has prospects for a minimally flourishing life, individuals should be allowed to enjoy the fruits of their labour in pursuit of their conception of the good. More specifically, they should be allowed to work in the profession of their choice and to raise income by so working. They should also be allowed to raise income by other means, for example by buying, and then selling for a profit, or leasing, property.

The claims made in the last paragraph suggest yet another point in support of conferring on the able-bodied a right to sell their body parts. It is standardly accepted that a surgeon's interest in generating (part of) the income she needs to implement her goals and projects is important enough to confer on her the right to demand a fee for performing an operation, for example, and, most relevantly here, a transplant operation. By the same token, then, it should be accepted that a supplier's interest in generating income, for similar purposes, is important enough to confer on him a right to demand a fee for making his body parts available. In outlawing organ sales, we are endorsing a state of affairs where, in transplant operations, the *only* individual who is not paid for his contribution to the patient's operation is the supplier of the needed organ. At the bar of justice, this, really, is entirely arbitrary.

To be sure, the fact that someone has the right to make a living by providing x does not suffice to show that it is appropriate to regard x as a commodity. Thus, the fact that we allow midwives to make a living by delivering babies does not show that babies can properly be regarded as a commodity.[1] Similarly, the fact that we allow surgeons to make a living by transplanting organs does not *suffice* to show that organs can be regarded as commodities. In section 6.3.1, however, I shall argue that they can be so regarded.

Pending my argument to that effect, opposing as I have done the view that surgeons can, but organ suppliers cannot, be paid for their contribution to patients' recovery, raises some troubling questions in the context of the theory of justice which underpins my argument. If, as we saw in Chapter 3, freedom of occupational choice is an important value, then a surgeon should be allowed to make a living from her chosen profession (provided she complies with all due academic and professional standards and requirements) even when she operates on individuals who have a claim for help at the bar of justice (in which case her fees are paid out of general taxation). Why, then, should a donor have a right to sell only in those cases where the needy have forfeited their claim to help, or where the needed body parts are such that no one can be held under a duty to make them available for free? It would seem that, like a surgeon, the donor should have a right to charge the patient for her body parts, even if the patient is not responsible for his condition. If true, my case for the confiscation of body parts collapses.

However, the claim that doctors, unlike organ donors, should be entitled to payment for helping the deserving needy, is plausible if one bears in mind that the doctor's salary for those operations should be understood as compensation for years spent in training and for the time devoted to operating. Similarly, as we saw in Chapter 5, donors should receive compensation for making their organs available to those who need them. Yet, and to reiterate, the right to receive compensation for x is not the same as the right to sell x: the latter, unlike the former, is a right to divest oneself of x for a profit. To claim that a donor should receive compensation for transferring her organ(s) to the sick is to claim that she cannot demand whatever price she deems fit in exchange for transferring her body parts to individuals who have a claim to them; similarly, to conceive of the surgeon's salary for operating on the deserving needy as compensation is to imply that, even though she is not under an obligation to help the needy by becoming a doctor, she cannot extract whatever salary she deems fit in exchange for having decided so to help them.[2]

There is an important difference, of course, between the surgeon's deployment of his skills and the supplier's transfer of his organs, namely, that the latter, unlike

[1] I owe this example to S. Olsaretti.

[2] For the view that wages should be understood as compensation, see J. Lamont, 'Incentive Income, Deserved Income and Economic Rents', *Journal of Political Philosophy* 5 (1997): 26–46; G. Sher, *Desert* (Princeton: Princeton University Press, 1987); H. Milne, 'Desert, Effort and Equality', *Journal of Applied Philosophy* 3 (1986): 235–43. For the view that wages ought to be conceived of as a reward for one's contribution rather than as compensation for time and training, see, e.g., D. Miller, *Principles of Social Justice* (Cambridge, Mass.: Harvard University Press, 1999).

the former, irrevocably loses a part of his body. That might be thought by some to ground an objection to the argument made so far, to the effect that to confer on individuals a right to use their body to earn a living does not commit one to conferring on them a right to divest themselves of its part for a profit. As a preliminary point, though, note that there is no such difference between deploying one's skills and transferring regenerative body parts such as blood, bone marrow, and liver lobes, since in those cases the supplier loses them only temporarily; or, rather, he loses them for good, but will swiftly acquire new ones. Whilst his situation is not, therefore, identical to that of the surgeon (who does not lose a body part at all), it is sufficiently analogous to be relatively unproblematic. In all other cases, it is true that the loss of functioning arising from the loss of an organ is permanent.

However, the fact that transferring an organ to someone else is, in those cases, irrevocable, in a way that deploying one's life-saving skills clearly is not, does not support the view that the surgeon can be paid whereas the organ supplier cannot. Irrevocability matters, or so it would seem, because someone who divests himself of a non-renewable organ may subsequently suffer from a serious illness or disability. Yet, consider the case of a surgeon who, the more he operates, the more he aggravates his back condition or seriously impairs his eyesight. Can we disallow payment? It seems not, for, then, we should prevent people from receiving a salary for any dangerous and risky job they might wish to take. And yet we do not do that. But if someone's interest in raising income by engaging in very risky activities—such as being a full-time boxer or a building-site worker—is deemed important enough to confer on her the right to do so (even though she would not engage in such activities were it not for the money), there is no reason to deny her the right to make parts of her body available to others in exchange for money, even though she would incur similar risks in so doing.[3] Furthermore, if irrevocability is what matters, it supports not merely the view that organ suppliers should not receive payment, but the much more controversial view that they should not be allowed to *give* their organs.

Opponents of organ sales, thus, who subscribe to the views that the surgeon can be paid for his work, even though so working might impair his health, and that suppliers must give their organs for free as required by the principle of sufficiency, must provide a reason as to why they assign to irrevocability in commercial transfers a weight which they do not confer on it in free transfers; they must also be able to justify discriminating against organ suppliers as compared with surgeons. I shall examine such reasons in section 6.3, and argue that they fail.

---

[3] For an argument along similar lines, see, e.g., G. Dworkin, 'Markets and Morals: The Case for Organ Sales', in G. Dworkin (ed.), *Morality, Harm and the Law* (Boulder, Colo.: Westview Press, 1994). Note that having a right to engage in risky activities only means that the state ought not to prevent us from doing so. It does not imply that the state ought not to regulate those activities. I shall explore the issue of regulation in more detail in section 6.4.

To recapitulate, then, both surgeon and donor are entitled to compensation when helping the deserving needy, and my case for the confiscation of live body parts therefore stands. In addition, both are entitled to extract a fee when helping the undeserving needy and those who want, as opposed to need, an organ. But yet another issue now arises, which leads us further to analyse the relationship between the provision of rescue services and that of body parts. On the one hand, my arguments for the right of the imperilled to the personal services of potential rescuers and for the right of the sick to (some) of the body parts of the able-bodied suggest that personal services and body parts are relevantly analogous: they are resources which all individuals need in order to lead a minimally flourishing life. On the other hand, I have also argued here that individuals have the right to sell their body parts to those who need, but are not entitled to, them, on the grounds that the latter are responsible for their predicament. If so, though, does it not imply that not only am I not under a duty to help those who are in peril through their own fault, but in fact that I have the right to offer my help conditional on their paying me? Do I not have the right to make my help conditional on payment, when the imperilled are the bad swimmer who, time and again, knowingly risks his life going into choppy seas, or the person who collapses on the pavement from a heart attack, and who has been consistently ignoring his doctor's advice on diet, alcohol, and tobacco consumption?

I argued in section 1.3.2 that we should desist from applying the no-responsibility condition if doing so would imply treating the needy without the respect they are owed as persons. As I made clear in section 2.1, this is particularly so when we are called upon to act as Good Samaritans, since we cannot really know of the imperilled, who *ex hypothesi* are strangers to us, whether they are responsible for their predicament. Suppose, though, that we could know for a fact that they are so responsible, without breach of respect. Could we not then make our helping conditional upon payment?

At the bar of justice, yes. All things considered, no: for, when faced with someone who might incur serious harm unless we help them—someone with a need so immediate, so direct—there really would be something monstrous in not doing anything unless the imperilled pay us, *even if we know them to be responsible for their plight*. In those cases where the imperilled are responsible, although our failure to help is not a failure of justice, it is nevertheless a failure, that of showing basic compassion. However, being under a duty of compassion to rescue the imperilled in emergency situations is compatible with having the right to be paid (above and beyond compensation) for doing it. No price negotiation could and should take place prior to the rescue, but payment could be asked for *ex post*. Thus a number of ski resorts in Europe are setting up procedures whereby reckless skiers who ski off beaten tracks, and are thereby in difficulties, will be rescued by emergency services but will have to pay for the cost of their rescues. One could imagine similar procedures in the case of one-rescuer situations.

In sum, on the one hand, one is under a duty of justice to help those in need of organs who are not responsible for their neediness provided that one does not thereby jeopardize one's own prospects for a minimally flourishing life. On the other hand, one has a right to sell one's organs to those who need them and of whom it can be known, without getting them to make shameful revelations about themselves, that they are responsible for their predicament; one also has the right to sell one's organs to those who do not *need*, but rather want, treatment requiring body parts.

Does my defence of organ sales apply to cases where the organ seller would die as a result of the transaction—cases, thus, where he is prepared to sell his heart, lungs, and whole liver? Interestingly, the most anti-paternalistic of liberals stop short of advocating that the state should allow such drastic curtailments of one's autonomy, indeed of one's life. This, I suspect, is because they tend to assume that no rational and reasonable person could be said to consent to it. On principle, though, I do not see why one cannot consider the possibility that individuals may sometimes fully, rationally, consent to selling their organs, even at such cost to themselves. The question, then, is whether they have the right to do so, and, correspondingly, whether patients have the right to buy in such cases.

Now, in section 1.2.3B, I argued that it is morally wrong to consent to being treated by others as less than a person, and that we do not have the moral power to enter transactions where we are so treated. As I pointed out then, this implies that such transactions are morally null and void, which is to say that the state ought not to enforce them. But it does not imply that the state can criminalize them. Accordingly, if selling one's vital organs, and thereby dying as a result, amounts to consenting to being treated as less than a person, then it follows that we lack the power to do so, in other words, that such transaction should be regarded as null and void; but further argument is needed to show that its parties have a right that others not interfere with them.

I believe that *intra vivos* sales of the heart, both lungs, and the whole liver are almost always morally wrong, for the following reason. Imagine someone who has so little self-respect that he believes, wrongly, his life to be worthless. Suppose further that he decides to sell his heart, or his lungs, whilst alive, knowing that he will die in the process, but hoping that by giving away the proceeds of the sale to a charity, he will make something of himself, albeit posthumously: in other words, he sacrifices his life in order to raise money. By conferring on patients rights over those organs, he would allow them to destroy his opportunity for self-respect, and irreversibly so. As we saw in 1.2.3B, individuals who accede to someone's request that they destroy his opportunities for self-respect because they would benefit from it ought not to do so, on the grounds, precisely, that it is wrong to benefit from someone's lack of self-respect. Note, though, that if I am correct, individuals lack the right to make these kinds of organ sales, not because they are sales, but because such agreements destroy opportunities for self-respect. Accordingly, gifts of that kind are morally wrong too, and individuals lack the right to make them.

I said above that sales involving vital organs are *almost* always morally wrong.
Indeed there are two cases (that I can think of) where they are not, as follows:
(1) X will soon die from a terminal disease, and wishes to divest himself, for a
profit, of his heart—in so doing, he will merely hasten a certain albeit untimely
death; (2) X is not ill but does not see any purpose in his life and intends to
commit suicide—however, he wants to secure his child's financial future, and
is contemplating selling his heart as a means to do so. The latter case differs in
one crucial respect from that outlined three paragraphs ago, since it posits that X
actually wants to die anyway.

Many would undoubtedly argue that X in both cases lacks the right to sell his
vital organs, perhaps for reasons adduced three paragraphs ago. However, I am
not convinced that they would be right. If one thinks that terminally ill patients
who ask a physician for help in committing suicide are not guilty of wrongdoing,
then there does not seem to be any reason to accuse them of wrongdoing when
they ask to die earlier than they would anyway, for the sake not only of whomever
would benefit from the income they would thereby raise, but of whomever would
benefit from receiving their organ.

I have argued that, in some cases, individuals have the right to buy and sell
vital organs. In other cases, however, they lack that right, which is to say that
a seller does not acquire rights, powers, and liabilities over the buyer's money,
and the buyer does not acquire rights, powers, and liabilities over the seller's
vital organs. In so far as they all lack the right so to transact, they do not have
a right against third parties that the latter acknowledge those transactions as valid. For, if no interest of theirs is important enough to be protected by a moral
power to make a particular transaction, then no interest of theirs can be important enough to be protected by a right that the state turn that moral power into a
legal power.

Do they also lack a claim-right that third parties not interfere with the transaction? That is, do they lack a right that the state not make the transaction
unlawful? As I argued in section 1.2.3B, if making a transaction unlawful would
seriously jeopardize an interest of one or both of the parties, that may count as
a very good reason for not doing so, which in turn would imply that the parties
whose interest is so protected have a right that the state not interfere with their
doing something which they lack the power to do. In the present context, in so
far as the seller would die (*ex hypothesi*), no serious interest of his could be jeopardized by making the transaction unlawful. But even if the operation were not
to be completed, and even if the seller were thus to survive, the state could legitimately charge him with attempting to do something which he would lack the
power to do. For I doubt, that is, that the best way to deal with someone whose
lack of self-respect is so crushing is to put them in jail; it might, instead, be better to get them to undergo psychiatric treatment (just as individuals who attempt
suicide are, in the UK, automatically referred to a psychiatrist). From the point
of view of the buyer, however, as we saw in section 1.2.3A, failing to treat others

with equal concern and respect is not the kind of wrong that can be protected by a claim-right. Accordingly, buyers of vital organs who are prepared to treat sellers merely as instruments of their own survival do lack a claim-right that the state not interfere with those transactions—which suggests that, unlike sellers, they are liable to state sanctions.

6.3 TWO OBJECTIONS AGAINST ORGAN SALES

So much, then, for my defence of the right to sell and buy body parts. Now, there are two standard objections against such transactions. According to the first objection, which has its source in Kantian moral theory, it is morally wrong to treat organs as commodities. According to the second objection, transactions involving the sale and purchase of organs are inherently exploitative of sellers and thus morally objectionable. If those objections are correct, they point to good reasons as to why the medical staff, but not organ donors, should receive payment for contributing to a transplant operation. However, neither of these two objections, I argue in sections 6.3.1 and 6.3.2, are strong enough to undermine my case, although they do point to the necessity of regulating organ sales—an issue which I address in section 6.4.

6.3.1 The Commodification Objection

Throughout this book I have argued that body parts are analogous to wealth in that they can be detached from us and constitute fungible resources which we need to pursue our conception of the good. This, I argued in Chapters 4 and 5, supports the view that they can, in some cases, be confiscated from the able-bodied so as to enable the sick to lead a minimally flourishing life. Moreover, as I pointed out in section 6.2, it supports the view that, in some cases, we have the right to buy and sell them. Now, as we saw in Chapter 5, many dispute the view that body parts can be confiscated by denying that they are relevantly analogous to material resources; likewise, many dispute the view that they can be bought and sold by issuing the same denial: such is the commodity objection to the commercialization of body parts.

Interestingly, opponents of organ sales are not committed to rejecting confiscation. They can concede the point that body parts are resources, and, because they are *in that respect* similar to material wealth, accept the argument, of which that point forms the first premiss, that they can be confiscated, and yet reject the view that they can be treated as commodities—that is, as goods, the production, distribution, and enjoyment of which can be regulated solely by market norms. For, they might note, the fact that body parts are a resource which we need to implement our conception of the good and which can be detached from us, does not mean that they are commodities. In this *other* respect, they would claim, organs do differ from material resources. Furthermore, they might point out that in so arguing, they need not deny that body parts are fungible. A good is fungible, you recall, if it is possible to replace it with another good—either a similar one, or a different one—without loss of significant value. But the replacement good need not be money: and so it is possible to hold the view that one's kidney, say, is fungible in that it can be replaced with another kidney without loss of significant value to oneself, but that it could not be exchanged for a sum of money without such loss.

Thus, proponents of the commodification objection to organ sales need not deny that body parts are fungible, detachable resources. Rather, their point is that body parts ought not to be treated as commodities. Their reasons for so objecting to organ sales are twofold: (1) the commodification of organs hampers the development of an altruistic, and therefore desirable, social ethos; and (2) it violates the requirement that persons treat one another with the respect owed to persons as such.

Let me start with the first strand of the commodification objection, whose best-known advocate is Richard Titmuss. In his seminal *The Gift Relationship*, Titmuss argues that allowing individuals to sell their blood contributes to the creation of a society where individuals become unwilling to engage in altruistic exchanges. As he puts it, 'The decline in the spirit of altruism in one sphere of human activities will be accompanied by similar changes in attitudes, motives and relationships in other spheres.'[4] In so far as altruistic gifts are essential both to a flourishing society and to furthering various individual freedoms, the state should avoid dilating the sphere of commercial exchanges and, correspondingly, leave as much as space as possible for what Titmuss calls 'gift relationships'.

Properly reconstructed,[5] Titmuss's argument against markets in blood (and, by implication, against markets in organs) consists of the following two claims: some goods have a meaning such that they ought not to be exchanged for money; if they are so exchanged, their meaning will be contaminated, that is, individuals will come to see those goods mostly in monetary terms, which in turn will make it harder for them to be willing to give them, as opposed to sell them.[6] On that view, whatever interest individuals may have in deriving a profit from transferring their body parts to others is outweighed by the importance of fostering altruistic relationships; accordingly, it is not important enough to be protected by a right.

---

[4] R. Titmuss, *The Gift Relationship*, eds. A. Oakley and J. Ashton (London: LSE, 1997), p. 263.

[5] As done by D. Archard in his 'Selling Yourself: Titmuss' Argument against a Market in Blood', *Journal of Ethics* 6 (2002): 87–103.

[6] The view that the commodification of a good can 'monetarize' the hitherto non-monetary meaning of that good and thereby change the motivations of the agents when exchanging it is sometimes called the domino theory. For a brilliant criticism of that theory, see E. Mack, 'Dominos and the Fear of Commodification', in J. R. Pennock and J. W. Chapman (eds.), *Markets and Justice: Nomos XXXI* (New York: New York University Press, 1989).

Titmuss believes, then, that altruism is essential to a flourishing society, in so far as, absent altruistic relationships, the bonds of community are broken. Relatedly, he also believes that the less space there is for such relationships, the harder it is for individuals to exercise their freedom to give or not to give blood, and the less likely it is that other individual freedoms will remain intact: once the forces of the market are allowed a free rein in the medical sphere, he argues, the rights of individuals, as patients, donors, and doctors, are undermined.

The first thing to note, here, is that Titmuss's objections apply both to the *ante-mortem* and to the *post-mortem* sale of body parts. The second thing to note, *pace* Titmuss, is that the non-monetary meaning of a good can coexist with its monetary meaning. Accordingly, to confer on individuals the moral right to sell is entirely compatible with conferring on them the moral right to give. Coexistence between those meanings obtains in two ways. First, a good can be given in some contexts with no importance attached to its monetary value, and in other contexts be treated merely as a commodity. For example, in giving my partner a present for Christmas, I give him something which has monetary value; but the fact that I do not give him the cash equivalent of that present suggests that I am able, in that relationship, to ignore its monetary value.[7] In other contexts, I might instead give a cash equivalent of that present.

Someone might counter-argue, obviously, that we can desist from conferring a monetary value on commodities in personal relationships, but cannot do so in impersonal relationships such as those that obtain between strangers—for example, and relevantly here, between a needy individual and someone who is in a position to help by giving him an organ without even meeting him. Those relationships are fragile, the argument goes, and therefore more vulnerable than personal relationships to the contamination of the meaning of the good thus exchanged.[8] That may be true, but the fact that, in a given context, the exercise of the right to sell impinges on the exercise of the right to give at best tells against its legalization; it does not tell against its being a requirement of justice. Or, rather, it does tell so *only if* one can show that allowing, in practice, individuals to sell their organs will *necessarily* result in others not being able, or finding it very difficult, to exercise their right to give. For the record, in the USA, where blood sales are permitted, slightly under 5 per cent of eligible donors give (as opposed to sell) their blood; in the UK, where blood sales are outlawed, slightly above 5 per cent of eligible donors do so. The difference does not strike me as significant enough to suggest that permitting sales discourages people from giving, or vice versa.[9]

---

[7] See Mack, 'Dominos and the Fear of Commodification', p. 209.

[8] Archard, 'Selling Yourself', at 100–2.

[9] Sources: for recent census and blood donation figures in the USA, see, respectively, <www.census.gov> and <www.aabb.org>. For similar figures in the UK, see, respectively, <www.statistics/gov.uk/census2001> and <www.blood.co.uk>.

The monetary and non-monetary meanings of a good can coexist in yet another way, to wit, in the act by which the good is transferred. Take blood: to many, its meaning is that of a life-sustaining good. On Titmuss's view, to distribute it in exchange for money crowds out its meaning, at the expense of fostering altruistic relationships. However, it is doubtful that such a process of crowding out takes place. For, in demanding money for giving my blood, I can at the same time be very aware that in so doing I contribute to saving the lives of some individuals. And that might well be one reason why I decide to sell my blood (as opposed to selling something else). Similarly, a surgeon who deploys her skills at performing difficult operations and extracts a fee for so doing may well do so not merely because she needs or wants to raise income but also because she thereby saves lives.

The foregoing suggests another point against Titmuss. On his proto-Walzerian view, goods should be distributed according to their meaning. And so blood, which is life-sustaining, should be distributed for that purpose, and not for the purpose of earning money (just as sex, many would argue, should be given out of love, sexual desire, or a desire to reproduce, and not as a way to raise income). Yet it does not follow from the fact that a good has a certain meaning that it ought to be distributed solely in accordance with that meaning. The meaning of a service such as the performance by a surgeon of difficult operations is to sustain life. Ought the surgeon work for free, then, and only for free? Surely not. But if she can extract a fee (other than as compensation) for saving the life of the undeserving needy—thus offering her services for reasons not merely to do with the meaning of those skills—then why cannot an organ supplier do so as well?

There is a deeper problem with Titmuss's opposition to organ selling. Of course, he might be right to assume that the greater the number of goods and services which are up for sale, the more market-minded our social ethos will be. Be that as it may, it seems clear that *some* goods and services must be up for sale, unless of course we want to do away altogether with conferring on individuals the rights to control, and to derive some income from, their property and themselves, and, in turn, unless we want to do away with the value of individual autonomy.[10] If, then, we must be allowed to sell *some* goods and services, an argument is needed as to why we cannot sell our blood (or other body parts) but can, for example, sell our flat to someone else, or food, or clothes—in short, other goods which serve to fulfil needs, and not merely wants.

At this juncture, I surmise that Titmuss, or those sympathetic to his views, would choose one of the following three responses. They would either invoke the second variant of the commodity objection, in virtue of which treating body parts as commodities violates the requirement that we treat one another with the respect owed to persons; or they would argue that the sale and purchase of blood

---

[10] That the value of autonomy requires private property is a commonplace in the literature on property.

(and more generally of body parts) is exploitative of the poor (who will sell their organs to the rich); or, finally, they would point out that it is extremely costly to the sick (who, in a privatized medical system, will have to pay for it). On the last two counts, commodification is, in short, highly detrimental to the interests of the most vulnerable members of society.[11]

I shall address the claim that it is exploitative of the poor in section 6.3.2. As to the claim that it is detrimental to the sick, it depends on the factual premiss that a medical system where blood is sold and bought is one which is almost entirely privatized, as is indeed the case in the USA. Yet it need not be so: one can imagine a health-care system where the state covers medical expenditures and, in order to control them, caps the price at which body parts can be bought and sold. I shall return to such considerations in section 6.4. Suffice it to say that a properly designed system for the sale and purchase of body parts would go some way towards alleviating Titmuss's worries.

The second variant of the commodity objection to organ sales holds that treating organs as commodities is incompatible with treating persons with the respect they are owed as such. As I pointed out two paragraphs ago, a Titmussean opponent to organ sales might be tempted to deploy that second variant in order to explain why some goods which are also needed by all to lead a minimally flourishing life—such as clothing, food, and shelter—can be treated as commodities whilst others cannot. Note, though, that one can endorse that second variant without subscribing to Titmuss's view that organ sales will drive out altruism. Note, also, that if the view that organ sales are incompatible with the respect owed to persons is correct, then it is devastating in the present context, since I aim to show that a just society *is* one where persons are given recognition respect as persons, and yet can sell and buy body parts. Note, finally, that the objection is all the more powerful as it takes as its starting point the view of the relationship between person and body which I posit in Chapter 1, which goes like this: our body is part of our person. In so far as our person is not a thing, our body itself is not a thing either. Thus, we do not own it, and cannot dispose of it, as if it were a thing. For, if we were to treat it as a thing, we would treat ourselves as a thing. In so far as selling something is to treat it as a thing, we cannot sell parts of our body.

Commodification is problematic, then, in so far as it implies objectification. Such, I believe, is Kant's view, as articulated in his *Lectures on Ethics*, and as deployed in similar terms by contemporary philosophers such as Charles Fried and Margaret Radin.[12] And yet this objection suffers from a number of weaknesses. First, although to treat something as a commodity is, indeed, to treat it

[11] Titmuss, *The Gift Relationship*, pp. 263–4.

[12] I. Kant, *Lectures on Ethics*, eds. P. Heath and J. B. Schneewind (Cambridge: Cambridge University Press, 1997), pp. 144, 147, 341, 349, and 371; C. Fried, *Right and Wrong* (Cambridge, Mass.: Harvard University Press, 1978), pp. 142–3; M. Radin, *Contested Commodities* (Cambridge, Mass.: Harvard University Press, 1996), pp. 126–7. Interestingly, Radin notes that her view does

as an object, to buy or to sell it need not be so.[13] For, to treat something as a commodity, you recall, is to treat it as something the production, distribution, and enjoyment of which can be regulated solely by market norms; to treat something in that way, in turn, is to treat it as an object. However, one can buy or sell something without treating it as an object—and by implication without treating it as a commodity. Such is the case, for example, when one buys an animal whose welfare one is concerned with, or when one sells an animal one has looked after for a while. Moreover, even if it is impossible to buy and sell something without treating that thing as an object, it is possible to buy and sell something without treating that of which it is a part as an object. Accordingly, one can sell *a part of* oneself without treating oneself as an object, for the simple reason that renouncing all rights over a part of oneself, a fortiori a detachable part such as an organ, does not mean that one is renouncing all rights over oneself. (In contrast, one cannot sell oneself without treating oneself as an object, in so far as selling implies a total renunciation of rights over the thing sold, including the right not to be treated as an object.)

Second, if objectification really is the problem, then, in so far as it is present in giving, the objection disallows the latter, as well as selling. Consider Fried's comments against sales: '[the] shame of selling one's body is just that one splits apart an entity one knows should not be so split. It is thus not the sale as such which is disturbing, but the treatment of the body as a separate, separable, entity. For I assume that buying and selling as such are not shameful activities.'[14] Fried's objection to organ selling proves too much, since it disallows *altruistic* organ and blood donations. Fried tries to deal with this counterclaim by pointing out that, '[in] a voluntary taking, I give up a part of myself not to satisfy some need or want, not to get anything and thus I do not trade myself for anything, as if my person were an item of commerce.'[15] The problem with his concession, of course, is that it is not clear at all that I do not get anything out of donating body parts: it may make me feel good about myself, or it may allow me to implement my conception of the good life, which is to live altruistically.

---

not commit her to banning organ sales in unjust societies; for, in imposing such a ban, she rightly notes, we would deny many very poor people the means to get the income they desperately need, and we would thereby also violate their personhood.

[13] For a study of what it means to treat someone as an object, see M. Nussbaum, 'Objectification', *Philosophy and Public Affairs* 24 (1995): 249–91.

[14] C. Fried, *Right and Wrong*, p. 142. Scholars disagree as to whether Kant is committed to rejecting not merely selling one's organs, but also donating them. See, e.g., R. Chadwick, 'The Market for Bodily Parts: Kant and Duties to Oneself', *Journal of Applied Philosophy* 6 (1989): 129–39; N. Gerrand, 'The Misuse of Kant in the Debate about a Market for Human Body Parts', *Journal of Applied Philosophy* 16 (1999): 59–67; J. C. Merle, 'A Kantian Argument for a Duty to Donate One's Own Organs: A Reply to Nicole Gerrand', *Journal of Applied Philosophy* 17 (2000): 93–201; S. Munzer, *A Theory of Property* (Cambridge: Cambridge University Press, 1990).

[15] Fried, *Right and Wrong*, p. 143.

In other words, one must show why the fact that money is exchanged corrupts the transfer of organs from one person to another. One rather common argument to that effect is that in selling, as opposed to giving, a part of oneself, one sees oneself as a commodity; similarly, in buying an organ from someone else one sees that person not as a person, but as a commodity. And that is obviously lacking respect for oneself as a person, and for others as persons. However, as we have already seen, it is simply not true that in treating a part of oneself as a commodity, one treats oneself as such. On the conception of personhood I sketched out in Chapter 1, one can be a person without having an intact body, and one can remain the same person over time if one loses a number of (non-vital) body parts: although the continuous occupancy of our body is a necessary condition for being a person, the continuous occupancy of *all* the parts that make our body is not. Thus, even if it is true that our body is constitutive of our status as persons, it is not true that, in selling *some* of its parts, we treat ourselves as commodities. Note, also, that although selling one's vital organs shows that (in most cases at least) one does not respect oneself, it is not tantamount to selling oneself: rather, in so doing, one destroys oneself, which is not the same as treating oneself as a commodity. Pending further argument to the contrary, then, the commodity objection to organ sales founders, and my case for the right to sell and buy organs stands.

6.3.2 The Exploitation Objection

The second important objection to organ sales adverts to the allegedly exploitative character of those commercial transactions. Many opponents of such transactions point out that, more often than not, organ sellers are recruited amongst the poor, who see selling one of their organs as the only or quickest way to improve their lot, whereas organ buyers are recruited amongst the rich. On that view, organ selling is exploitative of the poor and should therefore be disallowed.

Note that the claim that organ selling should be banned for those reasons implies that sellers do not have the moral right to sell; but it does not imply that, in selling, they are doing something which is morally wrong. If anything, it suggests that buyers, and not sellers, are guilty of wrongdoing, since they exploit the poor, even if, or so the objection might concede, their circumstances are such that they cannot be blamed for so acting (after all, they do need an organ, sometimes as a matter of life and death). In what follows, I shall argue that organ selling is not always wrongfully exploitative of sellers, and that, even if it is, it does not follow that the state should outlaw it. In fact, the state should forbear from interfering in those cases where the transaction does not destroy the sellers' opportunities for self-respect; in other cases, and as we saw in section 6.2, sellers and buyers lack the right to enter such transactions, but only the latter lack a right that the state not interfere with them.

The claim that organ sales are wrongfully exploitative—whether or not the sale is done *ante-mortem* or *post-mortem*—has a lot of intuitive appeal: most of us have heard stories of destitute people forced to sell a kidney or a cornea in order to survive. Yet it invites a number of critical replies: some familiar; others not so. Standardly, a transaction involving A and B is said to be wrongfully exploitative of B when the following three conditions—which are singly necessary and together sufficient—obtain: (a) A benefits from the transaction; (b) the outcome of the transaction is harmful or (in the case of a mutually advantageous transaction) unfair to B; and (c) A gets B to agree to the transaction by seizing on some features of B's, or of his situation, such that B would not agree to the transaction otherwise.[16] In order to work, then, the objection must show that a transaction whereby A is buying B's organs is one where A benefits from the transaction, where the transaction is harmful or unfair to B, and where A takes advantage of some feature of B's or of his situation. As I shall now show, such transactions do not always meet those three conditions.

Let us turn to the first of the aforementioned three exploitation conditions, which, one might think, all organ sales meet. For it seems uncontroversial after all that the patient—A—benefits from receiving an organ. However, A benefits only if the transplant operation is successful; if it is not, then B has not been exploited by him. To be sure, if A has bought B's organs through a for-profit procurement firm, the latter will have benefited from the transaction, whether or not the transplant is successful. In such cases, *if* the transaction meets the second and third conditions, it is indeed exploitative, but the firm, and not the patient, is the exploiter (of, potentially, both buyer and seller). Thus, only *some* organ sales are exploitative, to wit, those where the patient buys organs with the help of a for-profit firm, or where the patient buys them without using such a firm and where the operation succeeds. In cases where the organ has been brought through a not-for-profit centre and the transplant fails, in so far as there is no one who has benefited from it at B's expense, the sale does not meet the first of the aforementioned three conditions, and it cannot therefore qualify as exploitative.

Against the foregoing some might argue that, as A increases his chance for survival by buying an organ, he benefits from the transaction no matter what the outcome is. But I am not persuaded that merely increasing his chances does constitute a benefit. For suppose the operation fails: A is as badly off medically as (if not worse off than), and is worse off materially than, he was before the transaction took place. He clearly has not benefited from the transaction. All we can say is that in those cases where A does not in fact benefit from the transaction, he has attempted to exploit B and thus has engaged in exploitative behaviour towards him, but has not actually exploited him (just as someone who unsuccessfully

[16] See, e.g., A. Wertheimer's account of the idea of exploitation, in his *Exploitation* (Princeton: Princeton University Press, 1996); and D. Miller, 'Exploitation in the Market', in A. Reeve (ed.), *Modern Theories of Exploitation* (London: Sage, 1987).

attempts to deceive someone has engaged in deceitful behaviour but has not actually deceived them).[17]

The second condition states that the outcome of the transaction must be harmful or unfair to B. Now, it is important to note that, contrary to what is sometimes said, organ sales do not *always* harm B. Of course, uninterestingly, divesting oneself of one's heart and lungs is harmful. But giving a liver lobe, a cornea, or a kidney only *may* be so, in so far as general anaesthetics—which are necessary to remove those organs—are risky to the donors, and in so far as having to live with, say, only one kidney *may* constitute a serious handicap. The fact that donors incur the risks of such harms does not imply that they *do* indeed incur such harms. Moreover, giving blood or bone marrow under local anaesthetics is not harmful. Nor is giving one's organs posthumously: at the very least, it is obviously not physically harmful—a point worth noting, given that opponents of organ sales often point to the serious health risks incurred by sellers.[18]

In those cases where B receives money in exchange for divesting himself of a non-vital organ, and where he does so without incurring harm, the transaction, if exploitative, is at least mutually advantageous, in that B benefits from it too. In order to show that mutually advantageous organ sales are exploitative of B, one must show that their outcome is unfair to him. That is, one must show that, although B benefits, the distribution of gains between A and B is unfair. In what way, though, should it be unfair for the objection to go through? It cannot be because B always benefits from the transaction to a lesser extent than A does. For, in some cases, the benefits accruing to B may exceed those accruing to A, as when the latter can, post-operation, lead a life which is no more than minimally flourishing, whereas, thanks to the money he earned, the former is able to do more than that, and implement his preferred conception of the good.

At this juncture, a proponent of the exploitation objection might press that the money given by the buyer can *never* make up for, or be commensurate with, the loss of his organ: such transactions, he might hold, always involve a disparity in value, to the seller's detriment. However, whilst it is plausible to hold that no amount of money can make up for one's brain (for in giving one's brain one is annihilating oneself as a person), it is implausible to think that *no* amount of money can ever make up for the loss of a kidney, blood, or a cornea.

Could the worry be that the price obtained by B is much lower than he would have got had he not been in such need to sell? Generally, a transaction between a

---

[17] Suppose A buys from B a kidney which will enable him for two years not to go on dialysis, but which will then fail—failure which makes his condition worse. Has A really benefited from the transaction? In other words, at which point must it be the case that A benefits from the transaction for it to count as exploitative (assuming of course that the second and third conditions must be met)? I do not really have an answer to that question (which arises with any transaction, not merely with organ sales).

[18] I shall argue in section 8.3.2 that broadening the second condition so as to encompass the risk of incurring a harm will not do.

seller S and a purchaser P is exploitative of the purchaser if S gets from P a price which is higher than the price he would get in a hypothetical market where P would not be under pressure to transact.[19] Conversely, it is exploitative of S if P gets from S a price which is *lower* than the price he would get in a hypothetical market where S would not be under pressure to transact.

Strictly speaking, the foregoing points cannot apply to the case of organ sales. For whilst it is possible to compare market prices for, say, shovels bought and sold under normal conditions and prices for shovels bought under pressure,[20] it is not possible to compare market prices for organs bought and sold under normal conditions and market prices for organs bought and sold under pressure, as the market for organs is a pressurized market: those who want to sell their organs would not do so if they could raise money by other means; those who want to buy organs are (usually) in desperate need of them.[21] However, although one does not know what price organs would fetch in an unpressurized market, it might be possible to know how much people are paid who are willing to take similar risks for others, under unpressurized conditions. Accordingly, it might be possible to appeal to a baseline price in defence of the view that organ buyers exploit organ sellers, and should be denied the right to do so. By the same token, however, it might be possible to appeal to such a price in defence of the view that organ *sellers* exploit organ buyers, and should be denied the right to do so. In other words, the exploitation objection proves too much. For, just as purchasers may be in a position to impose too low a price on sellers, the latter may also be in a position to impose too high a price on purchasers. If there is exploitation, it is not only of the sellers by the buyers; it can be of the buyers by the sellers.

Finally, do organ sales meet the third condition that a transaction must meet in order to qualify as exploitative of organ seller B? That condition, you recall, stipulates that A, in that instance the organ buyer, takes advantage of B's situation, such as his poverty, so as to get him to agree to a transaction he normally would not agree to. Now, in support of their claim that B's consent to selling one of his organ to A is vitiated, proponents of the exploitation objection point out that organ sellers are recruited, overwhelmingly, amongst the poor, and argue that poverty vitiates consent: if sellers were not poor, if they really had a choice,

---

[19] Wertheimer, *Exploitation*, p. 231 ff.

[20] I allude here to a classic example in the literature on exploitation. Suppose a blizzard unexpectedly hits the area where P lives, at a time when shovels are in short supply; P goes to the hardware store to buy a shovel, expecting to pay the hitherto advertised price of 15 dollars. However, S, the store owner, has bumped up the price to 30 dollars upon hearing news of the blizzard. Has S exploited P?

[21] I say 'usually' for one could imagine an unpressurized market in, say, blood, involving buyers who need blood in elective surgery (such as plastic surgery). Then it would be possible to compare prices fetched by blood in such markets and prices fetched by blood in pressurized markets. On the whole, though, markets for organs are pressurized, which makes it impossible to assess whether the distribution of gains is unfair.

the argument goes, they would not choose to sell their organs and to expose themselves to the risks attendant on the removal procedure. In other words, they do not fully and freely consent to the transaction. And it is that which makes it objectionable.

Up to a point, the objection is correct. It is true, of course, that poverty seriously restricts the range of options available to individuals. As a matter of fact, organ sellers are taken advantage of by organ buyers, or by middle men, in the ways just described.[22] But it is no less true that in some cases, organ sellers could, in theory, take advantage of patients' desperate need for a life-saving organ. Here, again, it is not inherent in organ sales that they should be exploitative of sellers only: they might well be exploitative of buyers as well. This, of course, does not make them right. But, as I shall show presently, even if it is true that the potential seller or buyer has not given genuine consent to the transaction, even, that is, if the transaction meets the third wrongful exploitation condition, indeed, even if it is wrongfully exploitative—it does not follow that the state should ban it.

Before I defend this view, though, it is worth noting that the claim that the donors' poverty vitiates their consent and renders the transaction wrongfully exploitative loses some of its force if the principle of sufficiency obtains. For that principle, you recall, stipulates that individuals have a right to the material resources they need in order to lead a minimally flourishing life. More specifically, it stipulates that they have rights to minimum income, housing, education, and health care. In so far as, *ex hypothesi*, they have the material resources they need in order to live a minimally flourishing life, one cannot convincingly object to their wanting to maximize their income by selling their organs on the grounds that they are too poor for their consent to the transaction to be genuine.

Having said that, as we saw in section 1.3.1, sufficiency does not guarantee that everybody has those material resources, since there might be some individuals who, for whatever reason, have forfeited their claim for help at the bar of justice. The question then is whether those individuals, who do suffer from serious material deprivation and seek to remedy their situation by selling an organ, can be said genuinely to consent to the transaction, and ought to be allowed to take part in it.

In so far, then, as the sufficiency principle is in place, the exploitative but mutually advantageous transactions under scrutiny would involve either sellers who, although not poor, nevertheless are not well off enough to have a more than minimally flourishing life, or sellers who are poor and regard the sale of their

---

[22] See, e.g., N. Scheper-Hughes, 'The Global Traffic in Organs', *Current Anthropology* 41 (2000): 191–224; M. Goyal et al., 'Economic and Health Consequences of Selling a Kidney in India', *Journal of the American Medical Association* 288 (2002): 1589–93; L. Cohen, 'Where it Hurts: Indian Material for an Ethics of Organ Transplantation', *Daedalus* 128 (1999): 135–65; J. Zargooshi, 'Quality of Life of Iranian Kidney "Donors"', *Journal of Urology* 166 (2001): 1790–9.

organs as one way to raise the income they cannot get at the bar of sufficiency. Although such transactions may well be wrongfully exploitative, they should not be banned—which is another way to say that individuals have a claim-right against third parties, notably the state, that they not interfere with them. Consider first the buyer's point of view: to claim that he should not be allowed to buy because his extreme need for an organ vitiates his consent to the transaction implies that less needy individuals—who want, as opposed to need, an organ—can be allowed to buy. The more needy one is, the less, oddly, one is in a position to get the required organ.

Consider now the seller's point of view: reiterating a claim made earlier, to aver that the interest of the worse off in improving their lot in life by selling their organs is not strong enough to hold the state under a duty to let them do so and to protect them when they do so suggests, then, that they ought to be disallowed from taking *any* dangerous and unpleasant job, and that they receive no protection when doing so. This is problematic on two counts. For a start, it restricts the freedom of occupational choice of the worse off on the grounds that taking those jobs would jeopardize their health.[23] But such paternalistic concern for their welfare seems misplaced: if we, as a community, decide to withhold from them the extra resources they want on the grounds that sufficiency does not require that we do more than help them meet their needs, or if we decide that they have forfeited their claim for material help to begin with, *and* if we bar them from selling their organs, we penalize them twice, which seems unfair. If, as a community, we take their welfare to heart, then it is better to give them those resources, so as to enable them not to sell their organs.

Moreover, the objection also implies that individuals who already have the material resources they need to lead a more than minimally flourishing life could be permitted to sell their body parts as a way to increase their income even further and obtain, say, luxury goods, since the fact that they are well off protects them from being exploited. If that objection is correct, then, it allows, rather bizarrely, for a world where the interest of the worse off in helping themselves is not important enough to ground on the state a duty to let them sell their organs and validate such transactions, whereas the better off's interest in getting extra material resources, although much less acute than the worse off's similar interest, might be strong enough to hold the state under a similar duty. In short, on that view, the worse off lack, in virtue of being worse off, rights which the better off enjoy in virtue of being better off.

---

[23] At this juncture it has often been objected to me that the poor should not have to take those dangerous and risky jobs in the first instance: they should be able to take up better professional opportunities. Granted, a just society is one where individuals can choose their conception of the good from an adequate range of opportunities—including professional opportunities. But even in such a society, some (destitute) individuals will have no choice but to take up unpleasant and dangerous jobs, for they might simply be unable—through unavoidable lack of qualifications—to take up better jobs.

The proponent of the exploitation objection might be tempted to retort that, under his proposal, *everybody* should be denied the right to sell and buy organs: the materially worse off should be denied the right to sell on the grounds that organ sales are against their health interest, and the materially better off should be denied that same right on the grounds that it would be discriminatory to give them an opportunity to raise income denied the worse off. One might also argue that the medically worse off should be denied the right to buy on the grounds that organ sales are against their economic interest, and that the medically better off should be denied that same right on the grounds that it would be discriminatory to give them an opportunity to acquire an organ denied the worse off. One might also be tempted to defend the legal prohibition of organ sales on the grounds that it would be impossible to implement a law whereby only those earning above a certain income would be allowed to sell, and only those above a certain threshold of medical need would be allowed to buy.[24]

These retorts, however appealing they may seem at first sight, nevertheless fail to explain why concern for discrimination against the poor and/or difficulties in implementing a fine-grained law warrant blanket prohibition as opposed to blanket permission. In advocating the former, rather than the latter, one supposes that the harm incurred by the materially worse off when selling is such as to justify forbidding them to do so. As we saw above, this supposition does not hold, first, because organ selling does not always harm sellers, and, second, because even if it does, then the supposition in question commits us to disallowing them to take up dangerous jobs in general, at the unacceptable cost of their freedom of occupational choice.

So far I have argued that individuals have the moral claim-right to sell their body parts or to buy body parts from others, that is, that third parties are under a duty not to interfere with them, even if the transaction is wrongfully exploitative. Do they have the power to do so, though? And do they have a claim-right against third parties that they recognize the transaction as valid? As I argued in Chapter 1, someone has the power to enter a morally wrong transaction if for her not to have that power would harm one or several important interests of hers. Suppose that someone who has forfeited his claim to receive material help from others can raise the income he needs to lead a minimally flourishing life only by selling one of his kidneys. Denying him the power to enter that transaction would harm a very important interest of his: indeed, there are few interests more important than our interest in leading such a life. Accordingly, that individual does have the moral power to transact. Imagine now someone who lacks a claim to a kidney (which he needs very badly) at the bar of justice—on the grounds that the able-bodied cannot be made to undergo general anaesthetics for someone

---

[24] Similarly, some opponents of the legalization of cannabis agree that cannabis is not harmful to a number of individuals; but, in their view, the fact that it is very harmful to some, combined with the fact that it would be impossible to implement a fine-grained legal prohibition, justifies a blanket prohibition on its sale and consumption.

else's sake. His only chance for a kidney is to buy one. Denying him the power to enter such a transaction would harm his interest in leading a minimally flourishing life: accordingly, he too has the moral right to enter such a transaction.

I shall not examine all kinds of organ sales to determine whether individuals have the right to perform them. Rather, I shall address a final question, namely, that of assessing whether individuals who have the power to sell their organs and a right against third parties that they not interfere with the transaction also have a right that the latter recognize it as binding on both parties. Now, as we saw in Chapter 1, in those cases where one does have the right to enter a transaction with someone else, one also has the right that the state recognize the transaction as valid. Does that point apply to cases where someone exercises her right to enter a morally wrong transaction, more specifically, a wrongfully exploitative transaction? I believe that it does.

Some philosophers disagree.[25] On their view, the reason why individuals' right to sell and buy body parts, sometimes at great cost to themselves, should not be recognized, is not that they would thereby harm themselves (for that would be unacceptably paternalistic). Rather, it is that we—the community—find such transactions exploitative, and for this reason morally wrong; given that there are many other, and worthy, projects and endeavours for which resources are needed, we are at liberty, as citizens, to refuse to help individuals engage in that transaction by enforcing the resulting contract.

One can see the intuitive force of that argument. For, if it does make sense (as most would agree) for someone to refuse to lend his hand to a deed which he plausibly finds deeply objectionable, then it does make sense for us as a political community to refuse to lend our judicial apparatus to enforce transactions which we plausibly find deeply objectionable. However, as we saw in section 1.2.3B, individuals have the moral power to enter morally wrong transactions as well as a moral claim that it be regarded as legally valid, if not having that power or that claim would unacceptably jeopardize some important interest(s) of theirs. Consequently, then, the objection cannot, pending further argument, support the view that *any* organ sale ought to be regarded, legally, as null and void. Moreover, it may well be possible to regulate the commercialization of body parts in such ways as to eliminate their most seriously exploitative aspects, just as it is possible

---

[25] See S. Shiffrin, 'Paternalism, Unconscionability Doctrine, and Accommodation', *Philosophy and Public Affairs* 29 (2000): 205–51. J. Feinberg persuasively argues that although a liberal state cannot punish individuals for enslaving themselves, it can refuse to recognize slavery contracts, not on the paternalistic grounds that they are harmful to the self-enslaved, but on the grounds that a society in which they would be enforced would not be the kind of society in which we should want to live (for in such a society, slaves changing their mind would have to be dragged back to their owners, those who helped them escape would have to be prosecuted, the public at large would most probably feel greatly demoralized as a result, etc. (see Feinberg, *Harm to Self*, pp. 79–81)). Unlike Feinberg's, the objection under study does not point to the public costs attendant on the enforcement of contracts such as a slavery contract. Rather, it points to the state's prerogative not to devote scarce resources to help wrongdoers pursue their conception of the good.

to regulate the job market so as to protect destitute workers from being exploited by their employers. To exploring this issue I now turn.

6.4 REGULATING THE SALE AND PURCHASE OF BODY PARTS

A regulatory framework for the sale and purchase of body parts must deal with at least four different questions. First, as noted above, potential sellers are, as a matter of fact, recruited largely amongst the worse off: it is likely that they will continue to be so even under ideal conditions. In so far as they might be under considerable pressure to sell, care must be taken to ensure that they consent to the transaction in full knowledge—or at least in as full knowledge as is humanly possible—of all the risks attendant both on the removal operation and on living without the organ which they wish to sell.[26] Note that similar considerations apply to buyers, who also incur risks when having such major surgery. Just as sellers must be protected, at least up to a point, from buckling under the pressure of their material needs, purchasers must be protected from buckling under the pressure of their medical needs.

Second, as we saw in section 6.3.2, whilst the fact that organ sales can be exploitative does not constitute a good reason to outlaw them, it nevertheless constitutes a good reason to regulate them. So does the fact, mentioned in section 6.3.1, that organ sales are detrimental to the sick, in so far as they are part of a wider drive towards the privatization of health-care services. I pointed out in that section that price-capping would go some way towards addressing that concern. In fact, price-*fixing* in general would do that, as well as addressing the concerns raised by the exploitation objection.[27] For consider: a transaction is mutually advantageous where patient P desperately needs an organ, say, a kidney, and where donor D does not desperately need the money he will get from the sale, but it could be exploitative of P. P would be protected from being grossly exploited if the cost of kidneys were capped. Conversely, a transaction where donor D desperately needs the money he could get from selling, say, his blood, and where P does not desperately need to undergo cosmetic surgery during which blood would be needed is mutually advantageous, but it is exploitative of D. D

---

[26] Prohibiting them altogether from selling would constitute a full protection. However we have ruled that out, on anti-paternalistic grounds, in section 6.2.1. Some might be tempted to argue, at this juncture, that regulation actually does constitute a paternalistic interference with sellers and buyers, and should be ruled out for the reasons given in that section. Regulation is not paternalistic, however, when justified, not on the grounds that sellers and buyers ought to be protected against their wishes from ill-effects of pressurized transactions, but on the grounds that it helps buyers and sellers further their interests in, e.g., not having to pay too high, or to receive too low, an amount for the good, ensuring that they have as full information as possible before agreeing to the transaction, etc.

[27] For scepticism on price-capping as a way to solve distributional problems, though, see A. I. Ogus, *Regulation—Legal Form and Economic Theory* (Oxford: Clarendon Press, 1994).

would be protected from being grossly exploited if he could be sure to get a minimum price for his blood.

Note that price-fixing is compatible with the claim that individuals have the right to buy and sell organs: for to say that someone has the right to sell something is to say that she has the right to transfer her rights and liabilities over that thing to someone else, for payment—and, moreover, as we saw at the outset of section 6.2, to make a profit from the transaction. But it is not to say that she has the right to get as much from the sale as an unregulated market would allow. Conversely, to say that someone has the right to buy something is to say that he can acquire rights and liabilities over that thing, in exchange for payment; it is not to say that he has the right to pay as little for that thing as an unregulated market would allow.

One may wonder why it is so important that prices should be capped so as to ensure that the sick are not exploited. For, after all, in the context in which I deployed my argument for the commercialization of body parts, the sick, *ex hypothesi*, have forfeited their claim for a body part (either they are known to be responsible for needing organs, or their need is not such that, were it not met, they would lead a less than minimally flourishing life). So why should one be concerned with their ability to purchase it? However, that we may have a right to ask them for money in exchange for our organs does not imply that we have a right to exact from them whatever income they are willing to pay. In fact, justice forbids us to charge them so much that they would not have enough material resources left to lead a minimally flourishing life. For, although they are responsible for their *medical* predicament, and although we therefore are not under a duty of justice to help them get out of it, we are under a duty not to take from them the material resources they already have, and without which they cannot lead a minimally flourishing life.

That prices should be fixed (set high enough to ensure that donors are not victims of gross exploitation, but not so high as to make buyers themselves vulnerable to gross exploitation) leaves open the question—the third of the four issues mentioned at the outset of this section—of how body parts should be provided. Three options come to mind: (a) prices are fixed, but donors and patients buy from one another, either directly, or through profit-making brokerage firms; (b) non-profit organ procurement agencies buy body parts from all sellers, and in turn allocate them to patients; or (c) one agency—the state—buys all body parts from all sellers, and in turn allocates them to patients.

Standard reasons for allowing organ brokers to operate appeal to the fact that, as they would want to sell as many organs as possible, they would have an incentive to devise efficient procurement strategies, to help sellers maximize their profits, and so on.[28] On the downside, however—and this, I believe, is a decisive

[28] See, e.g., A. Barnett et al., 'Improving Organ Donation: Compensation versus Markets', in A. L. Caplan and D. H. Coelho (eds.), *The Ethics of Organ Transplants* (Amherst, NY: Prometheus Books, 1998).

reason *against* them—they would also have an incentive to hide from donors the risks attendant on medical procedures, and to hide from patients the problems arising from having recourse to particular donors. Even if they could be regulated tightly enough, procurement firms, profit-driven as they would be, would have to charge all patients. In so doing, they would not discriminate between two kinds of patients, both of whom, *ex hypothesi*, lack a claim that the able-bodied provide them with body parts, but only one of whom also lacks a claim to material help towards the cost of health care.

Indeed, recall that those who need body parts get them for free at the bar of justice if they need them through no fault of their own, and if the body parts they need are such that the able-bodied would not lose their prospects for a minimally flourishing life by giving them. Against that background, there are two kinds of buyers: patients who are known to be responsible for needing an organ and who have therefore disqualified themselves from gratuitous help, and patients who, although they are not responsible for their predicament, nevertheless cannot get help because their need is such that the able-bodied cannot be expected to provide them with the relevant body part. The former not only do not have a claim for a (free) body part: they do not have a welfare right to the resources needed for their medical treatment. The latter, however, do have such a right, precisely because they are not responsible for their condition. Accordingly, it would be unjust to ask them to pay for the cost of the needed body part; by contrast, it would not be unjust to ask those who are responsible for their condition to pay. (It might violate the requirement to show basic human compassion, but that is another matter.)

Of course, it might be possible to devise a mechanism which would discriminate between those who can be made to pay, and those who ought not to be made to pay. For example, the state might decide to reimburse patients for the cost of buying organs from a for-profit firm, provided patients are eligible for such help at the bar of justice. However, to devise a system whereby sales of organs would be brokered by for-profit firms only would be analogous to making it compulsory for doctors to find placements in a publicly funded health-care system through for-profit firms. And it is very unclear why the state should have to pay for such costs when they include not merely the cost of the organ (which includes the profit realized by the donor), but also the profit realized by the firm—by someone who is nothing more than an intermediary.

Such considerations, together with the risks attendant on handing over transactions as portentous as organ sales to profit-making firms, suggest that two options—(b), non-profit-making centres buy body parts, and (c), the state buys body parts—would both be preferable to (a). Proposal (b), in turn, is preferable to (c), for the fact that, under (c), the same institution would be responsible for fixing the price, and for buying, would lead to a conflict of interest: the state as purchaser would want a low price, which in turn would influence its pricing policy, to the detriment of potential organ sellers. Not-for-profit firms would not be faced with such a conflict, and would therefore be in a better position to act as intermediaries between patients and sellers.

Furthermore, not only should prices be fixed and body parts sold and purchased through such firms; in addition, all care should be taken to ensure that potential sellers are fully informed of all the risks attendant both on the removal and loss of the organ of which they wish to divest themselves, are given enough time to think through the consequences of their decision, and are allowed to change their mind right up until the last minute.

Finally, it is worth considering whether the income which individuals generate by selling their body parts whilst alive should be tax free and discounted when assessing their eligibility for welfare benefits. John Harris argues that it should, on the twofold grounds that tax exemption would provide an incentive for more potential organ sellers to come forward, and that the poor should not lose welfare benefits if they sell their organs.[29]

In response to the first point, one can easily concede that a situation where very few sellers come forward is not desirable. But Harris's point may seem to prove too much: for why not, by the same token, offer tax exemption to *anyone* who does a dangerous and/or necessary job? Perhaps that is, in fact, the way forward, as a remedy to shortages in, say, nursing, school teaching, and so on. Should one be reluctant to go down that road, tax breaks, rather than tax exemption, would be preferable: they would seem to strike the right balance between, on the one hand, encouraging individuals to make available a scarce resource, and, on the other hand, minimizing tax discrimination in favour of some people and against others. One could set up a system whereby organ sellers would be given such tax breaks.

In response to the second point, one can also easily concede that a situation where an individual earns some income by selling his blood or a kidney, then as a result loses his welfare benefits and thus falls below the poverty threshold, is not one we should allow for. But note that such a situation would not arise in a just society. For, as we saw, organ sellers would be either needy individuals who are known to be responsible for their predicament (without having had to make shameful revelations about themselves) and therefore lack a claim for help at the bar of justice, or individuals who are not needy but seek to increase their income. In neither case would sellers be entitled to welfare benefits, and in neither case, then, would the question of their eligibility for receiving them post-sale be raised.

6.5 CONCLUSION

At the close of Chapter 5, I argued that to hold the able-bodied under an obligation to make some of their body parts available to the sick does indeed constrain

---

[29] Harris, *Clones, Genes, and Immortality*, p. 167.

their autonomy, but does not undermine it, since there are many restrictions on the cases in which they are so held. As we have seen in this chapter, individuals have the right to buy and sell organs from one another. By implication, then, the able-bodied have the right to do either: they can sell their organs to those who lack a claim to having them for free at the bar of justice; should they themselves want to buy an organ, for whatever reason (for example, to implement their specific conception of the good, such as being a top-class athlete, which requires two kidneys), they can do so as well. Neither the exploitation objection, nor the commodification objection, I claimed here, succeed against the view that individuals have a qualified right to sell parts of their body—qualified, that is, by the sick's claim to some of their body parts; they also have a qualified right to buy body parts from others—qualified, that is, by others' right to withhold their consent to such transaction. These claims constitute further reasons as to why the restrictions on personal integrity which justice imposes on the able-bodied merely constrain, but do not destroy, their autonomy.

7
Prostitution

7.1 INTRODUCTION

Let us take stock of what has been said so far. As Chapters 2–5 demonstrated, individuals need both body parts and personal services in order to live a minimally flourishing life, and (with qualifications) have rights to them against ablebodied (or, as the case may be, dead) third parties. In Chapter 5, however, we saw that sexual and reproductive services are not the kind of services which one can be held under a duty to provide as a matter of justice. In addition, it was argued in Chapter 6 that individuals have the right to sell their body parts in all those cases where they are not under a duty to provide them for free; conversely, they have the right to buy body parts from those willing to sell, in all those cases where they do not have a claim to get one for free. Can we infer from the foregoing claims that individuals have the right to hire their body for sexual and reproductive personal services, and to buy those services from those willing to provide them? To put the question in the starkest possible terms, on what grounds, if any, do individuals—women *and* men—have the right to prostitute themselves or to buy a prostitute's services? On what grounds, if any, do women have the right to lease their womb out to prospective parents who cannot, by themselves, have a child? And on what grounds, if any, do the latter have the right to buy their services?

In this chapter, I address the issue of prostitution. Section 7.2 argues that engaging in prostitutional acts, whether as a client or as a prostitute, is not inherently morally wrong, and that individuals have the moral right to do so. In other words, they have the power, as granted by a moral rule, to change their relationship with others by transferring some claims over their body to sexual ends, and such power is protected by claims that the state not only not interfere with them, but also recognize the transaction as valid. I thus offer a defence of the legalization of prostitution—that is, not merely of its decriminalization, but of its regulation under labour and contract law. In section 7.3, I examine and rebut some claims, mostly but not only put forward by feminists, to the effect that prostitution is morally wrong and therefore should be criminalized.

Before I start, a point of terminology, and three caveats. Defining prostitution is harder than it seems at first sight. Consider the *OED*'s definition (current online edition):

1.a. Of women: The offering of the body to indiscriminate lewdness for hire (esp. as a practice or institution); whoredom, harlotry.

1.b. *Personified*

†1.c. *transf.* A prostitute, a harlot. *Obs.rare.*

1.d. Of men: the undertaking of homosexual acts for payment.

Setting aside some odd disparities between its accounts of female and male prostitution (according to the *OED*, male prostitutes, unlike female prostitutes, do not, by definition, seem to offer their body *indiscriminately*), note that the *OED* counter-intuitively rules out from its definition (because of 'indiscriminating') the high-flying prostitute who carefully selects a small number of wealthy clients and only deals with them for a number of years. In addition, it does not quite capture what is involved in practices as diverse as offering manual or oral sex only, phone sex, Internet sex, and so on. To some, those practices are not similar enough to the paradigmatic definition of prostitution to count as instances of it. However, I take for granted that they do. Finally, the *OED* does not take on board the fact that, however rare they are, male prostitutes whose clients are women do exist.[1] In section 7.2.1, I shall offer an account of prostitution which does embrace many (although, as we shall see, not all[2]) of those various phenomena. When doing so, and indeed throughout the chapter, I shall call 'heterosexual' a prostitutional act which takes place between two individuals of opposite sex, irrespective of their sexual orientation; conversely, I shall call 'homosexual' a prostitutional act which takes place between two individuals of the same sex, again irrespective of their sexual orientation. Thus, a prostitutional act between a heterosexual male prostitute and a homosexual male client is a homosexual act; so is an act between two heterosexual men, who would both rather, and normally do, have sex with women, but cannot do so under the circumstances in which they find themselves.

And now the three caveats. First, in so far as my task, in this book, is to delineate the rights individuals have over their own and other people's bodies, I shall focus on prostitutes' and clients' rights, and ignore pimping. I shall only, and presently, dispose of some objections to it. It is sometimes argued that pimping is morally wrong because it amounts to making a profit on the back (so to speak) of the prostitute. But if that is morally wrong, then so is capitalism itself, no matter how it is structured and regulated. Could it be that pimping is wrong because pimps make a profit from prostitution without doing any work for it? Not so:

---

[1] For an interesting first-hand account of such a practice—from the point of view of the male prostitute—see R. Perkin and G. Bennett, *Being a Prostitute: Prostitute Women and Prostitute Men* (Sydney: Allen and Unwin, 1985), pp. 204–10. For a useful review of different kinds of prostitution, see Perkin and Bennett, *Being a Prostitute: Prostitute Women and Prostitute Men*, pp. 4–14.

[2] Prostitution is such a multifaceted practice that any attempt to give a general account of it is vulnerable to the charge of over-generalization. My aim is to capture its most central characteristics.

some pimps actually do protect their prostitutes from abusive clients, and thereby provide a service to them. Moreover, this particular argument proves too much, in so far as it condemns as morally wrong, and recommends the banning of, all forms of profit-making which do not involve work, such as having someone invest for us in the stock market. In so far as profit-making of that kind occurs with the consent of all parties, it is unclear to me that it should be banned (indeed, that it is even morally wrong). Perhaps the point is that one should not make a profit out of other people's sexual desires, period. But that too seems to prove too much: consider a movie producer whose (non-pornographic) profit-making movies have steamy sex scenes and for that reason (amongst others) attract vast audiences. Is he acting wrongly? Surely not. And so perhaps the point is that one should not make a profit from getting people to have commercial sex, for commercial sex is wrong, debasing, unconducive to human flourishing, and so on. I shall argue against that view of commercial sex (and, by implication, against this particular objection to pimping) in sections 7.2.1 and 7.3.1.

Second, my focus is on voluntary prostitution, to wit, on transactions whereby someone provides sexual services to some other person(s) against payment, without coercion. Nothing I say here should be taken to imply tolerance towards pimps who terrorize vulnerable individuals into prostituting themselves by physically or sexually abusing them, and/or getting them hooked on drugs, or towards clients who themselves abuse and rape prostitutes, or who, even though they are not themselves guilty of such wrongdoings, nevertheless know that the prostitutes they visit are not on the game voluntarily. This is not to say that, as prostitution under its current forms more often than not involves such acts of violence, it should be criminalized. In fact, as I shall argue in section 7.3.2, criminalization is one of the surest ways of ensuring that prostitutes remain vulnerable to both pimps and clients. Rather, it is to say that involuntary prostitution is morally unacceptable, and that abusive clients and pimps should be put behind bars.

Third, my argument, you recall, is located in ideal theory, which implies that individuals fulfil their obligations of justice to one another. More specifically, in most cases, individuals' needs for the material resources necessary to lead a minimally flourishing life are already met, so that they have access to housing, minimum income, or health care. Accordingly, prostitutes, in this chapter, are less likely to be individuals who find themselves, through no fault of their own, in desperate poverty (a claim which I shall qualify in section 7.3.1). One might think (and indeed this objection has been made to me) that prostitution under such conditions is unlikely to occur, for two reasons. For a start, it is mostly desperately poor, and unlucky, women who prostitute themselves. If so, one might press on, my argument in support of the right to sell sexual services loses much of its bite: for it may well be that prostitution under those conditions is legitimate, but what matters is whether prostitution as it occurs now, under non-ideal conditions, should be legalized.

In addition, one might object that we simply do not know how individuals would relate to their body in a society devoid of gender inequalities; in fact, one might insist, in such a society it is highly unlikely that women would consider providing sexual services as a way to raise income, or that men would deem it acceptable to engage in such relationships. On that second point, however, we simply do not know how individuals would relate to their own and other people's bodies in a society free from discrimination against women. And we have no reason to believe that in such a society, no one would want to sell or buy sex. In fact, in so far as the view that women ought not to sell sexual services is informed, more often than not, by patriarchal norms about what counts as acceptable womanly behaviour, it might be that an egalitarian society would be one where more women than is currently the case would raise some income through sex. Either way, it is worth considering whether individuals, in such a society, have the power to sell and buy sexual services.

Furthermore, although the issue of prostitution under non-ideal conditions matters a great deal, it nevertheless remains important to assess whether prostitution under ideal conditions should be protected by rights. For a start, as we saw in Chapter 1, a just society is not one where poverty is completely eradicated, and so whether or not the destitute, in such a society, should be allowed to sell sexual services is not moot. Moreover, it is false that only the very poor prostitute themselves. In addition, many objections against the legalization of prostitution would apply, if they do at all, in a society where distributive justice obtains—such as the objection that sex ought not to be regarded as a commodity. Thus, in so far as there is no reason to believe that no one would want to prostitute themselves in a society where distributive justice obtains, the question of the legitimacy of prostitution in such a society remains salient.

7.2 A CASE FOR THE RIGHT TO BUY AND SELL SEXUAL SERVICES

In what follows, I first make a case for the right to buy and sell sexual services in a just society, and I then sketch out some of its policy implications.

7.2.1 A Right to Buy and Sell Sexual Services

A number of philosophers have challenged the view that prostitution is morally wrong and therefore should be criminalized. Their challenge, unlike mine, rests on the view that prostitution is just like any other kind of service work, and should accordingly be treated as a contract between a worker, to wit, the prostitute, and a buyer, to wit, the prostitute's client. Their argument can be formalized as follows:

(1) We all use our body to earn a living, and many individuals do so by providing services to others.

(2) Prostitution is simply one way to use one's body so as to provide a service and thereby earn a living.

(3) Using one's body to earn a living, including providing services to others, is morally permissible, and is protected by a moral right. Therefore:

(4) it is morally permissible, and individuals have a moral right, to earn a living by providing sexual services, provided they do not violate other people's rights in so doing. [3]

My case for the right to buy and sell sexual services differs from the contractual argument I have just sketched out. To be sure, it is true that, as per (1), individuals use their body to earn a living. In that sense, an employment contract is a contract over the use of the worker's body. However, as Pateman notes, the prostitution contract differs from other employment contracts: 'The employer is primarily interested in the commodities produced by the worker; that is to say, in profit . . . In contrast to employers, the men who enter the prostitution contract have only one interest: the prostitute and her body.'[4] And, indeed, the employer of a chicken-factory worker whose work involves considerable bodily effort is interested not in the worker's body, but in the chickens she helps produce. The same can be said about service work. Consider the cases of a masseuse and a colonoscopy model.[5] At first sight, one might think that their body is central to their relationship with the other party: the former provides relaxation and relief from pain to her client, through the use of her hands and arms. The latter provides the medical student who looks into her body through her anus with the means to acquire knowledge about the colon. Is not the employment contract, in those cases, over the masseuse's and colonoscopy model's body itself? And are not those employment and the prostitution contracts similar in that respect?

And yet, *pace* claim (2), prostitutional contracts differ, on the whole, from most other employment contracts. For the masseuse's client and the medical student are indifferent as to how they acquire, respectively, relief from pain and knowledge of the human colon: if they could get what they want by other means (say, a particularly good massage robot in the former case, and computer simulation in the latter), they would be willing to do so. It is not inherent in their relationship with the model and masseuse respectively qua student and patient, that they derive satisfaction (physical or intellectual) from their use of her body. By contrast, it is inherent in the prostitutional relationship that the client should seek, and expect to get, sexual pleasure from his interaction with the prostitute.

---

[3] M. Nussbaum, ' "Whether from Reason or Prejudice": Taking Money for Personal Services', in M. Nussbaum, *Sex and Social Justice* (Oxford: Oxford University Press, 1999); L. Ericsson, 'Charges against Prostitution: An Attempt at a Philosophical Assessment', *Ethics* 90 (1980): 335–66.

[4] C. Pateman, *The Sexual Contract* (Cambridge: Polity, 1988), p. 203.

[5] Those three examples—the chicken-factory worker, the masseuse, and the colonoscopy model—are borrowed from Nussbaum, ' "Whether from Reason or Prejudice": Taking Money for Personal Services'.

And in many such relationships it is the body, hands, and mouth of the prostitute he wants (or of whomever he imagines her to be): otherwise, he would simply masturbate on his own, or be content to use an inflatable doll.

This, I believe, can often be true even in prostitution which revolves around phone sex, that is, which does not require that the client actually see and touch the prostitute's body. For even then, it can be, indeed often is, about her body that the client fantasizes; it is her body that he imagines doing things to him. In other words, it can be through the body of the prostitute as mediated by the latter's voice that he derives sexual satisfaction. In fact, some people engage in phone sex not (merely) because it is safer than actually going to see a prostitute, or because, for those of them who are in a committed relationship, it is not as morally wrong (on the grounds, for example, that one is more unfaithful to one's partner by having actual sex with someone (whether or not that involves penetration) than by having phone sex with them). They do so primarily because they derive more pleasure from fantasizing about the prostitute's account of how she would use her body to pleasure them than they would from actually engaging directly with her. In some of those prostitutional phone encounters, the body of the prostitute can in some ways be more central *as body* to the sexual relationship than it is in actual sex, since it can be much more easily divorced from the person whose body it is.

To be sure, some clients do not want the prostitute's body as such: they want it because there does not exist a mechanical vagina which could 'do the work' as well; should such a vagina exist they would be happy to resort to it. Other clients want the prostitute to sit behind a screen and tell them how worthless they are: it is not from the use of her body (as opposed, trivially, to her voice) that they get sexual pleasure. Yet others pay prostitutes to watch them masturbate without touching them: there too the prostitute's body may not matter at all. Others still are fascinated not by the prostitute's looks, but by her personality, her intelligence, and so on. As I pointed out at the outset of this chapter, prostitution is too diverse a phenomenon to be accounted for in general terms. It remains the case, though, that the body of the prostitute is the locus and focus of most prostitutional encounters.

There is another difference between many prostitutional relationships and other service relationships. Not merely can the client often get what he wants only from interacting with another person, to wit the prostitute; in most cases his relationship with the prostitute, unlike (most) relationships between buyers and purchasers of services, is gendered. Of course, this is not so in all cases: for (to put it bluntly) some clients may want only a hole to penetrate, be that of a man or a woman. Still, usually, the prostitute's gender is central to his or her relationship with the client: a male client seeking a female prostitute wants a woman, as a woman, as a means to his sexual gratification; similarly, a male client seeking a male prostitute wants a man, as a man, as a means to his sexual gratification. A male client who would rather have sex with a woman but who has to resort to a male prostitute (for example, in prisons, where homosexual prostitution is rife) cannot but see his interaction with him as gendered, precisely because his sexual provider is, from his point of view, of the wrong gender.

In short, in many cases hiring one's body out for sex is not just like any other service. Accordingly, any argument in favour of the moral permissibility and legalization of prostitution has to take into account the characteristics it displays in those cases where the body of the prostitute is central to the encounter. What do prostitutes sell, then, if anything? We have just seen that the contractual approach to prostitution overlooks the fact that many (although admittedly not all) clients in a prostitution contract, unlike in other employment contracts, are interested in the body itself of the prostitute. However, so to object to the contractual approach cannot be taken to imply that the prostitute, in those contracts, sells *her body itself*: for to sell a thing consists in the complete transfer to someone else, against payment, of the rights, duties, and liabilities over that thing. Needless to say, the prostitute does not sell her body: prostitution is not sexual slavery (where slavery is understood as the complete relinquishing of rights over oneself). Rather, the prostitute in those contracts hires her body out; and if she sells anything, it is time and labour, over which she gives her client exclusive rights (but over which she does not necessarily give him *unlimited* rights: some prostitutes will not, for example, do anal sex). In those prostitutional encounters where the body of the prostitute plays no role at all (other than in the trivial sense that she uses, for example, her voice to excite her client, or her eyes to watch him masturbate), what she sells is merely time and labour.

Thus, prostitutes who actually have sex with their clients sell a service, and in many cases a service which consists in granting access to their body, for certain sexual purposes and/or for a certain amount of time. Prostitutes who operate phone lines also sell sexual services—a service whereby they facilitate, against payment, clients' sexual fantasies; and they often do so by describing what they look like, what they can do, or indeed are (allegedly) doing with their body, and so on. In sum, what makes prostitution different from other occupations, whatever the background conditions under which it takes place, is the fact that prostitutes sell sexual services, which in many cases cannot but be provided through (non-trivially) the use of the body, and cannot but be gendered. And *that* is what clients pay for. Accordingly, when defending the view that prostitutes have the right to sell, and that clients have the right to buy, sexual services, one is not committed to the claim that bodies can be sold and bought; but one cannot merely invoke the claim that prostitution is just one branch of the service industry. To reiterate, one must take on board the fact that it is often through the direct, sought-after, and gendered use of their body that prostitutes provide their services. And one must therefore ask whether buying and selling *that kind of* service is morally wrong, and if so, whether one might nevertheless have the moral right to do so.

It is hard to see why using one's body or parts of it in sexual ways, to earn a living, is morally wrong, unless one invokes either the view that sex should only be given out of love, or at least out of desire, or the view that any prostitutional act reinforces discrimination against women. I offer detailed rejections of those claims in sections 7.3.1 and 7.3.2 respectively. To anticipate, it simply is not true that sex should be so given because it is the only way to flourish as a human being. As a matter of fact, we do experience sex in a myriad of different ways in the course of our lives. Why should we think, for example, that a Franciscan monk who has given up on sex so as to better worship God leads a less flourishing life than someone who finds sexual fulfilment in a loving relationship? Why should we think that a superb poet who chooses to make a living by writing cheap airport novels of the worst kind alienates less of himself than a woman who could enjoy emotionally meaningful sex but decides to prostitute herself instead?[6] There is no reason to think that sexuality in general and emotionally meaningful sex in particular play a more central role to the formation of our identity, and are more important to our flourishing, than many of our other capacities. To claim that it is morally impermissible to have sex with someone unless one loves, likes, or desires them, smacks of moral fanaticism.

To be sure, prostitution consists in letting one's body be used in more or less invasive ways; and so, in many of its instances, it differs from many professions. But it also differs from them in another crucial respect. Although it can be more physically invasive, it need not be correspondingly more intimate. In fact, many people earn a living by engaging in activities which are much more emotionally and psychologically demanding than prostitution, and the performance of which touches to a greater degree on their sense of themselves. For example, although a philosophy professor does use her body to work—as we all do, in a trivial sense—she does so in ways which are not central to the work itself: it is not inherent in teaching, for example, that one may have to walk to a lecture theatre (one can lecture by video link); nor is it inherent in researching that one should use one's hands to write (one can dictate one's thoughts to a recorder, or indeed a computer). What is central to her work, though, is the fact that she is using her brain to communicate and defend her beliefs—sometimes very deeply held beliefs. And that is a very intimate thing to do, whether she does so in the solitude of her study or in the presence of her students.[7] For those reasons, a long-term relationship between a professor and her student, even a strictly professional one, is more intimate, in many ways, than the ten-minute relationship—if one can call it that—that obtains between a prostitute and an occasional client. However invasive sex can be, it is not necessarily the only, or the most, intimate way to earn a living.

[6] I owe this example to Argyrios Papaefstathiou.
[7] Nussbaum, ' "Whether from Reason or Prejudice": Taking Money for Personal Services'.

It is, however, and admittedly, a potentially harmful way to do so. Prostitutional sex often impairs prostitutes' ability to enjoy sex, and more widely, to enter committed, loving and long-term sexual relationships, as it becomes extremely difficult for them to divorce sex from the mercenary context in which they routinely have it.[8] Furthermore, unlike other professionals, prostitutes tend to find it hard to think of their work as something to be proud of, as something which it matters to do well. Besides, female prostitutes are more vulnerable to abuse—both from clients and from pimps—than their male counterparts. In addition, many prostitutes are drug addicts and/or alcoholics, caught as they are in a never-ending, vicious circle whereby they resort to prostitution as a means to pay off their addiction to substances, the consumption of which inures them to the difficulties inherent in their work. Finally, female prostitutes, unlike their clients (and male counterparts), incur the risk of being pregnant, and in turn the risks attendant on pregnancy itself. Prostitution is undoubtedly a risky business. But then again, many jobs are psychologically harmful to individuals, incompatible with a successful love life, physically harmful, or tightly linked to drug and alcohol abuse. If we deem it morally permissible to choose them, then there is no reason to deem prostitution impermissible.

In a nutshell, then, it is not morally wrong for someone to earn a living by hiring his or her body for sex. Accordingly, they have the moral right to do so. Moreover, if individuals generally ought to have the legal right to earn a living through the intimate use of their body, and in ways which can be harmful to their health, prostitutes too should have that right.

So much, then, for the right to sell sexual services. What about the right to buy them? It is hard to see how one can deem buying sex morally wrong unless one invokes the view that one is morally allowed to have sex only with those who are willing to do it for free—out of love, desire, or affection. But why should that be? Of course, it may be *preferable* for individuals to have sex under those circumstances only. But it does not follow that it is morally mandatory for them to do so, unless one thinks that prostitutional sex debases not merely the prostitute, but also the client, and that one is under a moral obligation not to debase oneself.

As I argued in Chapter 1, debasing oneself is morally wrong. As I also argued there, though, one does have a right that others not interfere with self-debasing acts. In any event, that prostitutional sex *necessarily* debases the client is doubtful. To be sure, many purchasers of prostitutional sex think that they are engaging in demeaning acts, that there is something pathetic, really, about someone who simply is not attractive, or manly enough, to get sex for free. That clients should regard themselves as such is one thing; that we should endorse their judgement is

---

[8] For testimonies to that effect, see, e.g., Perkins and Bennett, *Being a Prostitute*, pp. 28–9, 224–8. Studies of male prostitution by and large concur. See, e.g., D. J. West and B. de Villiers, *Male Prostitution: Gay Services in London* (London: Duckworth, 1992).

quite another. Let me quote, here, from a reader's letter published in the British weekly the *Observer* on 6 April 2003:

as a single man who visits prostitutes, I object to being branded ... a sad creature who must pay for his thrills. Most clients of these patient, sympathetic and compassionate ladies are, like me, disabled, elderly, disfigured, ugly or socially or sexually inadequate. The prostitute provides the only opportunity for a brief, life-enhancing taste of physical affection. God bless her! (Name and address withheld)

It is not true, of course, that the 'disabled, disfigured, elderly, ugly or socially or sexually inadequate' can only get sex by paying for it. What is true is that they do not want to have sex with other disabled, elderly, disfigured, ugly, socially, or sexually inadequate individuals: they want to have sex with persons whom they regard as desirable. But what is wrong with that? To the extent that these clients would rather be in loving sexual relationships with such persons, the fact that they have to resort to prostitutional sex should, if anything, elicit compassion and sympathy, rather than moral condemnation.

Having said that, there is strong evidence that, contrary to what the letter's author asserts, the majority of prostitutes' clients are married or in long-term relationships. Is it not wrong on *their* part to engage in prostitutional sex? After all, some opponents of prostitution may press, they cannot invoke disability or lack of social skills as a justification for seeking prostitutes. Nor, in fact, can many of them invoke the fact that they are not in a sexual relationship. For them, qua married clients to pay for sex is morally wrong, I believe, if and only if they do so without their partner's knowledge, or if they do so with their partner's knowledge but in full awareness that he or she will not leave them for so doing, no matter how difficult they find it to bear. However, the fact of their visiting prostitutes is not morally worse than their having an adulterous affair unbeknownst to their partner, or with her knowledge and notwithstanding her resulting unhappiness. What is morally objectionable in the client's behaviour is not the fact, per se, that he is paying for sex. Rather, it is the fact that he lies to his partner, or exploits her love and emotional dependence to get what he wants: the stability and companionship one finds in a long-term relationship, and the thrills—such as they are—of extra-marital sex.

Thus, the mere act of paying for sex is not morally wrong: its permissibility or wrongness depends on the reasons why one does so. Accordingly, clients have the moral right to do so in all those cases where their reasons for paying do not taint the act of paying. In fact, there is a further point in support of this claim. If it is true that, as was argued in Chapter 5, those who do not have a claim for body parts at the bar of justice can nevertheless buy them from those willing to sell, then there does not seem to be any good reason to deny those who need or want sexual services but cannot get them for free the possibility to pay for them. In fact, it would be arbitrary to deny it to them. For consider: we saw in Chapter 5 that someone who, for example, has lost one of his kidneys and wants a second one so as to be able to engage in competitive sports cannot get one for free, but should be allowed to buy one. We also saw that someone who would like to undergo non-reconstructive plastic surgery and would need a blood transfusion during the operation does not have a right to that blood, but should be allowed to pay for it. In the first case, the buyer wishes to meet an important need. In the second case, the buyer wishes to satisfy a want. Now, for many, if not most people, having sex is a need, certainly not as basic as the need for food and water, but a need nonetheless, and quite an important one at that. Accordingly, it would be odd to allow the athlete to meet his need and the surgery patient to satisfy his want, but to disallow the sexually deprived the possibility to do either.

I claimed two paragraphs ago that the permissibility of paying for sex depends on the reasons why one does so. I believe that the only instance where paying for sex is in itself morally wrong is where the client regards payment as a means to humiliate and degrade the prostitute (whether or not she actually feels humiliated or degraded). Conversely, it is also morally wrong for a prostitute to demand payment in exchange for her sexual services as a way to humiliate and degrade the client. For in so treating the other party, the prostitute, or the client, treats them merely as a means to their ends; they fail to confer proper weight to the fact that the other is a moral and rational agent, with his or her own ends, and thereby deny them an opportunity for self-respect.

In those cases, then, where exchanging and getting sexual services for money is morally wrong for the reason just adduced, do prostitutes and clients have the right to do it? In Chapters 1 and 6 I argued that, although we have the right not to treat ourselves as persons worthy of equal respect, we do not have the power to let ourselves be so treated by others. A fortiori, we do not have the power willingly to enter transactions where we will be so treated. Accordingly, selling sex to someone who pays for it as a means to treat us as unworthy of respect cannot be protected by a power. The point applies, *mutatis mutandis*, to buying sex from someone who sells it as a means to humiliate us.

That we lack the moral power to buy and sell sex in those cases entails that we lack a right that the state recognize such transactions as valid, since, as we saw in section 1.2.2C, if no interest of ours to enter such a transaction can justify conferring on us the moral power to do so, then no interest of ours can justify conferring on us a right that the state turn our non-existent moral power into a legal power. However, it does not follow that parties in those transactions lack legal protection of any kind. Suppose that a prostitute agrees to have anal sex with a client for £200, and that the transaction is entered by both with the intent to humiliate the other. Once the sex has taken place, the client leaves without pay-ing. To consider the transaction as legally null and void is to say that the state does not recognize that the prostitute has a right to the money. It is not to say, however, that the prostitute cannot press charges at all: she can, in fact, do so, on the grounds that the client in fact had with her a kind of sex which she made very clear she would not agree to—to wit, anal sex for free. It is that right of hers, to enter a sexual encounter only on her own terms (provided the other party gives every evidence that he agrees to it), which warrants protection, not her right to get £200 in exchange for acceding to the client's desire to humiliate her. Suppose, conversely, that the prostitute accepts the money and runs off without submitting to anal sex: to say that the client lacked the power to enter such a transaction in the first instance is to say that he lacked a right to have anal sex on those terms with the prostitute. But this does not amount to denying him any legal recourse: on principle, he can, in fact, press charges, on the grounds that the prostitute took money from him which he would not have given otherwise.

Thus, that parties lack the moral power to enter that kind of prostitutional encounter is not tantamount to denying them legal protection altogether. Moreover, that they lack that power does not imply that the state can interfere with such transactions. Indeed, there are some good reasons against interference. Put simply, it would be impossible to enforce a law against paying for sex with intent to humiliate, since we could not tell when either party is guilty of that charge or innocent of it. Even if one were to scrutinize every single prostitutional act—at the unacceptably high cost of undermining clients' and prostitutes' interest in privacy—one would not be able to establish intent to humiliate in all cases where it would be present, since prostitutes and clients would not necessarily express such intent. In so far as the law could not discriminate between prostitutional encounters which violate the requirement of respect and those which do not, and in so far as there are good reasons, as we have seen, to desist from interfering with the latter, the former will, in effect, be legally protected. Thus, although we lack the moral power to buy and sell sex when payment is meant to humiliate the other party, we nevertheless have a right that the state not interfere with our prostitutional encounters in general.

To recapitulate, using one's body to earn a living through prostitutional sex, and buying sexual services, are morally permissible, and should be protected by rights, at least in those cases where payment is not meant to humiliate. In those cases where it is so meant, parties nevertheless have rights that others not interfere with them and recognize the transaction as valid. I shall examine some objections to that view in section 7.3. For now, I want to deal with two questions which some opponents of the legalization of prostitution sometimes ask. Would one really want to live in a society where prostitutional sex becomes the norm? Would one really want to consider prostitution as a career option suitable for one's children? To the extent that one would not want either, the approach taken here, it is argued, is irredeemably flawed.[9]

But that argument is simply wrong. Consider the first question. One may consistently claim, on the one hand, that prostitution should be legalized, indeed that it is morally permissible, and, on the other hand, that a society where

⁹ See S. E. Marshall, 'Bodyshopping: The Case of Prostitution', *Journal of Applied Philosophy* 16 (1999): 139–50, at 140.

prostitutional sex is the main form of sex is not a particularly attractive one to live in. Reasons standardly advanced in support of the latter claim include, amongst others, the uncontroversial view that non-prostitutional sex is more emotionally meaningful than prostitutional sex: it would be a shame, the argument goes, to end up in a society where most people would not experience such potentially glorious fulfilment. So far, so good. But that cannot constitute a reason for criminalizing prostitutional sex—any more than the claim that an attractive society is one where haute cuisine is available constitutes a good reason for prohibiting the sale of hamburgers.

Some opponents of the legalization of prostitution also ask, rhetorically, whether we would want our children to work as prostitutes, and assume, without argument, that we would not, from which they conclude, again without much argument, that prostitution should be illegal. Now, it is true that most of us would not want our children to embark on such a career, for all sorts of reasons. I for one would not want my son to work as a prostitute, because it may hinder him in finding emotional fulfilment: but then again, nor would I want him to engage in any profession which would carry a similar risk. Or perhaps we would not want our children to work as prostitutes because we regard it as degrading of human beings. But then presumably we should not want them to work as a corporate raider either, and thereby lose their ability to regard individuals as ends in themselves, and not merely as means to making a profit. Or perhaps we do not want our children to work as prostitutes because of the social, legal, and economic conditions under which prostitutes are currently forced to work: it is physically unsafe, unrewarding, and so on. But then presumably we would not want our children to do mind-numbing factory work either; indeed, nor should we want them to expose themselves to the dangers inherent in, say, professional motor racing. In other words, there are many careers we may not want our children to pursue, for a host of reasons. If those reasons are not strong enough to justify outlawing those careers, then they cannot be strong enough to justify outlawing prostitution. At best, they justify regulating it: to this I now turn.

7.2.2 In Practice: Prostitution as a Job

Advocates of the decriminalization of prostitution are divided on the ways in which society should treat that phenomenon. Some recommend complete deregulation, whereby consensual sex between adults simply falls outside the remit of the law, whether it is commercial sex or not; others favour regulation, whereby commercial sex is regulated just as any other kind of service work.[10] If, however, prostitution is to be regarded as work, as I have argued that it should,

---

[10] Regulatory approaches are advocated with some qualifications by the English Collective of Prostitutes, the US Prostitutes Collective, and the International Committee for Prostitutes' Rights. The English and US collectives are against legalized brothels, on the grounds, amongst

deregulation is not an option, any more than deregulation of working practices in general is.

That leaves us with regulating it. Some countries already do so, in somewhat alarming ways. In Germany, prostitutes have to work in designated areas; in Turkey, they are required to register with commissions for the prevention of venereal diseases; once they do so, they are compelled to submit themselves to regular check-ups, and must exchange their national identity card for one which brands them, explicitly, as prostitutes. Brothels are legal, provided that they obtain a state licence, pay taxes, and report to the police prostitutes who move to another brothel and fail to undergo medical checks. The state, however, does not regulate relationships between brothel owners and employees: whereas all employees are guaranteed a statutory minimum wage, brothel owners can take as much off prostitutes' earnings as they want and control most aspects of the transaction, with the effect that prostitutes, crucially, have very little leeway to turn clients down and are therefore extremely vulnerable to sexual and physical abuse.[11]

The case of Turkey illustrates a kind of regulation which is entirely incompatible with the approach taken here; for it is one where prostitutes, but neither clients nor brothel owners, are regarded as second-class citizens, and where prostitution is viewed as a shameful, albeit ineradicable, activity which warrants tight state control over prostitutes but no control at all over the ways in which they are treated by brothel owners. Regulation should not take that form. Moreover, it should cater for independent prostitutes as well as prostitutes who work as employees in brothels or massage parlours. In the former case, we have a ready model in the UK in the form of massage parlours owned and operated by one person, which act as a front for prostitution. (Although prostitution in the privacy of one's home is not illegal, advertising for it is, which is why those prostitutes have to portray themselves as masseurs/masseuses.) Some of those prostitutes actually do register their massage business, and pay taxes on it. There does not seem to be any good reason why they could not openly declare themselves as 'prostitution practices'. This, in turn, would mean that those who want to establish themselves as independent prostitutes should be able to buy business premises for sex openly and wherever they want, without being subject to tighter zoning laws than apply to all other commercial establishments.

Prostitution in brothels and massage parlours where prostitutes are employed by an owner should also be regulated in the way other businesses are. Most

---

other things, that they 'prioritize employers' profits at the expense of sex workers' rights'. (Sources: <http://allwomencount.net>; <http://bayswan.org/ICPRChart.html>). For testimonies by prostitutes who are calling for regulation, see, e.g., Perkins and Bennett, *Being a Prostitute*. For examples of the regulation of prostitution in various countries, see, e.g., J. West, 'Prostitution: Collectives and the Politics of Regulation', in R. Matthews and M. O'Neill (eds.), *Prostitution, The International Library of Criminology, Criminal Justice, and Penology* (Burlington, Vt.: Ashgate, 2002).

[11] J. O'Connell Davidson, *Prostitution, Power and Freedom* (Ann Arbor: University of Michigan Press, 1998), pp. 25–6.

importantly, those places should be subject to health and safety regulations. This is not to say that prostitutes themselves should be checked against their will for sexually transmitted diseases. Some other writers on the subject might disagree. After all, in some countries, such as Canada, surgeons are under a contractual obligation to undergo HIV tests every few months. But the difference between surgeons and prostitutes is that we have much less of a choice as to which surgeon will operate on us than as to which prostitute to see, and, relatedly, that our need for an operation is likely to be more acute than our need for sex (and so we are in a much weaker position to refuse an operation at the hand of an HIV-positive surgeon than we are to refuse sex with an HIV-positive prostitute.) Accordingly, whereas we may have a good reason to protect patients from HIV-positive surgeons by asking surgeons, under employment laws, to take regular tests, we may want to let prostitutes decide whether or not to take a test, and simply ask them to provide a health certificate if their clients request one.

To insist that brothels and parlours should be subject to health and safety regulations, then, does not imply that prostitutes should undergo compulsory health checks. Nor is it to say, *pace* Shrage, that clients should do so, by way of blood tests taken from them on the premises by the prostitutes themselves, who in turn would enforce a waiting period until the results come through:[12] the idea of a client turning up at a brothel for sex, having to undergo a blood test, and being told to come back three weeks later seems rather bizarre. In any event, it would be impossible to ensure that the client has not had unsafe sex during the three-week waiting period. Rather, one could apply some of the provisions included in numerous health and safety acts throughout the world to the specific case of brothels and parlours. To advert to the British case, the Health and Safety Act of 1974 stipulates that employers are responsible for ensuring that their employees are not subject to violence, intimidation, and harassment, which would mean that brothel and parlour owners and managers should support prostitutes who are abused by their clients. The Act also dictates that working conditions for expectant and new mothers should be adjusted, which would mean, for example, that managers should support a prostitute's request not to engage in penetrative sex if she is pregnant.[13] Other clauses in the Act provide for various safety measures such as fire escape and salubriousness, which would mean that managers should take care not to let their employees work under squalid conditions. They also provide for breaks during the day, as well as for restrictions on the number of hours worked, particularly at night, which would render illegal current practices whereby prostitutes work up to sixteen hours a day, with hardly any break between clients. And so on.

---

[12] L. Shrage, *Moral Dilemmas of Feminism* (London: Routledge, 1994), p. 161.

[13] I am not implying, of course, that brothels' managers can coerce or even pressurize a prostitute into having penetrative sex if she is not pregnant or recovering from childbirth. They most emphatically cannot. Rather, I am suggesting that a prostitute who was willing—and hired—to do so until she got pregnant should be allowed not to once she is pregnant.

Not only should brothels and parlours be subject to health and safety regulations: prostitutes, as employees, should be paid a wage by the brothel's owners, under the protection of minimum wage legislation, on which they would pay exactly the same taxes and National Insurance contributions as other employees. Such a wage system is less exploitative, in some ways, than current practices, whereby prostitutes have to give to the brothel owner anything between 40 per cent and 70 per cent of the money they get for each transaction. Prostitutes typically have to work very long hours, and/or take more clients than they can endure, and/or consent to sexual demands they find repugnant, in order to make a living (many, in fact, do not make a living, and often get into debt to the brothel owner, which makes it that much more difficult to get out of prostitutional work). A guaranteed decent wage would protect prostitutes from having to work under those exploitative conditions.

Note, though, that a decent-wage system is more exploitative in some ways than current practices because, unless it is accompanied by further legal safeguards, it makes the prostitute more vulnerable to clients' demands. In section 7.2.1, I argued that prostitutes who engage in 'body to body' sex with their clients sell a service which consists in granting access to their body, for certain sexual purposes *and/or* for a certain amount of time. Indeed a distinction must be made between contracting with a client for the use of one's body for, say, an hour, and contracting with a client for the performance of specific sexual services. The former contract is more open to abuse than the former, as clients may tend to interpret it as allowing them to do whatever they want with the prostitute. Accordingly, prostitutes who are paid a wage to work a certain number of hours a day in a brothel or a massage parlour should by law be allowed to refuse to perform certain sexual acts (such as unprotected sex) or to be used by their clients in ways harmful to them.

Independent prostitution and brothels are not the only ways in which one should be able to work as a prostitute. There is evidence of what one may call collectives of prostitutes, that is, houses or flats shared by two or more sex workers, who each work independently, and who share expenses such as mortgage, electricity, wages for receptionists and cleaners, and so on: rather like (tongue in cheek) barristers' chambers. Collectives are, for many prostitutes, better than street work (for the presence of other prostitutes on the premises offers some protection against abusive clients) and brothels (for they have complete control—or at least as much control as independent workers in general—over the number of hours they work, the kind of clients they take, and the kinds of service they provide). Again, there is no reason why collectives should not be allowed, and why their members should not pay taxes and National Insurance contributions.

One might think that the regulation approach to prostitution has the following, and to many, odd, implication. If prostitution is a service, and should be regarded as such by all parties, then does it not mean that, just as a customer can sue a service provider for harming her, or for unsatisfactory performance, a client could sue a prostitute, for example, for passing on an STD to him, or for failure to please him? I do not think that he could. To be sure, for a prostitute to produce a certificate of good health is no guarantee that he or she is healthy. A client could sue a prostitute whose certificate was not genuine, on the grounds that he would not have run the higher risk of contracting an STD by having intercourse with a prostitute who does not undergo tests, or does not undergo them frequently enough. But he could not sue a prostitute from whom he believes he has contracted an STD even though she had produced a genuine health certificate.

Nor would it be wise to enable clients to sue a prostitute for non-performance, or failure to provide a good service, for two reasons. First, sex being as complicated as it is, it would be impossible for the courts to establish the facts of the case. A client who pays a prostitute to masturbate him, but does not climax, may be left dissatisfied not because the prostitute is bad at manual sex, but because for some obscure reason he was unable to reach an orgasm on that particular occasion. How on earth is the court to know? Second, and more importantly, it is a well-established principle of contract law that one cannot be forced to perform a personal service one has agreed to perform.[14] Thus, a singer who has agreed to give a number of performances at a given theatre and who, halfway through her run, goes to sing elsewhere because the pay is better, cannot be forced to go back to the first theatre to sing. All she can be forced to do is pay damages. One can see that this principle is particularly apt in the present context. As we saw in section 5.4, individuals have the right to decide whether or not to have sex, which includes the right to change their mind at any time should they have already agreed to have sex with someone. Failure to stop at one's sexual partner's request constitutes a rape; so does forcing her to have sex even though she had consented, earlier on, to have sex. The fact that money may have changed hands is irrelevant.

That prostitutes should not be forced to perform is one thing; that they owe nothing to the client for non-performance is quite another. Should the latter, for example, be able to claim damages, above and beyond simple restitution of the money he gave? Or should we let losses go? It all depends on the kind of prostitutional encounter at issue. One could conceive that a prostitute hired by a parlour ought, and can be made, to pay damages to her employer if she decides to stop working before the end of her contract (if her contract is temporary); one cannot conceive that a prostitute who finds her clients on street corners can be made to pay damages if she stops halfway through a prostitutional act.

Entering into the details of legal prostitutional contracts lies beyond the scope of this book. By way of a final word on those practical issues, regulation as

[14] I am not contradicting my claims, in Chapters 2 and 3, that the able-bodied are under an obligation of justice to provide personal services to those who need them. In both those cases and the case of prostitutional contracts, one party is under an obligation (in one instance contractual, in the other instance, not contractual) to provide a service. But in neither case ought the penalty for failure to perform be specific performance (army deserters are not punished by being forced to serve: rather, they are sent to jail, or dishonourably discharged).

sketched here would not suffice for prostitution to be regarded as a kind of work acceptable to a just society: wider programmes are needed to change attitudes towards, and prejudices against, commercial sex in general and prostitutes in particular. But, although regulation is not sufficient, it is a necessary step towards making prostitution a just way to earn a living.

7.3 TWO ARGUMENTS AGAINST THE RIGHTS TO BUY AND SELL SEXUAL SERVICES

Proponents of the view that prostitution is morally wrong and therefore should be criminalized standardly advance three arguments. The first argument claims that prostitution is wrong (and should be prohibited) on the grounds that prostitutes, just like wage workers, are the product of the exploitative economic and social conditions under which they are forced to sell their services. The second avers that prostitutes sell their body, and thereby themselves, and that in so far as the sale and purchase of human beings is morally wrong and should be (indeed is) criminalized, prostitution too is morally wrong and should remain (as it is in most countries) a criminal offence. Finally, the third argument claims that prostitution takes place against a background of, and reinforces, fundamental inequalities between men and women. On that view, prostitution is morally wrong because it partakes in discrimination against women; and it is precisely for that reason that it should be outlawed.

In this section, I focus on objections to prostitution which are specific to it. Accordingly, I do not address the exploitation objection. Others have done so already;[15] moreover, my rebuttal of the exploitation objection to organ sales applies here, *mutatis mutandis*, and I shall not, therefore, revisit it.

7.3.1 Selling and Buying Sex; Selling and Buying Persons

On the view I consider and reject in this section, prostitution does not consist in selling sexual services; rather, it consists in a transaction whereby a client contracts for the use of the body, and therefore the person, of someone else, with a view to achieving sexual satisfaction. Carole Pateman, whose works on what she calls the 'sexual contract' offer the best exposition of such a view, argues that in so far as there is 'an integral relationship between body and self' and 'identity is inseparable from the sexual construction of the self', 'in modern patriarchy, sale of women's bodies in the capitalist market involves sales of a self in a different manner, and in a more profound sense, than . . . sale of command over the use of the labour (body) of a wage slave'.[16]

---

[15] See, e.g., Ericsson, 'Charges against Prostitution: An Attempt at a Philosophical Assessment'.

[16] Pateman, *The Sexual Contract*, pp. 206–7. See also E. Anderson, *Values in Ethics and Economics* (Cambridge, Mass.: Harvard University Press, 1993). Interestingly, Anderson notes that, in a just

Pateman's objection, in effect, is that the client treats the body of the prostitute, and therefore the prostitute herself, as a commodity. One may think that my reply to the commodification objection to organ sales applies here. That, however, would be too hasty. For, whereas, in expelling waste from our body, our *kidneys*, not we, are doing something; in contrast (as I noted in Chapter 5), it is *we* who write, and not our hands, and it is *we* who smile, and not our mouth. Similarly, it is *we* who have sex, not our penis or vagina. At first sight, the claim that in selling sex one is selling oneself is more plausible than the claim that in selling one's kidney or blood one is also selling oneself.

Now, *if* prostitution really involves the sale of selves, it is morally wrong and it should be criminalized. For, after all, selling oneself and buying persons are generally thought to be morally wrong, from which it would seem to follow that, if prostitution involves the sale of persons, prostitution too is morally wrong. Moreover, in so far as the sale and purchase of human beings is outlawed, and rightly so, it would seem to follow that prostitution too should be criminalized.

However, as I shall argue presently, prostitution does not involve selling oneself, procuring human beings for sale, or buying them. And even if it did, it would not follow that it is always morally wrong from the point of view of all concerned; and even if *that* did follow, further argument than is offered by the objection under study is needed to establish the claim that prostitution should be criminalized.

The objection's central tenets, you recall, are the following:

(1) The transactions of buying and selling persons are egregiously wrong and cannot be protected by rights.

(2) The object of the transaction between prostitute and client, unlike that of the transaction between workers and capitalists, is the prostitute's body itself.

(3) There is an integral relationship between body and self.

(4) One cannot separate one's identity from the sexual construction of one's self. Therefore:

(5) In selling sex, the prostitute sells not only her body, but also herself. Similarly, in buying sex, the client buys not merely the prostitute's body, but also the prostitute herself. Therefore:

(6) The transactions of buying and selling sex are egregiously wrong and should not be protected by rights.

Claim (1) is obviously not in dispute. And, as we saw in section 7.2.1, it is true that prostitution differs from other kinds of labour, even the most intensely

---

society, there might be scope for professional sex therapists whose aim would be to help 'people liberate themselves from perverse, patriarchal forms of sexuality' (p. 156). Although those therapists would be paid for their work, their practice would not be governed by market norms (or so she claims), and would not, therefore, fall foul of the objection under scrutiny here.

physical kinds, such as working in a factory: there is a point to claim (2). However, as we also saw in that section, it is not true that a prostitute sells her body itself, and, even if she does, it does not follow that she sells *herself.* For *pace* (3), although there is, to be sure, an integral relationship between body and self, in that we cannot conceive of ourselves unless we have a body distinct from that of other people's bodies, that relationship is not all there is to say about the self: the self is not reduced to corporeality. And if that is correct, then in selling our body (assuming that this is what one does in prostitution[17]), we do not sell ourselves.

Claim (4) would seem to suggest otherwise. For, if our identity is bound up with the sexual construction of our self, in selling our body for sex, are we not selling that which constitutes us as distinct, separate individuals? Are we not, in fact, selling ourselves? Not really. It is true, of course, that we construct our identity, our sense of ourselves, as sexual beings; but just as there is much more to ourselves than our body, there is much more to our identity than our sexual construction, such as our moral beliefs, our relationship with our family, our long-term plans and attachments, and so on. If that is correct, then in selling our body *for sex*, we only sell a part of what constitutes us as distinct selves.

At this juncture, some proponents of claim (4) might be tempted to reply that our perception of ourselves as sexual beings is more central to our self than our moral beliefs, long-term plans and attachments, and so on: for it is only by experiencing sex as something which must be given freely—not necessarily out of love, but at least out of desire—that one can truly flourish as a human being.[18] Accordingly, as D. Satz puts it in the course of rebutting that claim, 'the sale of sex is taken to cut deeper into the self, to involve a more total alienation from the self'.[19]

On the one hand, testimonies from some prostitutes lend credence to that view. As we saw in section 7.2.1, it appears that engaging in prostitution diminishes one's capacity to experience sexual desire, to give oneself to sexual intimacy, to engage in meaningful relationships, and so on. On the other hand, some prostitutes report acquiring a tremendous sense of sexual empowerment through prostitution.[20] Moreover, as we also saw in section 7.2.1, individuals experience their sexuality in a wide variety of ways; indeed, some of them simply do *not* regard it as the fundamental determinant of their identity, or do not put such a premium on sexual intimacy and romantic love. It is unclear, then, that they would sell themselves were they to sell their body for sex.

---

[17] I argued in section 7.2.1 that prostitutes do not sell their body. My target here is the inference from selling one's *body* to selling *oneself.*

[18] For example, Radin, *Contested Commodities*, p. 100.

[19] D. Satz, 'Markets in Women's Sexual Labor,' *Ethics* 106 (1995): 63–85, at 70. For another good rebuttal of what one may call the 'sentimentalist charge' against prostitution, see Ericsson, 'Charges against Prostitution: An Attempt at a Philosophical Assessment'.

[20] The best-known examples come from prostitute activists from the movement COYOTE (Call Off Your Tired Ethics), founded by Margot St James in 1979.

Suppose that they would, though. Would prostitution thus understood be morally wrong? Proponents of the objection under study here believe that it would. However, the claim 'prostitution is morally wrong because it involves the sale and purchase of selves' is made up of two rather different statements the truth of which must be assessed independently: (a) it is morally wrong for someone to sell herself for someone else's sexual gratification; and (b) it is morally wrong for someone to buy another person for his sexual gratification, even if that person consents to the transaction.

Now, purchasing humans is wholly incompatible with treating them with respect, even if they consent to it. This is because for A to consider buying B means that A is willing to put himself in a position of exercising all the rights B is currently holding over herself. That is, A is willing to enter a moral relationship with B where B's autonomy and personal integrity would be entirely within A's command. It is hard to see how being willing to enter such a relationship with other human beings could ever be compatible with treating them with respect, even if they consent to it, indeed even if the buyer decides not to exercise those rights over his purchase. My claim, note, is not a paternalistic one to the effect that A would be acting against B's fundamental interest in purchasing him; rather, in line with my argument about self-respect and the right to do wrong, as deployed in Chapter 1, it is that there is something wrong about one's willingness to enter a relationship to which the denial of B's moral status as a person is central.

Accordingly, claim (b) is correct. However, claim (a) is not always so. That is, although a prostitute, in selling herself, fails to treat herself with respect, she is not always guilty of moral wrongdoing. To see why, we must distinguish between four states of affairs: (1) prostitutes sell themselves as the only way to meet their needs; (2) they sell themselves to meet their needs, even though they could do something else (i.e. take a factory job); (3) they are not needy but sell themselves in order, broadly speaking, to implement their conception of the good, and prostitution is the only way for them to do so; and (4) they sell themselves to implement their conception of the good, even though they could do something else.[21]

The first state of affairs, I submit, would most probably not obtain in a just society, since most needy individuals would get the material resources they need in order to lead a minimally flourishing life. Those few that would not do so, on the grounds that they can clearly be shown responsible for their predicament, would nevertheless not act wrongly in resorting to prostitution so as to meet their needs. For they would be presented with the following alternative: either they do not get the resources necessary for a minimally flourishing life, in which case they do not live as befits persons; or they get those resources by selling themselves,

---

[21] Not all prostitutes do sex work out of financial need. See, e.g., Perkins and Bennett, *Being a Prostitute*, pp. 220–2; and Davidson, *Prostitution, Power and Freedom*.

even though they will thereby surrender their right to be treated as persons. As I argued in 1.2.3B, in a just society it cannot be deemed impermissible for them to seek to secure their own survival in the only way available to them. Note that such a claim is compatible with the view that it is wrong for *a client* to buy a prostitute for his sexual gratification, since the client, unlike the prostitute, is not in a desperate situation.

Suppose, though, that prostitutes could meet their needs by taking a factory job, or that they sell themselves to raise a surplus of income, because it is the only, or the fastest, way for them to do so. They are not, *ex hypothesi*, in a desperate situation: they do have a choice as to whether or not to sell themselves. In such cases, just as it is morally wrong for their client to acquire those rights over them, it is morally wrong for them to forfeit their rights over themselves. For, in selling myself, I forfeit my right to be treated by all as a rational and moral agent worthy of equal respect, and I thereby destroy opportunities for self-respect. As we saw in Chapter 1, we lack the moral power so to act, and therefore a right that the state recognize such transactions as valid.

On the assumption that prostituting oneself does amount to selling oneself, only in some cases, then, is prostitution morally wrong, but only in a few of *those* cases do individuals lack the power to engage in it. In none of those cases, though, ought prostitution to be made unlawful. To say that it ought to be criminalized amounts to conferring on the state a right to interfere with prostitutes and clients, which in turn amounts to denying that the latter have a right to engage in prostitutional sex. Now, although one sometimes has an enforceable right to act wrongly, particularly in those cases where one does not harm other people's fundamental interests, one lacks such a right in those cases where one does so harm them. If clients do indeed buy the prostitute herself, they harm her fundamental interest in being treated with equal respect. That she may consent to being treated as something to be bought is irrelevant since, as we have just seen, she does not have the power to waive her right to be treated with equal respect. Thus, clients do not have the right to engage in prostitution so understood, which implies that the state is under no obligation *to them* not to interfere with them.

However, there are good reasons not to make prostitution unlawful, which appeal to some important interests of prostitutes themselves. For a start, criminalization is likely to make them very vulnerable to both clients and pimps, as it would deprive them of police protection. Moreover, a blanket prohibition on prostitution would affect not merely prostitutes who wrongly sell themselves, but also those who sell themselves as the only way to meet their needs and who, we have seen, are not acting wrongly when doing so. A discriminating prohibition, one which would seek to target the former and not the latter, could only be enforced at the cost of intolerable invasions of all prostitutes' privacy, since the police would have to arrest all prostitutes, then scrutinize their lifestyles, income, expenditures, and so on, in order to assess whether each one needed to go into prostitution to meet her basic needs. Making prostitution unlawful, in short, would further weaken prostitutes' self-respect.

Some activists suggest that the state should penalize clients and not prostitutes—in other words, that prostitution should be made unlawful but that prostitutes should not be prosecuted.[22] This would solve some of the problems identified above; in particular, it would encourage prostitutes to seek police protection against abusive pimps and clients; it would also free them from police scrutiny. However, the proposal is problematic in two respects. First, penalizing clients would not protect prostitutes from abuse at their hands (even though it might help them seek redress *ex post*): laws against kerb-crawling in the UK have not met with favour with prostitutes, as clients are so intent on not being spotted by the police that they leave very little time for prostitutes to negotiate a price and, more importantly, to assess how safe they are.

Moreover, in penalizing clients, the state would prevent prostitutes from selling sex (and thereby, or so the objection would have it, from selling themselves). For, to say that individuals have the right to sell something but that nobody has the right to buy it is incoherent, since a right to sell is not just a right to divest oneself of one's claims, powers, and liabilities over that thing: it is a right to transfer them to someone else. If no one has the right to get those entitlements, powers, and liabilities over it, then it simply cannot be sold. Accordingly, if no one has the right to get entitlements, powers, and liabilities over the prostitute, then the latter simply cannot be sold, and her right to sell herself is not respected. The problem, of course, is that, as we saw above, some prostitutes have the right to sell themselves, when doing so is the only way to meet their basic needs. In those cases, then, neither party should be interfered with when entering the transaction.[23]

To recapitulate: one cannot object to the claim that prostitution is morally permissible and should be legalized on the grounds that it consists in the sale and purchase of human beings, first because it simply does not consist in such transactions, and second because even if it did, it would not always follow that it is impermissible (at least from the prostitutes' standpoint) or subject to criminalization.

7.3.2 Prostitution and Gender Inequality

A second, important, objection to prostitution notes that prostitutes are overwhelmingly women, that clients are overwhelmingly men, and that

---

[22] I thank Clare Chambers for pressing me on that point.

[23] Note that I am not contradicting my earlier claim that clients do not have a right to engage in prostitutional sex even if the latter involves the purchase and sale of prostitutes themselves. On the interest-based theory of rights, you recall, X has a right to do A if his interest in doing A is important enough to ground some duties on third parties. In so far as the state's duty to let clients enter the transaction is grounded, not in the clients' interest in so doing, but in the prostitutes', the former do not have a right.

prostitution takes place against a background of, and reinforces, considerable inequalities between men and women. Most women who choose to go into prostitution do so only because they have few opportunities on the job market, and indeed fewer such opportunities than men; moreover, it is because prostitution rests on negative, stereotypical views of women as men's sexual servants that the former see it as a route out of poverty. Relatedly, men who seek out prostitutes often do so out of a desire to exercise power over women. And even if such desire is not what leads them to visit prostitutes, the very nature of the prostitutional relationship enables them to exercise power over them.[24] Most, but not all, authors who so object to prostitution believe that it is morally wrong, and should be criminalized, precisely for that reason. On that view, prostitution in all its forms, whether or not accompanied by coercion, far from being a victimless crime (as some proponents of legalization aver), is one whose victims are the prostitutes themselves, and whose perpetrators are clients, indeed anyone who benefits from it.[25]

It is not always clear whether proponents of that objection believe that prostitution cannot but have the aforementioned deplorable features. In the present context, whether it does or not is crucial; for, if prostitution by definition rests on, and reinforces, gender inequalities, it is wholly incompatible with the requirement that we give one another opportunities for self-respect, and therefore has no place in a just society. However, I shall argue here that prostitution need not have the foregoing features. As a preliminary point, though, it pays to reiterate that, under ideal conditions, where individuals' needs would be met, the objection under study would lose some of its strength, since the majority of women would not live under conditions of extreme poverty—conditions which, as we well know, are propitious to entry into prostitution.

Setting that point aside, the objection is problematic in six respects. For a start, even though some clients seek prostitutes as a way to exercise over those women a kind of power which they could not exercise otherwise, or at least not as easily, it is not inherent in prostitutional sex that they should do so. Moreover, even though it is obviously true that prostitution as it occurs at present rests on, and reinforces, prejudices against women, it is worth noting that it is also shaped by negative stereotypes of men, which prostitutes themselves often endorse, as enslaved to their sexual desire, stupid, idiotic, sexually pathetic, and so on.[26] This is not to deny that female prostitutes are usually held in greater contempt than

[24] For arguments to that effect, see D. Satz, 'Markets in Women's Sexual Labor'; L. Shrage, 'Should Feminists Oppose Prostitution?', *Ethics* 99 (1989): 347–61.

[25] See, e.g., C. Pateman, *The Sexual Contract*, pp. 192 ff; Satz endorses this objection to the claim that prostitution is morally permissible, but denies that it entails the view that prostitution should be criminalized. See Satz, 'Markets in Women's Sexual Labor'. For a similar argument, see E. Anderson, *Values in Ethics and Economics*, pp. 154–6.

[26] For testimonies by prostitutes who do have that view of men, see, e.g., R. Weitzer (ed.), *Sex for Sale: Prostitution, Pornography and the Sex Industry* (London: Routledge, 2000), pp. 47–8.

their male clients; but one should not overlook the fact that prostitution can be, and often is, demeaning to all parties. In those cases where it is, where prostitutes and clients dehumanize one another, it is morally wrong, in so far as it violates the requirement that we treat one another with equal respect. But it does not follow that it should be criminalized, if only because criminalization, as we saw in section 7.3.1 and as I shall stress again below, renders prostitutes more vulnerable than they already are.

Second, many an institution and many a profession take place against a background of, and reinforce, discrimination against women: consider nurses, secretaries, cleaning staff, supermarket cashiers, nursery and primary school teachers. The overwhelming majority of members in those professions, all of which involve serving others in some capacity or other, are women. To be sure, unlike prostitutes, they do not serve men primarily; but they do tend to be directly subordinate to male bosses, or to work in professions the upper echelons of which are usually occupied by men (consider nursery school teachers v. university lecturers, GPs v. hospital consultants, etc.). Women enter those professions, instead of more prestigious ones, partly because of restricted educational and professional opportunities, the reason for which in turn lies in conventional views of women as care providers. If the institutions which use women in those ways—in corporations as secretaries, in hospitals as nurses, in schools as teachers—are not morally wrong per se, and should not be banned (as we all agree—I hope!), why should prostitution be?

The reason, or so some would reply,[27] is that prostitution rests on, and reinforces, deeper prejudices against women than nursing or teaching. Most people think that prostitutes degrade themselves; very few believe that nurses and secretaries do. Moreover, and relatedly, unlike other female workers, prostitutes are considered by other parties in the transactions as objects, not as persons.

Now, I concede—who would not?—that prostitutes are seen in a far worse light than nurses and secretaries. But there are many more nurses and secretaries than there are prostitutes; and whilst most people—men and women—do, at some point in their life, come across secretaries and nurses, relatively few, in comparison, will come across prostitutes. Accordingly, the gender stereotypes which are conveyed by the prevalence of women in, say, the nursing profession are likely to have greater weight than those conveyed by the prevalence of women in prostitution. Moreover, the kind of stereotypes conveyed by prostitution can also be

---

[27] For example, Satz, 'Markets in Women's Sexual Labor', p. 81. In addition to the two points mentioned in the text, Satz notes that prostitutes are subject to violence (assault, rape, abuse) at the hands of men to a greater degree than any other female worker. That is entirely plausible: but at best it tells, not against the moral permissibility of prostitutional acts per se, but against the license of such violence against prostitutes (for example, it tells against the view that prostitutes know what they let themselves in for and do not have a claim not to be beaten up by their pimp or clients; it also tells against the view that the police cannot be blamed for not pursuing prostitutes' complaints for assault and rape).

found in activities and professions which proponents of the sex-discrimination objection probably would not want to see criminalized: witness degrading sexual images of women in advertising, film, literature, fine arts, and so on. In fact, it is plausible that the prevalence of such images in those areas, and the prevalence of those areas themselves, contribute far more to negative stereotyping of women than does prostitution, which is far less visible. In so far as one would not want to ban advertising and literature, even those works which do project such images of women, one needs further reasons than those adduced so far to ban prostitution for projecting similar images.[28]

At this juncture, the opponent of prostitution would insist that none of the foregoing points adequately takes on board the claim that prostitutes, unlike nurses and secretaries, are more often than not treated as objects by their clients, in the manifold sense that they are seen as fungible (a prostitute is not seen as a distinct individual but is deemed as good as any other provided she does what the client wants), proper subjects for abuse and destruction, and instrumental to the clients' ends. However, it is not inherent in a prostitutional encounter that the client should abuse the prostitute. Nor is it inherent in it that he should see her as fungible. For a start, as a matter of fact some clients do not want just any prostitute, but instead would rather have sex with only one prostitute over time. Furthermore, just as fungibility does not imply commodification, commodification does not imply fungibility: that one can buy something does not mean that one regards it as interchangeable with a similar good, or that one regards that thing's seller as interchangeable with any other seller. Finally, it is not inherent in prostitution that the client should treat the prostitute purely as a means to his ends, any more than it is inherent in any market relationship that the purchaser treats the seller purely as a means to his ends. The important thing is that clients treat prostitutes not merely as means, but as ends as well.

A third problem with the gender inequality objection to prostitution is that it does not deal adequately with all forms of prostitution, since it applies mostly to heterosexual prostitutional relationships, where the client is male and the prostitute female. Whilst most prostitutional relationships are of such a nature, an increasing number are not: witness the considerable increase in male prostitutes who sell gay sex to other men (even though they might be straight themselves), the small, but apparently growing, number of male prostitutes whose clients are

---

[28] To be clear: I am not implying that prostitution is just like, for example, advertising cars by using naked women. Clearly prostitution can, and often does, involve more direct degradation of actual women—the prostitutes—than such advertising does. And that, someone might be tempted to object, constitutes a reason for criminalizing it which would not apply to advertising. That may well be true, of course; but my focus at this juncture is the claim that prostitution should be banned for resting on, and conveying, degrading images of women. Reasons in favour of criminalizing it, such as adduced a few sentences ago in this note, constitute that which I claim in the text above is needed, namely, *further* reasons than the negative stereotype argument. Which is not to concede that those reasons are good reasons: I dealt with them in section 7.3.1.

women,[29] the admittedly marginal but nevertheless persistent phenomenon of
lesbian prostitution. It is true, of course, that many male prostitutional relationships replicate traditional gender roles: the male prostitute gives pleasure at the
behest of his male client, and is often reduced, in the latter's eyes, to the status
of a woman (which in part explains why many heterosexual men who engage in
homosexual prostitution refuse to be subject to anal penetration). But there is
no reason to believe that *all* male and gay prostitutional relationships are of such
nature. To those, the objection would not apply. Nor would it apply to prostitutional relationships where the client is female and the prostitute male.

The foregoing points suggest that it is simply not true that prostitution *inherently* reinforces sex discrimination: some forms of prostitution may do so, indeed
do so, under current conditions; others do not. Accordingly, the objection does
not successfully show that prostitution as an institution is morally wrong and
should be criminalized. *If* it shows anything—which remains to be seen—it
only shows at best that those forms of prostitution which reinforce sex discrimination are morally wrong and should be criminalized.

Fourth, the objection seems to claim that any prostitutional act partakes of
sexual inequality. But so to condemn prostitution smacks of tainting all its actors, no matter what their behaviour is, by association. Consider the following
analogy: fast-food chains clearly exploit their staff. Now suppose that A, who
owns a fast-food restaurant, treats his employees very well: he pays them well
above the minimum wage, ensures that they get regular breaks during their working hours as well as decent holidays, and insists that managers treat serving staff
with respect and consideration. Does A act wrongly simply by investing in a sector which is known for its objectionable treatment of menial employees? Do his
employees act wrongly by seeking to work in that sector, even though they work
for him? It seems not. Should they be legally prevented from so doing? Even less
so. Similarly, a man who buys sex from a willing prostitute, pays her well, treats
her decently, and does not acquire or foster negative views of women in general, and a woman who sells sex to a man on the understanding that she will
be so treated, do not *thereby* act wrongly, and ought not thereby to fall within the remit of criminal law, even though they take part in a practice which is
standardly, and currently, degrading to women. Note that I am not contradicting
my earlier point in section 7.3.1 that purchasing another human being can never
be compatible with treating them with respect, even if the buyer decides not to

---

[29] It is estimated that a third of prostitutes in metropolitan cities such as London, New York,
and Paris are men. As to male heterosexual prostitution, where clients are women, it takes the
traditional form of the older woman–gigolo relationship, as well as the form—to be found mostly
in Italy and Greece—of the so-called 'wolf packs' of young local men who have commercial sex
with female tourists. Women's greater economic independence, and the fact that in some societies
they can now enjoy casual and promiscuous sex without eliciting moral disapproval, are thought to
account for the rising incidence of male heterosexual prostitution. See R. Perkins and G. Bennett,
Being a Prostitute.

exercise his newly acquired rights over his purchase. In such a purchase, one by definition acquires over the person one is buying all the rights she had over herself: the very act of acquiring those rights is itself incompatible with treating her with respect. By contrast, it is not inherent in a prostitutional transaction that the client acquires rights to degrade the prostitute.

In so arguing, I am making an assumption which many proponents of the objection would reject, namely, that one can assess single prostitutional acts in isolation from the wider context within which they occur. On the contrary, they would say, one must focus on the institution of prostitution, and realize that a standard prostitutional act (involving a male client and a female prostitute) *always* involves sex discrimination against women, no matter how both parties, and in particular the client, behave.[30] On that view, prostitution as an institution is wrong, and that, not individual prostitutional acts, is what matters. However—and this is the fifth problem with this variant of the gender discrimination objection to prostitution[31]—it is not clear that prostitution as an institution necessarily takes place against, and reinforces, inequalities between men and women. That it currently does so is beyond doubt: that it would disappear in a society where gender equality would obtain is doubtful. As I noted in my introductory remarks, there is no reason to suppose that, in such a society, individuals simply would no longer purchase sex from one another—although their reasons for so doing might differ from those which they might have in a society ridden with gender inequalities.

Let us suppose that I am wrong, and let us assume, for the sake of argument, that prostitution inherently involves discriminating against women. Still—and this is my sixth point—to say that it is wrong does not make sense unless one means that at least some of the agents implicated in it engage in morally reprehensible actions. Accordingly, in order to assess whether prostitution is morally wrong (a first step towards showing that it should be criminalized), one must assess whether clients and prostitutes act wrongly, on the assumption that, regardless of the particular nature of their individual prostitutional transactions, they contribute to reinforcing gender inequalities.

Now, the claim that clients are acting wrongly is plausible, for surely it cannot be morally right to contribute to reinforcing gender inequalities.[32] What about

[30] For example, Pateman, *The Sexual Contract*, p. 182 ff; K. Barry, *The Prostitution of Sexuality* (New York: New York University Press, 1995).

[31] I say 'this variant', for the gender discrimination objection need not claim that prostitution as an institution, as opposed to single prostitutional acts, is at issue.

[32] By the same token, indirect beneficiaries of prostitution such as tour operators and travel agents, who act as intermediaries in prostitution-related tourism, as well as, say, company executives who procure 'escort' services for important clients, are guilty of moral wrongdoing. By contrast, someone whose partner is a prostitute, and who materially benefits from his or her income, without involving himself in his or her work, indeed without condoning it, does not, I think, act wrongly. For an interesting review of different kinds of pimping, see Davidson, *Prostitution, Power and Freedom*, pp. 42–58.

prostitutes themselves, though? Although proponents of the objection under study are quick to point out that prostitutes should not be blamed, they shy away, on the whole, from assessing whether they can be deemed to act wrongly. Let us return to the four scenarios outlined in section 7.3.1: (1) prostitutes sell themselves as the only way to meet their needs; (2) they sell themselves to meet their needs, even though they could do something else (i.e. take a factory job); (3) they are not needy but sell themselves in order, broadly speaking, to implement their conception of the good, and prostitution is the only way for them to do so; and (4) they sell themselves to implement their conception of the good, even though they could do something else.

It would seem that in the first of those four cases, prostitutes are *clearly* not acting wrongly: under (1), in so far as prostituting themselves is the only way for them to meet their needs, their interest in so doing outweighs other women's interest in living in a society which does not discriminate against them. Furthermore, under (3), if everybody else can realize their conception of the good without recourse to prostitution, a woman who does not have other options can use prostitution as a way to do so without moral taint: for, if all other women can further their own interests by raising income through other means, it is hard to see how her own interest in resorting to prostitution can be outweighed by their interest to live in a society free from sex discrimination. Finally, even if women can meet their needs by some other means (as per (2)), or if prostitution is a way amongst others for them to raise income so as to implement their conception of the good (as per (3)), one needs to know why they do not use those other means in order to do so, before one can condemn their engagement in prostitution as morally wrong. Perhaps taking a factory job would enable them to raise as much income as prostitution, but would not afford them the same degree of control over their working lives; or perhaps they feel more demeaned by working on an assembly line than they do by selling sexual services, and so on. In those cases, it is hard to see why their choice to enter prostitution can be deemed morally wrong. In other cases, though, their choice might be so condemnable.

Thus, in so far as clients always act wrongly (again, on the assumption, which I accept as true for the sake of argument, that any prostitutional act partakes of gender discrimination), and as prostitutes themselves sometimes do so, prostitution as an institution is morally wrong. And, although we sometimes have the moral power to act wrongly, we lack that power in those cases where we are guilty of treating others as less than equal—which is exactly what clients do with prostitutes. In so far as clients lack the power to engage in a prostitutional transaction, prostitutes themselves lack that power too. However, none of this entails that prostitution should be criminalized, simply because (as we saw in Chapter 1) the fact that an act is morally wrong does not suffice to confer on the state the right to interfere with it or to punish those who commit it. Moreover, criminalization reinforces gender inequality, and further restricts prostitutes' opportunities for self-respect. It is easier, for example, to arrest streetwalkers than their clients, as they have to make themselves visibly available; single mothers who work as prostitutes and are sent to prison see their children placed in foster care if none of their relatives can take over, whilst their male clients will not, as they are more likely to share responsibility for their children—albeit usually unequally—with the latter's mother. And so on.

Imposing fines, as opposed to jail sentences, will not do either, as they will be harsher on prostitutes, who are typically financially worse off than their clients, than on the latter. In fact, evidence suggests that prostitutes who are fined for soliciting—as is the case in the UK—simply do not have the wherewithal to raise the required money other than, precisely, through prostitution. Moreover, as I noted in section 7.3.1, laws against kerb-crawling, which are supposed to penalize clients as well as prostitutes, mean that the latter have less time to assess whether the former are potentially dangerous, and so adversely affects women to a greater extent than men. Furthermore, criminalizing prostitution amounts to denying prostitutes police protection from the various hazards of street work, which in turn leads them to seek it from pimps, who themselves are very often violent. Bans on advertising sexual services, which some anti-prostitution activists advocate as a way to avoid punishing prostitutes more harshly than their clients, will not do either: all prostitutes have to do is advertise for massage services, which is not a criminal offence. Of course, everybody knows, including the police, that massage services as advertised in the back pages of, say, gay magazines are really sexual services. But prostitutes who so advertise their services can easily protect themselves against undercover police officers and prosecution by running a legitimate massage business (which includes paying taxes and National Insurance contribution for whomever they might employ), and never providing sex to their clients unless they ask for it (an undercover policeman who would ask for sex and get it could not use that as the basis for a successful prosecution, since he would be guilty of entrapment). And so on.[33]

To be sure, some of the problems I have just identified may not arise under all circumstances. Imposing a fine on both client and prostitute may not be harsher on the latter than on the former if she happens to be better off than he is; imposing a jail sentence on both may in some cases be harder on the client than on the prostitute if he is a single father whose children would be placed in foster care while he serves his time, and if she is childless. But this could not give grounds for the proponent of the objection under study to dismiss my argument: for that proponent's case rests on an understanding of prostitution as it currently exists—as a practice where prostitutes are impoverished women and clients (relatively) better off men. It is my contention that criminalizing *that kind* of prostitution reinforces gender inequality: it is not my contention that any legal prohibition of

---

[33] The foregoing points are well documented in Davidson, *Prostitution, Power and Freedom*; and D. J. West and B. de Villiers, *Male Prostitution: Gay Services in London* (London: Duckworth, 1992). See also D. Satz, 'Markets in Women's Sexual Labor'.

prostitution in general would do so (although, as we saw in section 7.3.1, there are good reasons not to criminalize it).

At this juncture it is worth asking, once again, whether one could penalize clients, and not the prostitutes themselves. Perhaps one could impose fines on the former but not on the latter; perhaps one could deny a client convicted of engaging in prostitution access to his children; perhaps one could arrest kerb-crawlers but not prostitutes. I rejected this proposal in section 7.3.1, on the twofold grounds that it would unacceptably interfere with prostitutes who have the right to sell themselves, and that it would make all other prostitutes vulnerable. It is worth returning to it here, if only to note that it fails at the bar of gender equality as well. For it assumes that prostitutes, no matter who they are and what they do, are always victims, whereas clients, no matter who they are and what they do, are always perpetrators of serious wrongdoing. It is true, of course, that in some cases, including under ideal conditions, a prostitute is a victim—when, for example, she resorts to prostitution so as to get the resources she really needs but which justice does not grant her by right. In other cases, however, she is not, as when she goes into prostitution to finance a high-standard lifestyle which she could not finance otherwise. In those cases, where the prostitute cannot be regarded as a victim, to allow her to sell sex and to punish her clients amounts to treating her as someone who cannot really be held responsible for their choices: not a state of affairs which proponents of gender equality should endorse.

7.4 CONCLUSION

The problem with prostitution, then, is not the act per se of providing sexual services for money: rather it is the background conditions under which prostitutes currently have to work, whereby women and gays are victims of deeply entrenched prejudices, a number of individuals lack economic and social opportunities to such an extent that prostitution seems the best of a bad set of options, and sex is regarded as something one should only engage in out of love, desire, or affection. Those conditions in turn make prostitutes, especially female prostitutes, and, to a much lesser extent, their clients (mostly in the case of male gay prostitution), vulnerable to blackmail, extortion, and violence. However, whilst prostitution can, indeed often does, take place against a background of violence and sex discrimination which in turn reinforces prejudices against women, it is not inherent in its nature that it should do so. Moreover, while it does not merely consist in selling one's labour, it nevertheless does not consist in selling oneself. Rather, it consists in hiring one's body out for sexual services. As we saw, there is no reason to believe that it is morally wrong to do so; assuming that it is morally wrong, there are good reasons for the state to desist from banning it, for to do so makes prostitutes, and thus those women who work as such, more vulnerable than their (male) clients, which is unjust. At the bar of justice, then, there is a strong case for conferring on individuals the right to sell and buy sexual services. This suggests, once again, that the coercive provision of personal services and the confiscation of body parts, compatible as they are with the aforementioned right, leave more scope for individual autonomy than is usually thought.

8

Surrogacy Contracts

8.1 INTRODUCTION

In Chapter 5, we saw that individuals cannot be held under a duty to provide their gametes and, in the case of women, to make their womb available, to the infertile. In this chapter, I defend the view that women have the power to enter surrogacy contracts, under the terms of which they are inseminated with the male parent's sperm, carry the resulting child to term, and transfer their rights over that child to the commissioning parents. Conversely, commissioning parents have the power to enter surrogacy contracts with willing surrogate mothers. I shall also argue that such power should be protected by a claim that the state not interfere with contracting parties, as well as a claim that the contracts so made be regarded as legally valid but voidable. Terminology-wise, and unless otherwise specified, here too I will use the word 'right' to mean 'claim' or 'power'.

This view of surrogacy contracts, which I shall defend in section 8.2, is controversial. Echoing opponents of organ selling and prostitution, opponents of surrogate motherhood routinely point to the exploitative character of such transactions and to the gender inequalities which shape women's willingness to engage in them, as well as to the fact that buyers in those transactions—in other words, the commissioning parents—objectify the surrogate mother, since they see her only as an egg provider and a womb. In addition, they argue that surrogacy contracts harm the children whom they create and, for that reason alone, should be banned. I shall rebut those objections in section 8.3, and assess in section 8.4 some of the policy implications of my arguments. Throughout the chapter, I shall point to morally relevant similarities and differences between selling one's body parts, selling sexual services, and leasing one's body for reproduction.

A few preliminary remarks before I begin. First, although unpaid surrogacy is known to exist, my concern is with cases where prospective parents pay the surrogate mother for her services and her ovum. Accordingly, unless otherwise stated, by 'surrogacy' I shall always mean 'commercial surrogacy'. Second, it is important to distinguish between partial surrogacy, where the child carried by the surrogate mother is genetically hers, from full (or gestational) surrogacy, where this is not the case. Full surrogacy in turn is divided into cases where the egg is provided by the commissioning mother, and cases where it is provided by an egg donor. In fact, one can imagine surrogacy arrangements where neither gametes are provided by commissioning parents and surrogate mother. In this chapter, I shall focus on partial surrogacy, and more particularly on contracts made between a surrogate mother and a heterosexual commissioning couple. In so far as the partially surrogate mother provides both a part of her body and a service, the philosophical issues raised by partial surrogacy dovetail nicely with those raised by organ sales and prostitution. Moreover, one could not do justice to the practice of full surrogacy without addressing the enormously complex questions it raises with respect to parental rights—a task which lies some way beyond the scope of this book.[1] Finally, although I see no reason in principle to exclude from surrogacy arrangements single infertile women, single men, and male gay couples, it is worth, for the sake of brevity, attending to those arrangements which are most often made as a matter of fact.

Third, when assessing the legitimacy of prostitution, I focused on prostitutes' and clients' rights against one another, and did not examine the specific issues raised by pimping. Likewise, in this chapter, I shall focus on commissioning parents' and surrogate mothers' rights against one another, and will not examine in great detail the issues raised by surrogacy firms. A number of concerns have been expressed over the role of those firms in surrogacy contracts—most notably over the pressure many of them exercise on surrogate mothers. Some of those concerns, which are well grounded, ought to be addressed by any law and policy seeking to regulate surrogacy contracts, and I shall say a few words to that effect at the close of 8.4. Meanwhile, I shall assume that, if surrogacy contracts are morally permissible and ought to be recognized as legally valid, then it is permissible for an organization to act as intermediary between surrogate mothers and commissioning parents, subject to the regulations outlined therein.

Finally, and to reiterate, my argument is located in ideal theory, and thus assumes that individuals fulfil their obligations of justice to one another. This in turn implies that individuals respect one another as persons; it also implies, less abstractly, that no one lacks the resources they need in order to lead a minimally flourishing life, unless they can be shown to be responsible for their predicament (again, without having to make shameful revelations about themselves). Now, we saw at the outset of Chapter 7 that, for many, prostitution is a salient phenomenon precisely because we live in a non-ideal world. Equally, they might say, surrogacy is salient precisely because we live in a world where some women are desperate enough to carry a child for nine months and relinquish it at birth, where it is appropriate to think of women as little more than wombs,

---

[1] For a detailed study of the custody issues raised by surrogacy, see J. Mahoney, 'An Essay on Surrogacy and Feminist Thought', in L. Gostin (ed.), *Surrogate Motherhood: Politics and Privacy* (Bloomington: Indiana University Press, 1990). For a study of the ways in which full surrogacy requires that we rethink our understanding of motherhood, see S. B. Rae, *The Ethics of Commercial Surrogate Motherhood* (Westport, Conn.: Praeger, 1994), ch. 3. And for a review of the ethical issues raised by full surrogacy, see R. Ber, 'Ethical Issues in Gestational Surrogacy', *Theoretical Medicine and Bioethics* 21 (2000): 153–69.

and where the pressure to have children is such as to drive the infertile to pay for it. Under ideal conditions, they might add, surrogacy would not pose any interesting moral problem. As we shall see below, however, under current, non-ideal conditions, although most surrogate mothers are less well off than commissioning parents, they are not, in fact, poor. Moreover, in so far as a just society is not one where poverty can be completely eradicated, it may well be that, even then, some women would be tempted to act as surrogate mothers in exchange for payment. Taken together, those two points suggest that, from the point of view of assessing surrogacy, the ideal and non-ideal world are not as different as is often thought. Furthermore, we have no reason to believe that, under ideal conditions, those who cannot have children will not yearn for them and be prepared to pay for the privilege of being a parent. For all these reasons, it matters greatly to assess whether women should, in such a society, be allowed to sell gametes and reproductive services, and whether commissioning parents should be allowed to buy them.

8.2 A CASE FOR THE RIGHTS TO SELL AND BUY REPRODUCTIVE SERVICES

I begin this section by offering an account of the practice of surrogacy. I then argue that although reproductive services differ in important ways from other services which we have the right to buy and purchase, including sexual services, they are sufficiently similar to them that individuals have the rights to buy and purchase them.

8.2.1 Defining Surrogacy

The provision of a gamete and of a reproductive service is a central feature of partial surrogacy (henceforth, surrogacy). In Chapters 6 and 7, I argued that in so far as we have the right to use our body to earn a living, we have the right to divest ourselves of parts of our body, and to prostitute ourselves, for the same purpose. I also argued that we have a right to buy body parts and sexual services from those willing to sell them. It might seem, then, that *mutatis mutandis*, everything I have said so far applies to surrogacy contracts.

And, indeed, my argument in favour of their permissibility will be brief. Still, surrogacy differs enough from both organ sales and prostitution to warrant closer scrutiny than may seem necessary in the light of the last two chapters. It differs, quite obviously, from the sale of organs such as kidneys and corneas, first, because it does not only consist in providing a resource, and, second, because the resource to be provided, namely an egg, will serve to create another human being. On that latter count, and no less obviously, it also differs, as a service, from the provision of sexual services.

The foregoing points raise the question of how properly to understand commercial surrogacy—as the sale and purchase of a service and a resource, or as the sale and purchase of a child. Some of its opponents argue that it involves the latter, and that surrogacy therefore consists in viewing the child thus created as commodified property, from which it follows, or so they conclude, that, as so viewing children is morally wrong, surrogacy itself is morally wrong.[2] If they are right, surrogacy is morally impermissible *by definition*, and to such a degree that it cannot be protected by rights to engage in it. Were that the case, any argument in favour of conferring on prospective parents and surrogates the right to contract with one another is doomed to fail.

Now, it should be clear that, although the surrogate mother, in partial surrogacy, provides her egg, commissioning parents are not buying that egg as well as her service, any more than in buying bread from my local bakery I thereby buy the flour which goes into the bread. This obvious point raises a troubling question, though: granted, I do not buy the flour from the bakery, but do I buy the baker's service? That seems an odd way to characterize the transaction: what I buy is the bread, into which go a whole range of ingredients, together with the baker's labour. If so, then, is it not the case, by analogy, that what commissioning parents buy from a surrogate mother is neither her gamete nor her services, but the child itself?

At this juncture, one can adopt one of the following two strategies: one can either deny that surrogacy contracts stipulate terms under which children are sold and bought; or one can concede that they do so, but deny that it matters much.

Consider the first strategy. It is sometimes said, in response to the claim that a surrogate mother condemnably sells her child, that she is in fact paid to relinquish her parental rights over her.[3] However, this move to counteract the disturbing claim that she sells her child will not do, for selling an entity precisely consists in relinquishing, against payment, one's rights, powers, and liabilities over that entity. It is also sometimes said that the surrogate mother does not sell a child, but rather her services.[4] This move will not do either, for the surrogate mother is not paid merely for carrying a child to term: she is paid to relinquish her rights over the child. And in so far as that is what selling something amounts to, there is a sense in which she does, indeed, sell the child and that the commissioning parents buy it.

[2] See, e.g., E. Anderson, 'Is Women's Labor a Commodity?', *Philosophy and Public Affairs* 19 (1990): 71–82; Radin, *Contested Commodities*, pp. 136 and 140; Rae, *The Ethics of Commercial Surrogate Motherhood*, ch. 2.

[3] See, e.g., A. van Niekerk and L. van Zyl, 'Commercial Surrogacy and the Commodification of Children: An Ethical Perspective', *Medicine and Law* 14 (1995): 163–70.

[4] See, e.g., R. J. Kornegay, 'Is Commercial Surrogacy Baby Selling?', *Journal of Applied Philosophy* 7 (1990): 45–50; H. V. McLachlan and J. K. Swales, 'Babies, Child Bearers and Commodification: Anderson, Brazier et al., and the Political Economy of Commercial Surrogate Motherhood', *Heath Care Analysis* 8 (2000): 1–18.

My argument against the aforementioned two attempts to rescue surrogacy from the charge that it is tantamount to baby selling rests on the claims that surrogacy consists in relinquishing one's rights over the child in exchange for payment, and that selling something precisely consists in relinquishing one's rights over that thing in exchange for payment. Taken together those two claims entail that surrogacy does, indeed, amount to baby selling. Many would resist this conclusion, by noting that selling something consists in relinquishing one's *property* rights over that thing, and that, in so far as one does not have property rights over one's children, the act of relinquishing those rights against payment is not tantamount to a sale.[5] However, it is not true that one cannot be said to sell something unless that thing is the kind of entity over which one has property rights, that is, unless that thing is a piece of property. Indeed, it is possible to buy an entity which it is impermissible to treat as property, such as an animal, precisely because it is not a property. Accordingly, that we lack property rights over our children (a claim I am not disputing) does not establish that relinquishing one's rights over our children against payment is not tantamount to a sale.

Even if surrogacy contracts do set the terms under which children are bought and sold, not only does it not follow that the parties in those contracts thereby treat the children themselves as property; it does not even follow that they treat them as commodities. For, as we saw in section 6.3.1, it is possible to buy an entity which it is impermissible to treat as a commodity. The important question, then, is not whether a child is bought and sold, but whether the parties in the contract are thereby committed so to treat him. As a matter of fact, we know that they do not do so, but that is irrelevant to the issue at hand, just as the fact that a husband does not regard his wife merely as a means to his ends in a traditional marriage does not make such a marriage any less unjust. Rather, in so far as whether an entity is properly conceived of as a commodity depends on the rights one has over it, the issue at hand concerns the rights held by commissioning parents in respect of the child born from the contract. As it happens, one does not have rights to use, enjoy, and treat a child as permitted by the norms of the market (for example, by selling her to the highest bidder), from which it follows that one cannot regard her as a commodity. That one pays for being entrusted with rights and responsibilities over her is compatible with not so regarding her *and* does not matter much from a moral point of view, provided one turns her into an autonomous, rational, moral human being—which is (in part) what parenting is about.

Note, incidentally, that the foregoing points are compatible with the view, articulated in 6.3.1, that to sell oneself is to treat oneself as a commodity. For, in selling oneself, one is transferring to the buyer all the rights one has over oneself, including the right not to be so treated. In virtue of this transaction, my new owner acquires a right against third parties that they not treat me as a commodity,

---

[5] See, e.g., S. Wilkinson, *Bodies for Sale* (London: Routledge, 2003), p. 147.

but I lose my right against him that he not so treat me. By contrast, and to reiterate, in selling a child, one only loses whatever rights one has over that child, and those rights do not include a right to treat him, or her, as a commodity. Accordingly, one cannot deem surrogacy contracts impermissible on the grounds that they treat children as commodities.

Is this to say, then, that it is permissible for parents to relinquish their rights and responsibilities over their one-year-old child, against payment, provided that they have not used her only as a means to their ends, and have not harmed and neglected her? One might think that it is, in the light of the foregoing considerations. Is this also to say, then, that it is permissible for individuals, say a celebrity couple, to create children *with a view to* selling them, for quite a substantial amount of money (for they are, after all, a celebrity couple), again provided that they have treated them in the ways just mentioned? Again, one might think that it is.[6]

And yet, my argument against the view that surrogacy contracts necessarily involve treating children as commodities does not commit me to accepting those deeply unpalatable practices. For, whereas those who would buy the one-year-old baby and the celebrity couple's children would not, in so doing, necessarily treat them as commodities, the selling parents would. In relinquishing their rights over their baby against payment, after having cared for and looked after her for one year, they would show that they treat her as nothing more than a mere means to their ends, to be enjoyed and disposed of as market norms allow, when she no longer fulfils whatever purpose they had in initially conceiving and rearing her. Likewise, in creating children with a view to disposing of them against payment, and in marketing them as children of a celebrity couple, the latter would also make it clear that they view their children as nothing more than commodities. As is clear, treating individuals, including children, as commodities, violates the requirement that we treat one another with the respect owed to persons (or, in the case of children, to persons-to-be). By contrast, to sell one's egg and gestational labour does not inherently suggest that one views the resulting child as a commodity—a point borne out by many testimonies from surrogate mothers, hardly any of whom agree to act as surrogates for financial reasons alone. To be sure, some of them do, in which case they ought not to be allowed to do it, for reasons similar to those adduced above. But that is no reason to impose a blanket prohibition on surrogacy contracts; for were we to do so, we would unfairly penalize surrogate mothers who do not view and treat the resulting children as a commodity. As I shall stress below, it is worth paying the price of not 'catching out' the very, very few who do. In contrast, imposing a blanket prohibition on selling one's children later than a few weeks after they are born, or on selling children one has conceived for that purpose, would catch out parents who, as evidenced by their behaviour, clearly view their children in such a way.

---

[6] I am grateful to T. McDonald and D. McDermott for pressing me on these issues.

8.2.2 In Favour of Surrogacy Contracts

As we have just seen, parties in surrogacy contracts are not thereby committed to regarding the resulting child as a commodity, and so we can embark on the task of addressing the question of their legitimacy. A number of arguments have been deployed in support of conferring on women the right to act as surrogate mothers. It is sometimes claimed, for example, that, in so far as women have the right to decide whether, and how, to procreate, they have the right to do so by contract and against payment.[7] It is also sometimes argued that a woman who decides to bear a child for the sake of someone else is performing an altruistic act (even though she claims expenses), and should not be prevented from so doing.[8]

Whilst I have some sympathy for both arguments, my defence of the permissibility of surrogacy contracts takes a different form. As we saw above, the surrogate mother provides an egg and a service. The latter point is crucial: whereas the provider, in organ sales, is not wholly engaged in the transaction, surrogacy, like prostitution, makes demands on the person of the provider herself. In that respect, a surrogate mother is like (almost) any other person who works for a living. Now, to reiterate, according to the autonomy principle, provided sufficiency obtains, individuals should be allowed to pursue their conception of the good and to enjoy the fruits of their labour in pursuit of such a conception. If, then, they are allowed to work as models in medical schools, as philosophy professors, masseuses, prostitutes, and sex therapists, there seems to be a good, *pro tanto*, reason to confer on them the right to raise income from the use of their body in reproduction, pending successful rebuttal of objections to the contrary. In addition, it is worth noting that surrogacy is closer to a number of professions than prostitution, in that women who undertake to carry a child for someone else often do so not merely for reasons of financial gain, but also out of altruism, and/or desire to atone for the mistakes they believe themselves to have made (having had an abortion, having given up a baby for adoption, and so on). In other words, whereas a decision to enter prostitution (or to sell an organ, for that matter) is, more often than not, based on purely financial motivations, a decision to be a surrogate mother seldom is, but instead stems from a whole range of complex emotional and psychological factors, just as most professional decisions do.[9]

---

[7] Judge H. Sorkow, ruling *In Re Baby M*, 217 N. J Super 313. See also J. A. Robertson, 'Procreative Liberty and the State's Burden of Proof in Regulating Non-Coital Reproduction', in Gostin (ed.), *Surrogate Motherhood*.

[8] The *Warnock Report on Human Fertilisation and Embryology* notes that this is a possible defence of surrogacy contracts, but condemns the practice on other grounds (see M. Warnock, *A Question of Life: Warnock Report on Human Fertilisation and Embryology* (Oxford: Oxford University Press, 1985)).

[9] For fascinating insights in surrogate mothers' motivations, see H. Ragonné, *Surrogate Motherhood: Conception in the Heart* (Boulder, Colo.: Westview Press, 1994), ch. 2.

Prostitution and surrogacy differ in other important ways. First, recall that when making an argument in favour of the right to sell sexual services, I claimed that the contractual approach to prostitution was defective. On that approach, in so far as prostitution is simply one way to use one's body so as to provide a service and thereby earn a living, and in so far as using one's body to earn a living, including providing services to others, is morally permissible and protected by a moral right, prostitution is morally permissible and is protected by a moral right. As I noted, though, prostitution is not just like any other kind of service work, since what the client wants, at least in most cases, is the body of the prostitute itself. By contrast, and I believe interestingly, it is unclear that a surrogate mother's clients are interested in her body itself. To be sure, in so far as they cannot, *ex hypothesi*, have a child unless she makes her womb available to them, what they want is access to her body. However, their interest in it is contingent on the state of medical technology—just as the student's interest in the colonoscopy model's body is contingent on there not being alternative ways for him to learn about the colon. If it were possible to bring an embryo to term in an artificial womb, without in any way adversely affecting it, prospective parents who cannot, for some reason, have a child 'naturally' themselves, would no longer have an interest in appealing to a surrogate mother. In most (although admittedly not all) prostitutional relationships, however, a client's interest in the prostitute's body is not contingent on there being as yet no inflatable doll, or mechanical vagina, which could 'do the work' well enough to satisfy him. If I am correct, the contractual approach seems to fit surrogacy better than it does prostitution, at least in that respect.

Second, surrogacy involves the purchase and sale not merely of a service, but also of a body part, to wit, a gamete. The prostitute, in contrast, does not divest herself of a part of her body. However, in so far as individuals have the right to sell and buy gametes, the fact that surrogacy and prostitution are disanalogous in that respect is irrelevant to the claim which I make here. So too is the fact that surrogacy contracts involve a transfer of rights over the child: after all, surrogacy, albeit dissimilar to prostitution on that count, is similar to those services which consist not merely in using one's body or brain, but in using them so as to create something, rights over which are transferred to the purchaser in virtue of a sale agreement.

Finally, prostitution and surrogacy differ in yet another way: whilst a sexual transaction usually is punctual (even if it is part of a long-term agreement between a client and a prostitute), surrogacy requires of the mother that she make her body available for nine months. Moreover, unlike safe sex, childbearing, even at its safest, almost always affects the woman adversely—although to various degrees—and always presents a risk of serious disability. Pregnancy affects cardiovascular, digestive, muscular, and urinary functions; it causes sleeplessness and memory loss, which in turn may trigger profound behavioural changes—not always for the better; it can also cause fatal increases in blood pressure. In addition, childbearing may cause long-term, post-birth, troublesome conditions such as urinary dysfunction, joint and back pains; childbirth itself can be dangerous—indeed fatally so—to the mother. Regarding the dangers it poses to the surrogate mother, surrogacy is closer to organ sales (some of which are dangerous to the sellers) than to prostitution.

In some ways, then, surrogacy is much more demanding on surrogate mothers than prostitution is on prostitutes.[10] However, it is not more demanding than many other activities in which people engage in exchange for payment: think about those who work in factories, for eight or nine hours a day, standing, in the midst of deafening noise, with every inch of their body under strain; think of astronauts who live for several months in a very restricted environment, and subject themselves to constant monitoring, indeed, in some cases, to medical experiments; think of those people who risk their life, more or less routinely, in the course of their jobs. These activities are not the same as childbearing, of course, but they are extremely demanding on the body and person of those who engage in them. If we allow individuals to work in a factory, sign up with NASA, work in coal mines, as boxers, car drivers, and so on, so as to further their conception of the good, then there seem to be good, *pro tanto* reasons to allow women to hire their wombs out for the sake of the infertile.

There are also good reasons to allow prospective parents to enter such agreements. As I argued in Chapter 6, individuals who need a body part to which they lack a right because they need it so as to implement a specific conception of the good have a moral right to buy it from individuals willing to sell. Now, parenting is one of the most important, most fulfilling conceptions of the good life individuals may have; it is also one of the hardest to have to abandon in the face of enduring infertility. The emotional and psychological difficulties experienced by many individuals and couples who cannot have the children they want are well known, ranging from marital breakdown and loss of self-respect to severe clinical depression. In some cases of infertility, as when the woman has endometriosis and cannot carry a baby to term, the only way for those individuals and couples to have a child who is genetically related to them is to have recourse to a surrogate mother. Although those harms are not serious enough to warrant imposing on fertile individuals an obligation to provide their gametes and wombs for free, and although, as we saw in section 5.4, they do not warrant funding fertility treatments from general taxation, they are serious enough to confer on the infertile the

---

[10] In other ways, it is less costly: prostitutes often lose their self-respect, and the ability to enjoy sex to form emotionally meaningful relationships. By contrast, although some surrogate mothers report experiencing grief at abandoning their child, the overwhelming majority of them also claim to feel immensely proud at enabling someone to experience the joys of parenthood. See, e.g., Ragonné, *Surrogate Motherhood*, ch. 2. For a recent study of thirty-four UK-based surrogate mothers, which concludes that they do not appear to experience psychological problems as a result of the surrogacy agreement, see V. Javda et al., 'Surrogacy: The Experience of Surrogate Mothers', *Human Reproduction* 18 (2003): 2196–204.

right to enter surrogacy agreements with women willing to carry a baby for them in exchange for payment.

8.3 OBJECTIONS TO SURROGACY

To recapitulate, I have argued that surrogate mothers' and commissioning parents' interests in contracting with one another with a view to create children is important enough to confer on them the moral power to do so—a power which should be protected by a right against the state that it not criminalize those contracts, and that it should regard them as valid. In this section, I examine, and reject, the following four objections to surrogacy: it involves treating the surrogate mother's body as a commodity (section 8.3.1); it exploits her (section 8.3.2); it rests on, and reinforces, gender inequality (section 8.3.3); and it is harmful to the children born as a result of such contracts (section 8.3.4).[11] As we saw in Chapters 6 and 7, the first three objections are routinely deployed in debates about organ sales and prostitution, but it is worth revisiting them here for the purposes of assessing the legitimacy of surrogacy contracts.

Three preliminary points before I begin. First, it pays to note that one can coherently deny that organ sales and prostitution are vulnerable to the commodification, exploitation, and gender equality objections, *and* hold that surrogacy contracts are so vulnerable, on the grounds that gestational labour is special in such ways as to warrant protection from market norms. My aim, in the next three sections, is to show that my rebuttal of the commodification, exploitation, and gender inequality objections against organ sales and prostitution applies to the case of surrogacy.

Second, although I present and reject those three objections separately, they are sometimes interwoven. Thus, it can be, and is, argued, in defence of the view that surrogacy contracts should be banned, that they exploit surrogate mothers, and in turn, that they exploit them because, by commodifying their labour, or by reinforcing their situation of inequality vis-à-vis men, they harm them.[12] My points against the commodification and gender inequality objections apply, by implication, to this particular version of the exploitation objection.

Third, those who put forward those three objections do not always clearly specify whether they aim to show merely that surrogacy contracts are morally impermissible and should be regarded as legally null and void, or whether they aim to show, more strongly, that they ought to be made unlawful. If the latter, one needs to know whether surrogate mothers, as well as commissioning parents

---

[11] Those objections can be found in, e.g., Anderson, 'Is Women's Labor a Commodity?', p. 87; Warnock, *A Question of Life: Warnock Report on Human Fertilisation and Embryology*; G. J. Annas, 'Fairy Tales Surrogate Mothers Tell', in L. Gostin (ed.), *Surrogate Motherhood*; R. Macklin, 'Is there Anything Wrong with Surrogate Motherhood?', in Gostin (ed.), ibid.; B. Steinbock, 'Surrogate Motherhood as Prenatal Adoption', in Gostin (ed.), ibid.

[12] See, e.g., Anderson, 'Is Women's Labor a Commodity?'

and surrogacy firms, ought to be prosecuted. Opponents of surrogacy contracts who argue that they should be made unlawful usually claim that neither commissioning parents nor surrogate mothers, whom they regard as the victims in those transactions, ought to be punished. They all insist, however, that surrogacy firms should. We encountered a somewhat similar claim in Chapter 7, to the effect that prostitutes themselves should not be punished, whereas their clients and pimps should. One might think that my reasons for rejecting that claim apply to surrogacy, and one might accordingly mount the following argument: the proposal for differential liability wrongly assumes that surrogate mothers are always victims and that surrogacy firms are always guilty of serious wrongdoing; in those cases where the surrogate mother cannot properly be regarded a victim of her circumstances, and undertakes to carry a child for someone else in full knowledge of the possible consequences this might have on her life, not to prosecute her, but to prosecute the surrogacy firm instead, amounts to treating her as someone who is not fully responsible for her actions—a state of affairs which opponents of surrogacy contracts should be wary of condoning.

However, it is possible on the one hand to hold that, *if* clients and pimps ought to be prosecuted then so should prostitutes, and on the other hand to deny that, *if* surrogacy firms ought to be prosecuted, then so should surrogate mothers and commissioning parents, simply because prosecuting surrogate mothers and commissioning parents would place the children born from their contracts in the highly damaging position of being parented by criminals. Were one to adopt that position, though, one would thereby concede, if implicitly, that individuals' power to enter a surrogacy agreement is not protected by a claim-right against non-interference, since non-interference in that case is grounded, not in an interest of theirs, but in the children's interest in the best possible start in life.

No one (that I know of) argues that surrogate mothers and commissioning parents ought to be prosecuted. Many, however, argue that surrogacy contracts ought at least to be regarded as legally null and void, on the grounds that they treat women's labour as a commodity, further gender inequalities, and exploit women. I shall argue that it is not inherent in surrogacy contracts that they should do any of those things, and thus that none of the aforementioned three claims supports the view that surrogacy contracts ought to be regarded as legally null and void. At this juncture, an opponent of surrogacy contracts might point out that surrogacy contracts harm the children which they create and that *that* is a reason, not merely to regard them as legally null and void, but to deem them unlawful. I shall reject that view in section 8.3.4.

8.3.1 The Commodification Objection

In Chapters 6 and 7, I examined what I called the 'commodity objection' to the sale of body parts or sexual services, which consists in claiming that selling one's body parts or sexual services is morally wrong, as it bespeaks the wrong kind of attitude to one's body, and therefore to oneself. As I argued there, the objection errs in assuming that, when we sell parts of our body or sexual services, we treat our body itself (and therefore ourselves) as a commodity. Such reply will not do, or so many will be tempted to claim, when the objection pertains to surrogacy: for surrogacy consists in doing for money what should be done out of love—just as prostitution consists in doing for money what should be done, if not out of love, at the very least out of desire.

Interestingly enough, whereas many opponents of the legalization of organ sales and prostitution castigate those practices because they consist in selling oneself, opponents of surrogacy do not use such language. And yet, as already noted, pregnancy involves not merely the woman's body, but her whole person, to a much greater degree, in fact, than prostitution does. However, to reject surrogacy contracts on the grounds that they regulate the terms under which a surrogate mother sells herself would be misguided, for reasons similar to those adduced against the view that prostitutes sell themselves: just as the prostitute does not sell, but 'merely' hires her body, so does the surrogate mother; and just as there is more to ourselves than our body, and to our identity than our sexual construction, there is more to a woman than her ability to carry a child to term. Womanhood, to point out the obvious, does not equate with motherhood. Accordingly, in deploying our reproductive capacities for nine months, we only hire out a part of ourselves.

Be that as it may, proponents of the commodification objection to surrogacy contracts would insist, commercial surrogacy ought to be rejected, for the following reasons.[13] It treats women's gestational labour as a commodity—that is, as something the production, exchange, and enjoyment of which can be regulated solely by market norms. Moreover, it denies them respect by requiring of them that they suppress whatever love they feel for the child they are carrying, and by denying legitimacy to their feelings of grief at the prospect of having to relinquish it. In so doing, surrogacy 'reduces the surrogate mothers from persons worthy of respect and consideration to objects of mere use':[14] it turns them into a mere means to the commissioning parents' ends, and a fungible one at that, since any womb will do.

As I noted in Chapter 1, we do not have the power to enter transactions where we will be treated with less than the respect that is owed to us as persons. If the commodity objection is correct, then, surrogacy contracts are morally impermissible, and for reasons such that we lack the power to make them. Were that the case, though, it would not follow that they ought to be outlawed, since in interfering with the parties, the state might in fact undermine another important interest of theirs—important enough, in fact, to warrant respecting.

---

[13] See, e.g., Anderson, 'Is Women's Labor a Commodity?', at 80ff; Annas, 'Fairy Tales Surrogate Mothers Tell', pp. 45–6.

[14] Anderson, 'Is Women's Labor a Commodity?', at 80.

In any case, the objection is not correct. For a start, although some surrogacy firms, commissioning parents, and indeed a few surrogate mothers seem to see the surrogate mother as little more than a vehicle for the child, most of them do not; and, indeed, the standard practice (at least in the USA) of *mutual* selection on the part of commissioning parents and surrogate mothers suggests that the interest of the latter in dealing with parents they can trust must be taken on board, and in turn that it is crucial for the success of the agreement that they regard one another as distinct persons, each with their own ends, aspirations, and desires.

Moreover, the claim that surrogacy contracts require that the surrogate mother not feel anything for her child and suppress whatever grief she may experience at the prospect of losing it derives much of its strength from the ways in which some contracts are phrased and some surrogacy firms operate. It is true that, in some of those contracts, the woman (and her husband) undertake not to attempt to form any sort of parental relationship with the child—in other words, not to bond with her. In addition, some surrogacy firms and specialized lawyers are known to manipulate, and trivialize, surrogate mothers' feelings about their pregnancy and the child they are carrying.

If this is what surrogacy is about, then it involves a more serious loss of respect for the 'seller' than prostitution and organ sales. For most organ sellers, I surmise, do not relate to their organs in such a way that divesting themselves of them for money requires that they not love them. Likewise, it is not central to prostitutional relationships that prostitutes not love their clients, nor is it central to them that they should so love them: love generally does not come into play at all. Of course, a situation may arise where a prostitute comes to love one of her regular clients, in which case she might feel that she has to silence that love in order to be able to continue taking money from him; yet she could take steps to stop herself loving him—for example, by not seeing him at all. In contrast, one cannot reasonably expect anyone to silence her love for her child, particularly not a gestational mother. For, although it is possible in some cases to take steps so as to weaken one's love for someone, for example, by not interacting with them in any way or by constantly reminding oneself of their undesirable characteristics, one simply cannot do so with the child one is carrying.

My point is not that one cannot but love the child one is carrying (indeed some pregnant women feel no such love); nor is it that it is impossible to stop loving the child one is carrying (it is entirely conceivable that a woman who was drugged unconscious and then raped, who becomes pregnant, and who realizes some time into the pregnancy that her baby is the result of a rape, might stop loving it).[15] Rather, my point is that if one already loves that child (and such attachment can be formed very early on in the pregnancy), it is impossible *to school oneself out of it*. This point, though, which I share with the commodification objection, at best

[15] I owe this example to D. McDermott.

only supports the view that it is morally wrong and ought to be impermissible for a couple to engage in a surrogacy contract which requires of the surrogate mother that she not love the child she is carrying. It does not support a blanket moral and legal prohibition of surrogacy contracts in general. Lurking behind many accounts of the commodification objection is the thought that pregnancy is a special kind of labour—to wit, a labour of love, which should not be subverted by financial considerations. But, just as many people do not regard sex as something that one ought to do out of love or even desire, some women do not regard childbearing, even when they are engaged in it, as something one ought to do only out of love. And just as one ought not to charge those who regard sex as divorced from love and desire for failing to understand one of the deepest facts about human nature, one ought not to charge those who regard childbearing as divorced from love for failing to understand one of the deepest facts about womanhood.[16]

To be sure, it is undoubtedly easier for a surrogate mother to relinquish her child—and thereby fulfil her part of the contract—if she does not love it. But, first, we have no reason to believe that it is impossible, or, indeed, too costly for her to do so if she loves her child. Second, even if it were impossible, or too costly for her to fulfil her terms of the contract, even if, then, she would let herself be treated with less than the respect owed to her as a person, she nevertheless ought not to be interfered with: for, as I have consistently argued, one has a moral right not to be interfered with when harming oneself.[17] Moreover, it is not inherent in surrogacy contracts that they be overseen by for-profit firms who have a strong interest in ensuring that surrogate mothers' perspective on their pregnancy and decision to relinquish the child is silenced. Concerns at such practices ought to be taken seriously, but, again, they at best constitute reasons to reform surrogacy, not to deny individuals the right to engage in it.

Assuming that I am wrong, that pregnancy cannot but be a labour of love, it still does not follow that it ought not to be done for money. As we have seen in connection with organ sales and prostitution, a good can be imbued at the same time with a non-monetarized and a monetarized meaning. Indeed, surveys of surrogate mothers show that only very few of them (less than 1 per cent, according to some studies[18]) do it solely for the money: the overwhelming majority of them do it out of the altruistic desire to help infertile couples, out of guilt for having had an abortion, out of the desire to get the social recognition granted to pregnant women, and so on. Granted, guilt and lack of self-esteem are troublesome reasons for wanting to carry a child for someone else's sake—a point to which I

[16] For an extended criticism of the 'labour of love' objection to surrogacy contracts, see D. Satz, 'Markets in Women's Reproductive Labor', *Philosophy and Public Affairs* 21 (1992): 107–31, at 110 ff.

[17] It may be that surrogacy contracts harm the children born from surrogate mothers, to a sufficient extent to justify prohibition. I shall address such concerns in 8.3.4.

[18] See Anderson, 'Is Women's Labor a Commodity?', at 83.

shall return in 8.3.2. Suffice it to say, at this stage, that it is coherent for a woman to carry a child and demand money for it, just as it is coherent for a surgeon to perform risky operations out of the altruistic desire to save lives and at the same time ask to be paid for doing it.

In the end, the commodification objection is the stronger for supposing that the surrogate mother must be contractually bound to relinquish the child. As a matter of fact, courts have held (at least in partial surrogacy cases) that she is not so bound, and that custodial disputes such as may arise post-birth must be resolved in the best interest of the child. I shall revisit this issue in section 8.4.

8.3.2 The Exploitation Objection

In Chapter 7, I desisted from addressing the exploitation objection to the moral permissibility of prostitution, on the grounds that my rebuttal of that very same objection as deployed against organ sales applied there *mutatis mutandis*. However, it is worth considering whether the charge of exploitation is successful when levelled against surrogacy contracts. That charge has two variants. The familiar, *economic exploitation* variant notes that a sizeable proportion of aspiring surrogate mothers come from a background of socio-economic deprivation (and warns of surrogacy firms' intention to recruit surrogate mothers from Third World countries, as a way to drive the costs of surrogacy contracts—but not their profit margins—further down). The *emotional exploitation* variant notes that a sizeable proportion of aspiring surrogate mothers suffer from emotional and psychological difficulties. On both variants, commissioning parents take advantage of those women's economic and emotional difficulties to further their own interests in parenting. Moreover, they do so in two ways: first, they benefit from those women's willingness to do something—carrying a child in exchange for money—which they would not do but for their circumstances; and, second, they use those very circumstances to impose on surrogate mothers terms and conditions to which, again, they would not agree but for those circumstances.[19]

Now, as we saw in section 6.3.2, a transaction involving A and B is said to be wrongfully exploitative of B if the following three conditions obtain: (a) A benefits from the transaction; (b) the outcome of the transaction is harmful or unfair to B; and (c) A gets B to agree to the transaction by seizing on some features of B's or of her situation—features or situation such that, were B not to have those features, or were her situation different, she would not agree to the transaction.

---

[19] For the charge that surrogacy contracts exploit surrogate mothers, see Anderson, 'Is Women's Labor a Commodity?'; A. Capron and M. Radin, 'Choosing Family Law over Contract Law', in Gostin (ed.), *Surrogate Motherhood*, p. 72; M. Field, *Surrogate Motherhood* (Cambridge, Mass.: Harvard University Press, 1986), p. 25; Warnock, *A Question of Life: Warnock Report on Human Fertilisation and Embryology*, p. 46; Rae, *The Ethics of Commercial Surrogate Motherhood*. For a good account of the exploitation objection to surrogate motherhood, see A. Wertheimer, 'Two Questions about Surrogacy and Exploitation', *Philosophy and Public Affairs* 21 (1992): 211–39.

On either of its variants, then, the exploitation objection will not succeed unless it can show successfully that surrogacy contracts meet all three conditions. However, although some surrogacy contracts do indeed do so, and thus are exploitative of surrogate mothers, it is not inherent in them that they should do so—just as it is not inherent of organ sales that they should be exploitative of organ sellers.

Consider the first condition. It is met only if A—the commissioning parent—benefits from the transaction. Accordingly, it is met only if B, the surrogate mother, actually carries a child to term and relinquishes her rights over it. If B miscarries, has an abortion, or decides (and is allowed to) keep the child, A has not benefited from the transaction, and cannot be said to have exploited B, irrespective of the reasons why B entered the contract in the first instance, and of the terms of the contract. All that can be said of A, in that case, is that he, or she, has attempted to exploit B. Of course, if A and B contract with one another through a for-profit firm, if that firm receives some money from A irrespective of the outcome of the pregnancy, if the pregnancy fails or if the mother changes her mind, and if the other two conditions are met, the transaction is exploitative, but the exploiter, here, is the firm itself, which profits at the expense of both surrogate mother and commissioning parents. In all other cases, though, one cannot say that the commissioning parents exploit the surrogate mother.

The second condition stipulates that the transaction must be harmful or unfair to the surrogate mother. Now, as we saw in section 8.2.2, it is true that pregnancy and childbirth adversely affect women; it is no less true, however, that not all those adverse effects actually count as harmful, or as a setback to women's important interests. Moreover, just as some organ sales, as we saw in section 6.3.2, are not harmful but 'merely' impose a risk of harm on the sellers, in many cases pregnancy and delivery 'merely' impose a risk of harm—indeed of very serious, fatal harm—on surrogate mothers. Moreover, it is not always the case that surrogate mothers are harmed by the act of relinquishing the child to the commissioning parents. On the definition of exploitation I offer here, the mere fact that B incurs a risk of harm is not enough to render it exploitative (even if the first and third exploitation conditions obtain).

One could, of course, broaden such definition and posit that a transaction is exploitative of B if B risks incurring a serious harm (together with the first and third conditions). On that broader definition, though, a whole range of contracts would be deemed exploitative which under closer scrutiny seem not to be. For example, a wage contract under which B, who is psychologically driven to earn a lot of money, works for A, the owner of a nuclear processing plant, is exploitative of B, since B runs the risk of being seriously harmed, indeed of dying, should there be a leak of radioactive material. And yet that does not seem quite right. Even if it is right, it does not follow that B should be prevented from working for A, or that their contract should be regarded as null and void under labour law. To outlaw it would be unacceptably paternalistic (as per my arguments in section 1.2.3); to regard it as null and void would leave B open to further exploitative practices on A's part. Similarly, even if it is correct that a surrogate mother is exploited merely by running the risks attendant on pregnancy (assuming that the other two conditions are met), outlawing surrogacy contracts on those grounds would be unacceptably paternalistic towards her; regarding them as null and void would make her vulnerable to further exploitation on the part of commissioning parents—a point to which I shall return below.

Not all surrogacy contracts, then, are harmful to B.[20] Those which are not are in fact advantageous to her, since not only is she not harmed, but she also receives payment. Could they nevertheless be exploitative of her? Yes, the exploitation objection would go, in so far as they are unfair to her, that is, as the distribution of gain between her and commissioning parents is unfair. In section 6.3.2, however, I noted that organ sellers might benefit more from organ sales than organ purchasers, which suggests that such transactions are not always exploitative of the former. Likewise, surrogate mothers might well benefit from the contract to a greater degree than commissioning parents. Many people would doubt it, on the grounds that there is nothing more valuable, objectively, than bringing up a child. I do not think that that is true. But, even if it is true, the fact that a distribution of gain between A and B is unequal does not suffice to show that it is unfair. To show that the commissioning parents exploit the surrogate mother in that sense, one must establish that the latter accepted a price lower than the price she would have accepted had she not been under pressure to transact.

To be sure, one *may* be able to establish that. By the same token, though, one may also be able to establish that commissioning parents accepted a price higher than the price they would have accepted had they not been desperate to have a child: surrogacy contracts, if they are exploitative, can be exploitative of the parents as well as of the surrogate mother. Some of their critics are well aware of that possibility: if the surrogate mother is allowed to keep the child, they argue, this gives her immense leverage over the commissioning parents—leverage which she might use to make extortionate financial demands on them. But to conclude that surrogacy contracts should be totally prohibited testifies, here again, to an unwarranted lack of faith in possibilities for regulation.

Finally, surrogacy contracts are exploitative of the surrogate mother only if they meet a third condition, whereby commissioning parents take advantage of some feature of her, or of her situation, in order to get her to carry a child for them or to agree to terms and conditions she would not normally accept. It is at this juncture that the economic and emotional variants of the objection part company. The economic variant is familiar, echoing as it does the exploitation objection to organ sales which we examined in section 6.3.2. My rebuttal of it is equally familiar: true, poverty restricts women's options; true, those women

---

[20] For a more detailed rebuttal of the charge that they are, see Wertheimer, 'Two Questions about Surrogacy', at 214–22. For a defence of that charge, see S. Wilkinson, 'The Exploitation Argument against Commercial Surrogacy', *Bioethics* 17 (2003): 169–87.

perhaps would not agree to be surrogate mothers if they were better off.[21] First, though, note that the objection loses some of its force if sufficiency obtains: for, in so far as most prospective surrogate mothers have the resources they need to lead a minimally flourishing life, one cannot object to their consenting to surrogacy on the grounds that they are too poor to know better. In those cases where a woman decides to act as a surrogate mother in order to raise income which she desperately needs but is not entitled to at the bar of justice, to object to her decision on the grounds that her poverty vitiates her consent unacceptably deprives her of prospects for a minimally flourishing life.

Second, if the economic variant is correct, women who are worse off should be barred from taking any dangerous job, or at least—should one desist from criminalizing such transactions—should be left without the protection of the law if they decide to take those jobs, since they lack the moral power to enter such employment contracts in the first instance. That point will not convince many opponents of surrogacy who, at this juncture, standardly argue that the fact that women are already driven to take such jobs is no justification for giving them yet another dangerous option. However, such response is vulnerable to the charge that it singles out surrogacy, as opposed to other dangerous jobs, as a candidate for prohibition or non-regulation, and that it needs a reason for doing so—for example, that surrogacy commodifies women's reproductive abilities, that it partakes of gender discrimination, and that it harms children. I rebutted the first view in section 8.3.1; I shall reject the latter two in sections 8.3.3 and 8.3.4 respectively. Meanwhile, pending argument to the contrary, the economic variant of the exploitation objection fails.

In the context of surrogacy contracts, its emotional variant is equally misguided. It notes that some women want to be surrogate mothers because they believe that they can achieve self-worth only by being pregnant, or in order to put to rest their guilt at having had an abortion. Moreover, as one commentator puts it, 'most surrogate mothers are motivated by emotional needs and vulnerabilities which lead them to view their labour as a form of gift and not a purely commercial exchange'; this in turn enables surrogacy firms to exert considerable pressure on them to accept less advantageous financial terms than they might get, by impressing on them that if they were really generous and altruistic they would not ask for more money.[22] Although such concerns are targeted at surrogacy firms, they can be, and have been, raised at the behaviour of commissioning

---

[21] It pays to note, incidentally, that one of the most comprehensive studies on American surrogate mothers' economic profiles seems to show that they are not recruited, by and large, amongst the poorest women. That may well be because, in the USA at least, they are not recruited amongst black women (and that in itself is a cause for concern), who happen to be some of the poorest members of society. In any event, it seems that one cannot say of American surrogate mothers that they are driven by economic *necessity*. See R. Charo, 'Legislative Approaches to Surrogate Motherhood', in Gostin (ed.) *Surrogate Motherhood*, pp. 90–1.

[22] Anderson, 'Is Women's Labor a Commodity?', at 85.

parents. As concerns about the ways in which some firms and parents operate, they ought to be taken seriously. As grounding a blanket prohibition on surrogacy contracts, or indeed a blanket refusal to have them recognized as legally valid, they ought not. For a start, many individuals, indeed many women, take on difficult and dangerous jobs out of (partly) altruistic motives which in turn are shaped by emotional and psychological traumas: here, again, the exploitation objection proves too much since it would, by the same token, prohibit such wage contracts. In addition, just as many surrogate mothers are emotionally vulnerable, so are many commissioning parents, driven as they are by their desperate need for a child: again, exploitation can occur both ways.

To recapitulate, although, as a matter of fact, some surrogacy contracts are exploitative of surrogate mothers, it is not inherent in the practice that they should be so: as we have seen, it can be exploitative of commissioning parents as well. Of course, two wrongs do not make a right. But assuming, quite readily, that for commissioning parents to exploit a surrogate mother's vulnerability, and for the latter to exploit the former's need to parent a child, is morally wrong, it still does not follow that they lack the moral power to contract with one another. Accordingly, it still does not follow that surrogacy contracts should be forbidden, or even regarded as legally null and void. As I have noted on several occasions, individuals have a claim-right not to be interfered with as well as a claim-right to have their act of self-harm be deemed legally valid, in those cases where interference and lack of legal recognition would jeopardize a fundamental interest of theirs. In so far as interference and lack of legal recognition would, in that instance, harm surrogate mothers' abilities to raise income as well as make them more vulnerable than they are, and in so far as they would harm commissioning parents' deep-seated interest in raising a child and make them vulnerable to exploitation, both surrogate mothers and commissioning parents have a claim-right not to be interfered with, and to have the contract recognized as valid, even if it is exploitative of them. That individuals have those rights is entirely compatible, of course, with the view that surrogacy contracts should be regulated so as to make them as non-exploitative as possible.

8.3.3 The Gender Inequality Objection

Some authors agree that surrogacy contracts ought not to be deemed impermissible, and ought not to be made unlawful on the grounds that they commodify women's labour and exploit them. They claim, however, that they are impermissible, and ought to be regarded as null and void, on the grounds that they rest on, and buttress, deep inequalities between men and women. They are said to do so in two ways: first, they allow commissioning parents, and in some jurisdictions the commissioning father alone, rights of control over the surrogate mother's body, for example, by forbidding her to smoke, drink alcohol, or engage in supposedly risky activities, and by compelling her to have regular medical check-ups, or even to have an abortion if tests show that the baby suffers from genetic abnormalities. Second, they reinforce stereotypes about the proper place of women as nurturers and home-makers.[23]

There are obvious similarities between the gender equality objection to surrogacy and the gender equality objection to prostitution, most notably in that they both hold that prostitution, and surrogacy, are ways for men to use women to their own ends—sexual pleasure and reproduction respectively, and thus reinforce objectionable stereotypes about women. However, they differ in an interesting way. Some opponents of prostitution, you recall, deem it morally wrong on the grounds (amongst others) that men who seek out prostitutes often do so out of a desire to exercise power over women, indeed to humiliate and debase them. As a matter of fact many clients do so behave towards prostitutes. By contrast, one may plausibly surmise that men who enter a surrogacy agreement with a woman do not do so out of a desire to control and humiliate her. At the bar of gender equality, there is a sense, then, in which paying a woman for, say, oral sex might be worse, morally speaking, than paying her for carrying one's child, when one does the former not (merely) to seek sexual release, but (also) in order to humiliate her.

Before examining the view that surrogacy contracts discriminate against women, it is worth reminding ourselves briefly of a line of argument which was deployed in section 7.3.2 against the gender inequality objection to prostitution. There I noted that to say that prostitution is morally wrong because it fosters gender inequalities implies that some of its agents are acting wrongly. Similarly, to say that surrogacy contracts are morally wrong because they foster gender inequalities implies that parties in those contracts are acting wrongly. Now, in section 7.3.2, I argued that, on the assumption that prostitutional agreements partake of gender discrimination, it is always the case that clients, who are male, are guilty of wrongdoing, and sometimes the case that prostitutes are so guilty (in those cases, that is, where they could raise income by not doing prostitutional work). I also argued, though, that it does not follow that prostitution should be criminalized. When surrogacy is concerned, the picture is

---

[23] See, e.g., B. Brecher, 'Surrogacy, Moral Individualism, and the Moral Climate', in J. D. G. Ecans (ed.), *Moral Philosophy and Contemporary Problems* (Cambridge: Cambridge University Press, 1987); Satz, 'Markets in Women's Reproductive Labor'; Annas, 'Fairy Tales Surrogate Mothers Tell'; Pateman, *The Sexual Contract*, pp. 209–18. Satz also targets full surrogacy, and claims that in denying a full surrogate mother the right to change her mind and keep the baby, on the grounds that the child is not genetically hers, they resurrect the view that women are but repositories for men's offspring, and that their gestational labour counts for very little in the production of children (see Satz, 'Markets in Women's Reproductive Labor', at 127–8). A solution to that problem is to treat full surrogate mothers exactly on a par with partial surrogate mothers, and thus to allow them to change their mind and keep the child. (There are serious difficulties with this approach, though. Most worrisomely from the point of view of gender equality, in cases where the gametes are provided by the commissioning couple, it confers rights on the commissioning father *in virtue of* his biological connection to the child which it denies the commissioning mother *notwithstanding* her own biological connection to the child.)

not that straightforward. For, although it seems, if the objection is correct, that male commissioning parents are guilty of wrongdoing and are blameworthy, it is less clear that female commissioning parents are similarly guilty; and, if they are, it is not so clear that they are blameworthy, since their desire to have a child might result from prevalent and semi-oppressive views to the effect that a woman cannot fully realize her potential as a woman unless she is a mother (or so would many a proponent of the gender discrimination argue). Be that as it may, that commissioning parents and, in some cases, surrogate mothers themselves might be guilty of moral wrongdoing at the bar of gender equality does not entail that surrogacy contracts should be outlawed or unregulated, for reasons similar to those adduced against the criminalization and non-regulation of prostitution in Chapter 7.

Setting that aside, let us consider the claim that surrogacy contracts allow men to control women's bodies. To begin with, that claim clearly overlooks the fact that, in standard cases, commissioning parents include women who cannot carry a child to term: there is little reason to believe that in wanting, sometimes desperately, to have a child that is genetically related to their partners, those women merely submit to patriarchal norms.

Having said that, it is true that some surrogacy contracts do, as a matter of fact, impose considerable restrictions on surrogate mothers' lives. And to note, in reply, that such restrictions are acceptable because they are those of 'normal', non-contractual pregnancy anyway[24] will not do. For a start, some surrogacy contracts impose greater obligations on surrogate mothers than is thought to be necessary for the sake of the child's health. (For example, they prohibit drinking altogether, even though having a glass of wine from time to time is not considered harmful to the foetus; some contracts have prohibited the mother from cycling and eating certain kinds of food; others have sought to impose on the mother a number of non-routine medical examinations; and so on.) Moreover, although it is true that a pregnant woman who elects to give birth to her child is under a moral obligation not to endanger his health unnecessarily, she owes that obligation to the child itself, and not to his father.[25] A proponent of the gender equality objection to surrogacy contracts need not deny that she is under such an obligation to the child: the salient point is that surrogacy contracts bind her vis-à-vis the child's father, and that *that* reinforces gender inequality.

That some surrogacy contracts are unacceptably restrictive of surrogate mothers' lives is undoubtedly true. Those contracts are unacceptable, in that

---

[24] *Pace* R. Arneson, 'Commodification and Commercial Surrogacy', *Philosophy and Public Affairs* 21 (1992): 132–64, at 161.

[25] The clause 'who elects to give birth to her child' is important. For to claim that she wrongs her child by endangering his health does not entail that she would wrong him by having him aborted. Judging that she is wrong not to secure for her child, pre-birth, the conditions under which he will be able to live a minimally flourishing life neither implies nor presupposes that her child, *at the foetal stage*, has a moral status such that he should not be killed.

commissioning parents trade on, and benefit from, the surrogate mother's will-ingness in those particular cases to be regarded not as a rational and moral agent, but as a mere means to their ends. In so doing, they fail to enable her to act on the basis of the weight *she* gives to the fact that she is a moral and rational agent, aware of her obligations and responsibilities both to them and to the child—and thus deny her an opportunity for self-respect. As we saw in section 1.2.3B, that the surrogate mother consents to being so treated does not render it permissible for others to treat her in this way. In fact, in such cases, neither commissioning parents nor surrogate mother have the moral power to transact with one other. From this it follows that such contracts ought to be regarded as null and void, but not that they should be made unlawful, as interference would render parties in it—particularly surrogate mothers—even more vulnerable than they are.

However, this does not constitute a good reason for regarding *all* surrogacy contracts as morally impermissible, null and void, and warranting prohibition, since it is possible to regulate the practice in such a way as to allow room for non-restrictive contracts. I shall argue at length for this approach in section 8.4. Suffice it to say at this point that the first strand of the gender equality objec-tion to surrogacy contracts supports neither the view that they all are morally impermissible, nor the view that they all ought to be outlawed or at the very least regarded as null and void.

Nor, furthermore, does the second strand. It holds that surrogacy contracts reinforce the stereotypical claim that women are, above all, nurturers and home-makers. Now, it is true that available data on American surrogate mothers show that the latter are recruited overwhelmingly amongst women who are already married, and already have children, and whose life revolves around their domest-ic duties.[26] As a matter of fact, then, surrogacy attracts women who do conform to gender stereotypes. However, as I pointed out in section 7.3.2, many a pro-fession and many a practice take place against, and reinforce, stereotypes which are detrimental to women. To be sure, it may well be that surrogate mothers, like prostitutes, are seen in a worse light than nurses and secretaries. However, to reiterate, far more people will come across nurses and secretaries (and prostitutes, for that matter) than will come across surrogate mothers. Accordingly, the stereo-types conveyed by the former professions are likely to have greater weight than those conveyed by surrogacy. In so far as one would still confer on men the right to employ female nurses and secretaries, one should confer on commissioning parents—who are not men only—the right to hire a surrogate mother.

8.3.4 The Harm-to-Children Objection

So far I have examined objections to surrogacy contracts to the effect that they harm surrogate mothers. Were their proponents convinced by my, and

---

[26] See Ragonné, *Surrogate Motherhood*, ch. 2.

others', rebuttal, they could, and many of them would, still reject surrogacy contracts on the grounds that they are harmful to the children thus created. In so far as the objection's premiss is that harm accrues to vulnerable third parties, it can more convincingly conclude, not merely that surrogate mothers and commissioning parents lack the power to enter surrogacy contracts, but also that such contracts ought to be made unlawful, on the grounds that individuals generally can be interfered with when harming third parties without their consent.

If that objection is correct, then, it is at this juncture that surrogacy and prostitution, for all their similarities, part company. It would be tempting, at this point, to head off that objection by helping ourselves to something like Parfit's so-called non-identity argument. According to Parfit, a fourteen-year-old girl is not under a duty to her unborn child not to conceive it at time *t* if it would suffer from having such a young mother.[27] In the context of surrogacy, the argument would go like this:

(1) To exist is not a burden (assuming that one's existence is worth living).
(2) Those children exist thanks to surrogacy contracts. Therefore:
(3) they are not harmed by surrogate mothers and commissioning parents. Therefore:
(4) they are not wronged by surrogate mothers and commissioning parents.

However, this rebuttal of the harm-to-children objection to surrogacy contracts does not work, because its move from (2) to (3) rests on a concealed and problematic premiss, namely, that in judging whether P's doing A vis-à-vis R is morally wrong or permitted, one must assess whether A negatively or positively affects the quality of R's life *overall*. And yet it is entirely plausible to hold on the one hand that P acts in such a way as to not make R worse off overall—indeed, that he acts in such as way as to make him better off—and on the other hand to claim that in so acting, he harms a *particular* interest of R's.[28]

Consider Parfit's fourteen-year-old girl. She is told that if she gets pregnant now, she will not be able to give her child the degree of care and attention he will need in order to lead a minimally flourishing life (although his life will still be worth living). If she waits a few years, she will be able to give the (different) child she will have *then* a better start in life. Notwithstanding her parents' and doctor's objections, the girl decides not to wait, and has a child whose life, predictably, is less than minimally flourishing.[29] According to Parfit, the girl does not harm her

---

[27] See Parfit, *Reasons and Persons*, pp. 357–61. For a deployment of that objection in the context of surrogate motherhood, see B. Steinbock, 'Surrogate Motherhood as Prenatal Adoption'; and Robertson, 'Procreative Liberty and the State's Burden of Proof in Regulating Non-Coital Reproduction'.

[28] See J. Woodward, 'The Non-Identity Problem', *Ethics* 96 (1986): 804–31.

[29] Parfit, *Reasons and Persons*, pp. 358–9.

child by so acting.[30] On the contrary, I believe that the girl does indeed harm the child's interests and thereby wrongs him. For consider: if P is under an obligation to R to do A at time t_1, then surely he is under an obligation to R at time t not knowingly to do anything then that will make it impossible for him to do A at t_1. Now, assume that having a child at age fourteen makes it impossible for the girl to fulfil her obligations to her child once he is born, such as her obligation to provide him with the proper level of material and emotional care. In having that child at t, the girl harms him (in so far as she will not be able to further his interests in receiving such care) and to such an extent as to wrong him (since she has an obligation to him to provide him with such care).

Against the non-identity view, then, a proponent of the harm-to-children objection to surrogacy contracts could hold that although surrogate mothers and commissioning parents cause children to exist, they nevertheless harm them in so doing, and to such an extent that one cannot have the power to enter them; indeed, that they should be outlawed. The question, thus, is whether those children are indeed harmed, and if so to what extent. The commodification objection often reappears here: as we saw in section 8.2.1, it is sometimes said by opponents of surrogacy that both surrogate mothers and commissioning parents are committed to regarding the children born from those contracts as commodified property. I rebutted that view there, but to reiterate briefly, assuming, *arguendo*, that parties do indeed buy and sell a child, it does not follow that they treat her as property, simply because, in buying and selling her, they transfer to one another only those rights that they have over her; and those rights are *not* property rights. Rather, they are rights to look after her *in her best interest*.

Proponents of the harm-to-children objection to surrogacy contracts are not satisfied by the foregoing point. They insist that even if the surrogate mother and the commissioning parents do not regard the child as property, their relationship to her is contaminated, as it were, by the fact that payment was given and accepted: for, while it is possible for the parents and the surrogate mother to assign non-monetary value to the child, it is impossible for them not to assign her monetary value *as well*. After all, in selecting a particular surrogate mother, whose gamete, let us not forget, 'goes into' creating the child, they will have paid for the latter's attributes And that, it is said, will harm the child. For a parental relationship in which such value is assigned to the child, even in coexistence with a non-monetary value, violates the norms of parental love, whereby parents love their child unconditionally and passionately, always act in her best interest, and *only* do so. And violating those norms harms children, in two ways: first, to the extent that commissioning parents can pay for surrogate mothers with certain genetic characteristics, their attitude to their children is likely to be that of a

---

[30] Parfit believes, though, that she ought not to conceive, on the grounds that, 'If in either of two outcomes the same number of people would ever live, it would be worse if those who live are worse off, or have a lower quality of life, than those who would have lived.' (*Reasons and Persons*, p. 360.)

consumer satisfied (or not, as the case may be) with the 'product' he has bought, rather than of a parent who loves her child unconditionally; and, second, a child thus created is likely to be harmed by the knowledge that her birth mother abandoned her, not in her best interest, but because she was paid to do so.[31]

It will not do to deny, in response, that the foregoing considerations fail to justify prohibiting surrogacy contracts, on the grounds that very few children are born through such contracts, and that 'market trading in parental rights and duties will take place at the margin, not at the centre, of childbearing practices'.[32] For, if it is indeed the case that the children so created cannot but be given monetary value and that they incur serious harm as a result, that might be reason enough to outlaw the practice.

In the light of my argument against the commodification objection to organ sales in section 6.3.1, this objection to surrogacy contracts is particularly interesting.[33] The former, you recall, has it that the commodification of organs hampers the development of an altruistic, and therefore desirable, social ethos. In reply, I noted that the monetary and non-monetary meaning of a good can coexist: first, in that we can in one context pay no attention to its monetary meaning and pay it attention in another context; and, second, in that we can demand money in exchange for a good and at the same time exchange that good for non-money-regarding reasons. The commodification objection to surrogacy I am examining here holds, in effect, that the coexistence of both monetary and non-monetary meanings to the child thus created does harm her, and sufficiently so as to warrant moral, and legal, impermissibility.

However, the objection fails, for two reasons. First, it may be that some commissioning parents will indeed fail to love their child if she fails to display whatever desirable characteristics the surrogate mother is thought to have. But it may also be that many would not, just as parents who are disappointed because their child does not have a musical ear or lacks athletic abilities (usually) do not, as a result, fail to love her. Second, that a surrogate mother's reason for entering the contract should be (in part) financial does not mean that she will not come to develop an attachment to the child she is carrying; accordingly, she might end up

---

[31] Anderson, 'Is Women's Labor a Commodity?', at 75ff. See also A. Capron and M. Radin, 'Choosing Family Law over Contract Law as a Paradigm for Surrogate Motherhood' in Gostin (ed.), *Surrogate Motherhood*; G. J. Annas, 'Fairy Tales Surrogate Mothers Tell'; Radin, *Contested Commodities*, p. 137. Note that it is possible to deploy this objection to surrogacy contracts whilst at the same time conceding that they do not involve buying a child: for the objection need not deny that parents only have very limited rights over their children to drive home the point that they will tend to assign them monetary value if allowed to have them through a surrogacy contract.

[32] R. Arneson, 'Commodification and Commercial Surrogacy', *Philosophy and Public Affairs* 21 (1992): 132–64, at 142.

[33] As Arneson remarks, the objection applies to partial, not full, surrogacy, since parents who use their own gametes only pay for the surrogate mother's gestational service, and do not assign monetary value to the child's attributes, and thereby to the child itself. See his 'Commodification and Commercial Surrogacy'.

relinquishing her rights over the child not (merely) because she will get paid, but rather because she thinks that (for whatever reason) she is not the best person to bring her up.

Let us assume, for the sake of argument, that the surrogate mother does not so relate to her child, and that she relinquishes her rights over it not because it is in that child's interest, but because she will receive money for so doing (or indeed because she has altruistic concerns for the commissioning parents' welfare). To argue that she culpably fails to behave to her child as dictated by the norms of parental love assumes that genetic and gestational mothers are bound by those norms, even if they do not rear their child. But why should that be? Of course, children thus born may suffer psychological damage akin to that suffered by children who are given up for adoption, some of whom never fully recover from the fact that they have been abandoned by their birth mother. Be that as it may, we have no reason to believe that they will not receive love, care, and commitment from their rearing parents. To think that the benefit of being reared in a loving family cannot make up for the harm they might incur for having been abandoned by their gestational mother, and to insist that such harm is such as to render surrogacy contracts impermissible, seems to go one step too far, mostly because we do not have enough evidence to go on: indeed, we simply do not know the extent to which children are affected by the practice. Of course, as a matter of policy one ought to be sensitive to the welfare of those children. But, here again to me, at best this seems to tell in favour of regulating, rather than outlawing, surrogacy contracts.[34] To this issue I finally turn.

8.4 THE REPRODUCTIVE CONTRACT

To recapitulate, I have argued that, at the bar of autonomy, individuals have the moral right, and should have the legal right, to buy and sell reproductive services. In the course of making that argument I undertook on several occasions to tease out the policy implications of such a view, and it is now time to make good on my promise.

But why such concerns? Why not leave prospective surrogate mothers and commissioning parents free to contract as they wish? In fact, or so someone might be tempted to press, it would be unacceptably paternalistic, and thus autonomy-restricting, to deny them the legal power to do so, let alone to interfere with them should they attempt to make such an agreement. However, as we saw in section 6.4, regulating a practice by invoking some important interests of the

---

[34] I have prescinded from addressing other harm-to-children objections which target not merely surrogacy agreements but new reproductive technologies in general. Available research suggests that children so conceived suffer few, if any, psychological ill effects. See R. Edelmann, 'Psychological Assessment in Surrogate Motherhood', in R. Cook and S. D. Sclater (eds.), *Surrogate Motherhood: International Perspectives*.

parties need not be paternalistic. More specifically, regulation is compatible with an anti-paternalistic stand on those matters when grounded in the parties' interests in being paid, or having to pay, a fair price, having access to as much information is possible, and so on. In addition, regulation is not paternalistic if it is grounded in the parties' interest in being treated with the respect owed to persons. For a contract which would violate the requirement of respect is one which the parties lack the moral power to enter, and which should not, therefore, be regarded as legally valid, but it ought not to be made unlawful. In fact, for reasons adduced in sections 8.2 and 8.3, there are good grounds for not criminalizing surrogacy contracts of that kind, which is to say that individuals who wish to enter such agreements ought not to be interfered with. To regulate surrogacy contracts along the lines suggested below so as to help their parties preserve their opportunities for self-respect is not tantamount to paternalistically preventing them from entering contracts under the terms of which they would lose those opportunities.

In addition, although contracts which do conform to those guidelines ought not to be treated as void, they ought to be treated as voidable. A void surrog-acy contract is one where parties' rights and obligations vis-à-vis one another are left unaffected, so that the surrogate mother is deemed never to have undertaken to relinquish her rights over the child, and is not liable to repay the money she received for the child. In contrast, a voidable surrogacy contract is one where the parties are under (reasonable) contractual obligations to one another but can change their mind (e.g. the surrogate mother keeps the child but loses her enti-tlement to a fee, the commissioning parents do not take the child but have to compensate the surrogate mother for labour); it is also one where, if all parties comply with the terms of the contract, the state will confer on the commissioning parents full rights and responsibility over the child (provided, of course, that it is not against the child's best interest).

As we saw, opponents of surrogacy contracts raise a number of concerns which, as I argue here, can be alleviated in large part through careful regulation of the practice. One such concern pertains to the restrictions which many contracts impose on surrogate mothers' lives. I conceded in section 8.3.3 that, as a mat-ter of fact, some surrogacy contracts impose far greater restrictions on a woman's life than is thought to be necessary for the foetus's sake, most notably with respect to drinking, smoking, attending antenatal appointments, and so on. One might think that a contract stipulating that the surrogate mother should only drink reas-onably, should attend antenatal appointments once a month from the second trimester onwards, and so on, should be regarded as enforceable, in so far as it would only impose reasonable restrictions on her. Note, though, that it would be impossible to ensure that the surrogate mother complies with such obligations without unacceptably invading her privacy in the course of the pregnancy (such as making her medical records available to the commissioning parents or the surrogacy firm, for example). Accordingly, contracts imposing such restrictions should be regarded as imposing a duty to perform only in the sense of giving rise to action for damages (so that whereas a surrogate mother could not be monitored for excessive drinking, she might be liable for damages should the baby be born with foetal alcohol syndrome).

Another concern, raised by those who worry about exploitation, is that surrogate mothers are manipulated by commissioning parents and surrogacy firms (but mostly the latter) into regarding their childbearing as mostly an act of altruism, as a result of which they are under pressure not to demand as high a price as they could get for their labour. But here again, regulation, rather than prohibition, is a sensible way to deal with this problem. As a matter of policy, we could insist, for example, that a surrogate mother be paid a (decent) hourly wage for the whole duration of the pregnancy. For gestational labour is not a nine-to-five job: rather, it enacts constant demands on the mother, not merely in so far as it imposes constraints on the mother's life with respect to nutrition, activities, work, and so on, but also in so far as it imposes on her heavy health costs, such as sleeplessness, morning sickness, nauseas, cramps, heartburn, and incontinence, and this at any time of the day and night. It is hard to think of any kind of labour where the 'worker's' whole person—body and mind—is pressed into service, twenty-four hours a day, seven days a week, for nine months. Payment should reflect that.[35] To claim that it should not reflects the view that women somehow are not entitled to command high salaries—a view to which those who worry about exploitation should not be sympathetic.

But could payment be more than compensation for labour and expenses? Most commentators deny that it can be, on the grounds that to allow surrogate mothers to 'make a profit' out of their childbearing ability is tantamount to baby selling. Now, in so far as the fact that surrogacy may indeed involve the sale and purchase of babies does not suffice to render it impermissible, that objection to paying surrogate mothers as opposed to merely compensating them for labour and expenses fails. In any event, to insist that the surrogate mother can only be paid for labour and expenses is odd. For a start, in partial surrogacy, she is also paid for her egg; moreover, in all cases of surrogacy, the commissioning parents are not paying for her merely to create a child. Nor are they paying for being given joint rights—with her—over the child. Rather, they are paying for her to relinquish her rights over the child. Why should she not charge for that, given that she is not under a duty, at the bar of justice, to do it?

So much, then, for protecting the surrogate mother's financial interests. Those of the commissioning parents should not be overlooked either. In section 8.3.2 we saw that a surrogate mother who can credibly threaten not to relinquish her rights over the child unless the commissioning parents pay her more than was initially agreed is in a position to exploit the latter's emotional vulnerability. As I noted then, this is no reason to prohibit surrogacy agreements: rather, it is a

---

[35] See L. Andrews, 'Surrogate Motherhood: The Challenge for Feminists', in Gostin (ed.), *Surrogate Motherhood*.

reason to regulate them, for example along the lines adopted in Israel, whereby the Approvals Committee, which oversees all surrogacy contracts, is given notice of the financial terms agreed upon by the parties, and whereby attempts by either party to renege on those terms is deemed unlawful.[36]

However, a more important issue is the surrogate mother's right, or lack thereof, to change her mind. There are two ways in which she might want to do so: she might want to abort, or she might refuse to relinquish her rights over the child once it is born. In both cases, I believe that she should be allowed to change her mind—that is to say, that a contract under the terms of which she is bound to carry on with the pregnancy and give up the child should be regarded as null and void. For, in undertaking neither to have an abortion nor to keep the child, she forecloses the possibility of protecting herself from the serious physical dangers caused by her pregnancy, as well as from the emotional dangers caused by her alienation from her child, and in turn denies herself opportunities for self-respect.

Let us start with abortion. It is sometimes said, in the literature on surrogacy, that in so far as a husband does not have a right that his wife carry a pregnancy to term, a commissioning father does not have a right that the surrogate mother carry his child to term. However, those two cases are disanalogous in the crucial way that a woman is not bound by contract to have her husband's child, whereas a surrogate mother does enter a contract to that effect. In order to show, thus, that a surrogate mother ought to be allowed to change her mind, one must show that her interest in not going through with the pregnancy is strong enough to nullify any contractual obligation to continue with the pregnancy which she may have imposed on herself. Now, as we saw in Chapter 7, it is a well-established principle of contract and labour law that no one can be sued for specific performance of a personal service they have undertaken to perform. Thus, a worker can walk out of a job, on the grounds that he found it too dangerous, too unpleasant, too risky, and so on, without being dragged back to work. Likewise, a woman should be allowed to terminate a pregnancy on those grounds—all the more so as she, unlike most other workers, may be faced with the realization that, should she carry this child to term and relinquish her rights over it, she will incur emotional costs far higher, and far more destructive, than she had anticipated.

Relatedly, just as a surrogate mother should be allowed to have an abortion if she so wishes (under the constraints of what counts as a morally permissible abortion), she should also be allowed *not* to have one, irrespective of the commissioning couple's wishes. This is quite important, as there have been cases where a surrogate mother was contractually bound to terminate the pregnancy if the foetus were found to suffer from genetic abnormalities. Such contracts should, I believe, be deemed null and void: just as a woman ought not to have to subject her body to pregnancy even if she undertook initially to do so, she ought not to

---

[36] See R. Schutz, 'Surrogacy in Israel: An Analysis of the Law in Practice', in Cook and Sclater (eds.), *Surrogate Motherhood: International Perspectives*.

have to subject her body to an abortion for the sake of ensuring that the commissioning parents can implement their specific conception of the good (to wit, a life free of responsibility for a disabled child), all the more so as she might thereby jeopardize her own prospects for a minimally flourishing life. As it happens, abortion is not a risk-free procedure (although it is less risky than pregnancy and childbirth), as it can cause serious fertility problems. Moreover, most women who elect to have an abortion regard this as one of the most difficult decisions of their life, the psychological and emotional impact of which can be felt for decades. The costs of being made to have an abortion against one's will are far higher; so high, in fact, that no woman should be asked to incur them.

The question remains, of course, of the commissioning father's obligations in respect of this child he no longer wants. If one thinks (and, I believe, rightly so) that a man lacks a right to ask a woman who is pregnant by him to abort, and that he has an obligation to provide support for his child even though he did not want him to be born, then a commissioning father who would rather have the surrogate mother abort should not be exonerated from such obligations. To be clear: my point is not that the surrogate mother has a right against him that he support her even though she decided, against his wishes, to bring the child into existence. Rather, my point is that her decision does not extinguish his obligation *to the child* to support him. Fatherhood and its attendant obligations to one's offspring are a risk of both sexual intercourse and non-coital procreation through surrogacy.[37] Note, though, that fatherhood and its attendant rights in respect to one's offspring are also a consequence of either procreative act. If one thinks that an unwed father generally has parental rights vis-à-vis his children, the commissioning father ought to be given those rights if he so wishes: there is absolutely no reason to treat conception through surrogacy differently from conception (coital or otherwise) between two partners.

A surrogate mother ought to be allowed to change her mind not merely by terminating the pregnancy, but by refusing to relinquish her rights over the child. As a matter of fact, cases where the surrogate mother changes her mind and refuses to hand over the child are very rare.[38] Still, this is probably one of the most sensitive issues raised by surrogacy contracts, and one where the no-specific performance rule is of no help, since what is required of the surrogate mother is not the performance of her service (that performance finishes with the birth), but rather the handing over of the child whom she created by performing that service.

Interestingly, public opinion surveys suggest that, for a majority of people, 'a contract is a contract', and thus that the surrogate mother ought not to be allowed to keep the child.[39] At this juncture, some writers on the topic argue

---

[37] For the opposite view, see Field, *Surrogate Motherhood*, ch. 9.

[38] Studies quote figures of between 1 per cent and 5 per cent. See E. Jackson, *Regulating Reproduction* (Oxford: Hart, 2001), p. 282.

[39] See Field, *Surrogate Motherhood*, p. 67.

that adoption law, rather than contract law, should govern surrogacy contracts, in which case a surrogate mother can decide to keep the child, just as a woman who, whilst pregnant, has agreed to give up her child for adoption by a particular couple, can change her mind after birth.[40] However, one can also invoke contract law to support the view that a surrogate mother ought to be allowed to change her mind, for two reasons. First, contract law recognizes that some contracts are voidable on the grounds that one party engaged in it by mistake, without realizing the full impact of what they were doing. By that token, it can recognize that a woman who makes a surrogacy contract and later decides she cannot part from her child has made a mistake in not realizing that she would develop such strong attachment to the latter.[41]

Second, contract law recognizes unilateral contracts, that is, contracts of the form 'if you do this for me I will pay you £x', where the party who is offered the money retains the option to decide whether or not to proceed. Now, there are few things as viscerally important to most individuals as their relationship with their children. Accordingly, in the light of the emotional costs the surrogate mother would incur if she were made to abandon a child who is genetically hers and whom she has carried in her body for nine months, it makes sense to conceive of surrogacy contracts as unilateral contracts under the terms of which she can decide whether or not to give up the child. This would imply that, should she decide not to give it up, she would not have to pay damages to the commissioning parents, although she would, of course, forfeit her right to the fee.

In sum, 'a contract is a contract' indeed, but so to view surrogacy does not preclude the possibility of allowing the surrogate mother to keep the child. Does it allow commissioning parents to change their mind once the pregnancy is under way, or after birth, in cases where the surrogate mother is willing to do her part of the bargain and to relinquish her rights over the child? This situation has sometimes arisen when the child was found to be disabled. Some commentators believe that they should not, on the grounds that, since the child would not exist but for their having taken steps to that effect, and since it is in the interest of the child to have a stable family, they should assume responsibility for the child no matter what.[42] There are reasons to doubt the wisdom of such a policy, however, not least because it clearly is not in the interest of a child to be reared by parents who wish they had not created him. I confess not to know whether it would be

---

[40] See Capron and Radin, 'Choosing Family Law over Contract Law', in Gostin (ed.), *Surrogate Motherhood*.

[41] Field, *Surrogate Motherhood*, p. 82.

[42] For example, Field, *Surrogate Motherhood*, p. 103. A well-known American example of that kind is the Stiver–Mallahoff case: Mrs Stiver, who had agreed to act as a surrogate mother for the Mallahoffs, gave birth to a child who presented a very high risk of mental retardation. Initially, neither party wanted to keep the child. After it was proved that the child was, in fact, Mr Stiver's, the Stivers agreed to keep it. Such cases are, in any event, extremely rare. In the UK, no commissioning parents have ever defaulted on their contract.

better to regard them, and not the surrogate mother, as the child's parents. In any event, the fact that whoever has responsibility for the child's welfare might choose to exercise it by having the child adopted should not count as an argument against surrogacy contracts, any more than the fact that biological parents might decide to have their disabled newborn adopted should count against coital reproduction.

I should like to end with a few words on surrogacy firms. In countries where surrogacy contracts are allowed, those firms act as intermediaries between surrogate mothers and commissioning parents, and have been criticized for putting profit before the contracting parties' welfare. More specifically, they have been accused of failing to screen participants adequately, for showing excessive deference towards commissioning parents at the expense of surrogate mothers, for exploiting the latter, and so on.[43] In fact, many of the criticisms which are levelled against surrogacy contracts, and which we reviewed in section 8.3, target surrogacy firms rather than commissioning parents. Accordingly, advocates of the criminalization of surrogacy contracts often argue that, unlike commissioning parents and surrogate mothers, such firms ought to be liable to prosecution. However, although abuses such as described in the literature are unacceptable and should be checked, to make acting as intermediaries between parents and surrogate mother a criminal offence would not be appropriate, for at least two reasons. First, in so far as neither commissioning parents nor surrogate mothers would be prosecuted, it is likely that they would still enter a contract but would do so entirely privately, with very few guarantees of the other party's willingness and commitment to go through with it, and, most importantly, with no psychological support throughout the process (a worrisome implication of the criminalization approach; all experts on the topic, whether or not they approve of surrogacy, agree that such support is crucial to the success of the practice). Intermediaries are useful not merely in putting commissioning parents and surrogate mothers in touch, but in accompanying them throughout the whole process.

Second, the fact that important actors in a given practice behave appallingly does not on the face of it call for criminalization, unless one can show that regulation would not work. As it happens, it seems possible to regulate surrogacy firms in such a way as to avoid such abuses, at least up to a point. Thus, if one is concerned at the extent to which firms' conduct vis-à-vis their clients is shaped by the money they receive from them, one can envisage a system where surrogacy arrangements are entrusted to not-for-profit firms, such as the UK-based COTS (Childlessness Overcome Through Surrogacy),[44] or with a governmental regulatory body, as is the case in Israel. One can also envisage setting a statutory

---

[43] For an interesting study of some of the best-known surrogacy firms in the USA, see Ragonné, *Surrogate Motherhood*, ch.1.

[44] See G. Dodd, 'Surrogacy and the Law in Britain: Users' Perspectives', in Cook and Sclater (eds.), *Surrogate Motherhood: International Perspectives*.

minimum fee for surrogate mothers, to be reviewed from time to time, and which surrogacy firms could not challenge.

8.5 CONCLUSION

To conclude, I have argued that women have the power to make a contract with commissioning parents, whereby they undertake to have one of their eggs fertilized by the man's sperm, and to carry the resulting child to term, against financial payment. Contracts so made, I claimed, ought to be recognized as legally valid, as opposed to unlawful and void, but voidable. The surrogate mother thus retains the right to change her mind and terminate the pregnancy or to keep the child. Conversely, commissioning parents have the power to make such contracts with surrogate mothers. Under the terms of those contracts, the surrogate mother confers on commissioning parents some rights over her body, and has a right against the state that it let her do so. Commissioning parents, similarly, have a right against the state that it let them acquire some rights over the surrogate mother's body.

Objections standardly raised against the foregoing points have been shown to fail: regulation, as we saw, goes a long way towards alleviating concerns expressed over the commodification of women's labour, their exploitation, and gender equality. Of course, regulation will not fully protect surrogate mothers, in particular from emotional exploitation and vulnerability, since manipulative behaviour by firms and parents can take place behind closed doors. But the fact that regulation cannot fully protect surrogate mothers cannot be a reason for outlawing surrogacy contracts, simply because, generally, we cannot and will not ever be able to live in a risk-free society, particularly one free of the emotional risks attendant on parenthood. Nor, in fact, should we aspire to do so.

Conclusion

At the outset of this book, I took for granted, with sufficientist theories of distributive justice, that individuals have welfare rights to the material resources they need in order to lead a minimally flourishing life (that is, income, housing, and health care). As I noted there, justice is not thought to require of the comparatively well off that they provide the needy with resources other than material goods. In particular, it is not thought to require of the well off that they provide the needy with personal resources such as body parts and personal services: any such requirement, the argument goes, would constitute an unacceptable interference in their lives; it would, in fact, undermine their autonomy; indeed, if we are to believe Dworkin, it would destroy their personhood. At first sight, it seems that the argument is correct, particularly if the reason why justice requires of the well off merely that they meet the needy's needs (and not bring about material equality) is that those who are in a position to help have the prerogative to accord greater weight to their projects, plans, and goals than they do to those of others—once the needs of all are met. For if it is true, as many would argue, that the coercively directed provision of personal services does indeed undermine individual autonomy (let alone destroy personhood), then it cannot be mandated by a theory of justice which makes space for individual autonomy in the way just suggested.

My aim, in this book, was to show, first, that justice in fact requires the provision of personal resources such as body parts and personal services, and, second, that it can do so without undermining individual autonomy. On the first count, I argued in Chapters 2–5 that the rationale for conferring on individuals welfare rights to material resources also applies to the provision of emergency rescues and longer-term services in the welfare sector (Chapters 2 and 3 respectively), as well as (more controversially) to the provision of cadaveric and live body parts (Chapters 4 and 5 respectively).

On the second count, I showed that the coercive provision of personal services does not undermine the autonomy of the able-bodied (of those, then, who are comparatively well off, relative to the needy and imperilled, in the way that matters here). I also argued that it is compatible with the view that individuals in general (the needy and the able-bodied) have rights to sell body parts and personal services, under certain conditions. Even though the able-bodied do have to provide emergency rescues, work for a year in the welfare sector, make their organs available at death, and provide some organs whilst alive, they nevertheless have ample time and resources to devote to their plans, projects, and goals. Moreover, they are not required to provide body parts and personal services if doing so would render their own life minimally flourishing. There are, in short, limits to the sacrifices that they can be expected to make for the sake of the needy and the imperilled.

In addition, the able-bodied have rights to sell body parts and personal services in all those cases where they are not under a duty to provide them for free at the bar of justice, either because the body part or service in question is not one which one can be under a duty to help, or because those who need or want them are not eligible for help. Accordingly, the able-bodied have rights to sell (some of) their organs to some of those who need or want them; they also have the right to sell sexual and reproductive services. Note, furthermore, that the needy and imperilled also have such rights. As a result, the able-bodied are in a position to maximize their autonomy in two different ways: by selling body parts and personal services so as to generate the income they need in order to implement their conception of the good; and by having access to the body and persons of those who might themselves have been recipient of their help, but who can offer something (a body part, a service) which the able-bodied now want or need. By way of an example, we saw in Chapter 8 that women have the right to hire their body out for reproductive services, and that individuals who wish to be parents and cannot do so unless they resort to surrogacy have the right to purchase those services. This suggests that the able-bodied, who are sometimes under an obligation to provide personal resources to those who need them, do nevertheless have a number of autonomy-protecting rights—the right to use their womb as a source of income, and the right to purchase reproductive services so as to implement their conception of the good; in that instance, parenthood.

At the end of a long trail of arguments, then, we have reached the following conclusion. Not so long ago, being a liberal meant, amongst other things, upholding rights of private property and opposing coercive taxation for purposes other than their protection. To paraphrase Dworkin, it meant drawing a prophylactic line around individuals' property and person. That line, though, acted as a prophylactic not merely by preventing third parties from accessing individuals' property and person, but also by preventing those individuals themselves from making their person in general and body in particular available to others against payment in areas other than standard labour.

A good deal of liberal philosophical thinking over the last hundred years has consisted in redelineating individuals' rights over their property: nowadays, many philosophers who call themselves liberals would claim that we must ensure that the needy have a right against the well off to the material resources they need in order to lead a minimally flourishing life. They still insist, however, that the body and person of individuals be protected from the demands of the needy; some of them also stress that they should be protected from individuals' willingness to sell some of their organs or hire themselves out for sexual and reproductive services. As I have shown here, the liberal enterprise cannot stop at relaxing individuals' hold on their material resources: it must go further, and relax their hold on some of their body parts as well as on the deployment of their personal skills; at the same time, however, it must recognize that individuals do have rights to engage in organ sales, prostitution, and surrogacy contracts—in short, to make parts of themselves available against payment in areas hitherto confined to the spheres of altruism, love, and desire.

If I am correct, those who defend commercialization and reject confiscation on the grounds that we have an absolute right to control what happens to our person are misguided; and those who might be tempted to defend confiscation and reject commercialization on the grounds that the basic necessities of life ought not to be distributed through the market would be equally misguided. Surprisingly, perhaps, confiscation and commercialization do go hand in hand. More generally, one need not draw a prophylactic line around the body in particular and the person in general in order to be an egalitarian liberal.

Bibliography

Ackerman, B., *Private Property and the Constitution* (New Haven, Conn.: Yale University Press, 1977).

_____ and Alstott, A., *The Stakeholder Society* (New Haven, Conn.: Yale University Press, 1999).

Anderson, E., 'Is Women's Labor a Commodity?', *Philosophy and Public Affairs* 19 (1990): 71–82.

_____, *Values in Ethics and Economics* (Cambridge, Mass.: Harvard University Press, 1993).

Anderson, M., 'Comment: The Dirty Work Philosophy of National Service', in W. M. Evers (ed.), *National Service*.

Andrews, L., 'Surrogate Motherhood: The Challenge for Feminists', in L. Gostin (ed.), *Surrogate Motherhood*.

Annas, G. J., 'Fairy Tales Surrogate Mothers Tell', in L. Gostin (ed.), *Surrogate Motherhood*.

Archard, D., 'Selling Yourself: Titmuss' Argument against a Market in Blood', *Journal of Ethics* 6 (2002): 87–103.

Arneson, R., 'Equality and Equal Opportunity for Welfare', *Philosophical Studies* 56 (1989): 77–93.

_____, 'Commodification and Commercial Surrogacy', *Philosophy and Public Affairs* 21 (1992): 132–64.

Ascher, M. L., 'Curtailing Inherited Wealth', *Michigan Law Review* 86 (1990): 69–151.

Audi, R., 'The Morality and Utility of Organ Transplantation', *Utilitas* 8 (1996): 140–58.

Bandow, D., 'National Service Initiatives', in W. M. Evers (ed.), *National Service*.

Barnett, A., et al., 'Improving Organ Donation: Compensation versus Markets', in A. L. Caplan and D. H. Coelho (eds.), *The Ethics of Organ Transplants*.

Barry, B., *Political Argument* (London: Harvester Wheatsheaf, revised edition, 1990).

_____, *Justice as Impartiality* (Oxford: Oxford University Press, 1995).

Barry, K., *The Prostitution of Sexuality* (New York: New York University Press, 1995).

Ber, R., 'Ethical Issues in Gestational Surrogacy', *Theoretical Medicine and Bioethics* 21 (2000): 153–69.

Boddington, P., 'Organ Donation After Death—Should I Decide, or Should My Family?', *Journal of Applied Philosophy* 15 (1998): 69–81.

Brecher, B., 'Surrogacy, Moral Individualism, and the Moral Climate', in J. D. G. Ecans (ed.), *Moral Philosophy and Contemporary Problems*.

Callahan, J., 'On Harming the Dead', *Ethics* 97 (1987): 341–52.

Caplan, A. L., 'Living Dangerously: The Morality of Using Living Persons as Suppliers of Liver Lobes for Transplantation', *Cambridge Journal of Medical Ethics* 1 (1992): 311–17.

_____ and D. H. Coelho (eds.), *The Ethics of Organ Transplants* (Amherst, NY: Prometheus Books, 1998).

Capron, A. and Radin, M., 'Choosing Family Law over Contract Law as a Paradigm for Surrogate Motherhood', in L. Gostin (ed.), *Surrogate Motherhood*.

Carens, J., *Equality, Moral Incentives and the Market* (Chicago: Chicago University Press, 1987).

Chadwick, R., 'The Market for Bodily Parts: Kant and Duties to Oneself', *Journal of Applied Philosophy* 6 (1989): 129–39.

Chapman, B., 'Politics and National Service: A Virus Attacks the Voluntary Sector', in W. M. Evers (ed.), *National Service*.

Charo, R., 'Legislative Approaches to Surrogate Motherhood', in L. Gostin (ed.), *Surrogate Motherhood*.

Cohen, G. A., 'On the Currency of Egalitarian Justice', *Ethics* 99 (1989): 916–44.

——, *Self-Ownership, Freedom and Equality* (Cambridge: Cambridge University Press, 1995).

Cohen, L., 'Where it Hurts: Indian Material for an Ethics of Organ Transplantation', *Daedalus* 128 (1999): 135–65.

Cohen-Christofidis, M., 'Talent, Slavery and Envy', in J. Burley (ed.), *Dworkin and His Critics* (Oxford: Blackwell, 2004).

Cook, R. and Sclater, S. Day (eds.), *Surrogate Motherhood: International Perspectives* (Oxford: Hart, 2003).

Darwall, S. L., 'Two Kinds of Respect', *Ethics* 88 (1977): 36–49.

Davidson, J. O'Connell, *Prostitution, Power and Freedom* (Ann Arbor: University of Michigan Press, 1998).

Dickensen, D. and Widdershoven, G., 'Ethical Issues in Limb Transplants', *Bioethics* 15 (2001): 110–24.

Dillon, R. S., 'Self-Respect: Moral, Emotional, Political', *Ethics* 107 (1997): 226–49.

Dworkin, G., 'Markets and Morals: The Case for Organ Sales', in G. Dworkin (ed.), *Morality, Harm and the Law* (Boulder, Colo.: Westview Press, 1994).

Dworkin, R., *Taking Rights Seriously* (London: Duckworth, 1978).

——, 'What is Equality? Part II: Equality of Resources', *Philosophy and Public Affairs* 10 (1981): 283–345.

——, 'Comment on Narveson: In Defence of Equality', *Social Philosophy and Policy* 1 (1983): 24–40.

Eberle, C., *Religious Convictions in Liberal Politics* (Cambridge: Cambridge University Press, 2002).

Ecans, J. D. G. (ed.), *Moral Philosophy and Contemporary Problems* (Cambridge: Cambridge University Press, 1987).

Edelmann, R., 'Psychological Assessment in Surrogate Motherhood', in R. Cook and Sclater (eds.), *Surrogate Motherhood: International Perspectives*.

Enoch, D., 'A Right to Violate One's Duty', *Law and Philosophy* 21 (2002): 355–94.

Ericsson, L., 'Charges against Prostitution: An Attempt at a Philosophical Assessment', *Ethics* 90 (1980): 335–66.

Evers, W. M. (ed.), *National Service: Pro and Con* (Stanford: Hoover Institution Press, 1990).

Fabre, C., *Social Rights under the Constitution* (Oxford: Clarendon Press, 2000).

Feinberg, J., *Harm to Others* (Oxford: Clarendon Press, 1984).

——, *Harm to Self* (Oxford: Oxford University Press, 1986).

_____ , *Harmless Wrongdoing* (Oxford: Oxford University Press, 1988).

Field, M., *Surrogate Motherhood* (Cambridge, Mass.: Harvard University Press, 1986).

Flathman, R., *The Practice of Rights* (Cambridge: Cambridge University Press, 1976).

Fried, C., *An Anatomy of Values* (Cambridge, Mass.: Harvard University Press, 1970).

_____ , *Right and Wrong* (Cambridge, Mass.: Harvard University Press, 1978).

Garwood-Gowers, A., *Living Donor Organ Transplantation* (Aldershot: Ashgate, 1999).

Gaus, G., *Justificatory Liberalism* (Cambridge: Cambridge University Press, 1996).

Gerrand, N., 'The Misuse of Kant in the Debate about a Market for Human Body Parts', *Journal of Applied Philosophy* 16 (1999): 59–67.

Gorham, E., *National Service, Citizenship, and Political Education* (New York: State University of New York Press, 1992).

Gostin, L. (ed.), *Surrogate Motherhood: Politics and Privacy* (Bloomington: Indiana University Press, 1990).

Goyal, M., et al., 'Economic and Health Consequences of Selling a Kidney in India', *Journal of the American Medical Association* 288 (2002): 1589–93.

Harris, J., 'The Survival Lottery', *Philosophy* 50 (1975): 81–7.

_____ , *Clones, Genes, and Immortality* (Oxford: Oxford University Press, 1992).

_____ , *Property and Justice* (Oxford: Oxford University Press, 1996).

Haslett, D., 'Is Inheritance Justified?', *Philosophy and Public Affairs* 15 (1986): 122–55.

Hohfeld, W. N., *Fundamental Legal Conceptions as Applied in Judicial Reasoning* (New Haven, Conn.: Yale University Press, 1919).

Jackson, E., *Regulating Reproduction* (Oxford: Hart, 2001).

James, W., 'The Moral Equivalent of War', *International Conciliation* 27 (1910): 8–20.

Javda, V., et al., 'Surrogacy: The Experience of Surrogate Mothers', *Human Reproduction* 18 (2003): 2196–204.

Kagan, S., *The Limits of Morality* (Oxford: Clarendon Press, 1989).

Kant, I., *Lectures on Ethics*, eds. P. Heath and J. B. Schneewind (Cambridge: Cambridge University Press, 1997).

Kleinig, J., 'Good Samaritanism', *Philosophy and Public Affairs* 5 (1976): 382–407.

Kornegay, R. J., 'Is Commercial Surrogacy Baby Selling?', *Journal of Applied Philosophy* 7 (1990): 45–50.

Korsgaard, C., 'Personal Identity and the Unity of Agency: A Kantian Response to Parfit', *Philosophy and Public Affairs* 18 (1989): 101–32.

Kramer, M., 'Rights without Trimmings', in M. Kramer, N. E. Simmonds, and H. Steiner, *A Debate over Rights: Philosophical Enquiries* (Oxford: Clarendon Press, 1998).

Lamb, D., *Organ Transplants and Ethics* (London: Routledge, 1990).

Lamont, J., 'Incentive Income, Deserved Income and Economic Rents', *Journal of Political Philosophy* 5 (1997): 26–46.

Larmore, C., *Patterns of Moral Complexity* (Cambridge: Cambridge University Press, 1987).

Le Grand, J., 'Markets, Welfare and Equality', in J. Le Grand and S. Estrin (eds.), *Market Socialism* (Oxford: Oxford University Press, 1989).

_____ and Nissan, D., *A Capital Idea: Start-Up Grants for Young People* (London: Fabian Society, 2000).

Levenbook, B., 'Harming the Dead, Once Again', *Ethics* 95 (1985): 162–4.

Levy, M. B., 'Liberal Equality and Inherited Wealth', *Political Theory* 11 (1983): 545–64.

McIntyre, A., 'Guilty Bystanders? On the Legitimacy of Duty to Rescue Statutes', *Philosophy and Public Affairs* 23 (1994): 157–91.

Mack, E., 'Bad Samaritanism and the Causation of Harm', *Philosophy and Public Affairs* 9 (1980): 230–59.

——, 'Dominos and the Fear of Commodification', in J. R. Pennock and J. W. Chapman (eds.), *Markets and Justice: Nomos XXXI* (New York: New York University Press, 1989).

Mackie, J., 'Can there be a Right-Based Moral Theory?', in J. Waldron (ed.), *Theories of Rights* (Oxford: Oxford University Press, 1984).

Macklin, R., 'Is there Anything Wrong with Surrogate Motherhood?', in L. Gostin (ed.), *Surrogate Motherhood.*

McLachlan, H. V. and Swales, J. K., 'Babies, Child Bearers and Commodification: Anderson, Brazier et al., and the Political Economy of Commercial Surrogate Motherhood', *Heath Care Analysis* 8 (2000): 1–18.

McMahan, J., *The Ethics of Killing: Problems at the Margins of Life* (Oxford: Oxford University Press, 2002).

Mahoney, J., 'An Essay on Surrogacy and Feminist Thought', in L. Gostin (ed.), *Surrogate Motherhood.*

Malm, H. M., 'Liberalism, Bad Samaritan, and Legal Paternalism,' *Ethics* 106 (1995): 4–31.

——, 'Bad Samaritan Laws: Harm, Help, or Hype?', *Law and Philosophy* 19 (2000): 707–50.

Marshall, S. E., 'Bodyshopping: The Case of Prostitution', *Journal of Applied Philosophy* 16 (1999): 139–50.

Meikle, J., 'Tests Hold out the Hope of Cure for Diabetics', *Guardian*, 27 January 2001.

Merle, J. C., 'A Kantian Argument for a Duty to Donate One's Own Organs: A Reply to Nicole Gerrand', *Journal of Applied Philosophy* 17 (2000): 93–201.

Miller, D., 'Exploitation in the Market', in A. Reeve (ed.), *Modern Theories of Exploitation* (London: Sage, 1987).

——, *Principles of Social Justice* (Cambridge, Mass.: Harvard University Press, 1999).

——, 'But are they *My* Poor?', in J. Seglow (ed.), *The Ethics of Altruism* (London: Frank Cass, 2004).

Milne, H., 'Desert, Effort and Equality', *Journal of Applied Philosophy* 3 (1986): 235–43.

Moskos, C., *A Call to Civic Service—National Service for Country and Community* (New York: Free Press, 1988).

Mulgan, T., 'The Place of the Dead in Liberal Political Philosophy', *Journal of Political Philosophy* 7 (1999): 52–70.

Munzer, S., *A Theory of Property* (Cambridge: Cambridge University Press, 1990).

Murphy, L. and Nagel, T., *The Myth of Ownership: Taxes and Justice* (Oxford: Oxford University Press, 2002).

Muyskens, J., 'An Alternative Policy for Obtaining Cadaver Organs for Transplantation', *Philosophy and Public Affairs* 8 (1978): 88–99.

Nagel, T., *Equality and Partiality* (Oxford: Oxford University Press, 1991).

Narveson, J., 'On Dworkinian Equality', *Social Philosophy and Policy* 1 (1983): 1–23.

Nozick, R., *Anarchy, State and Utopia* (New York: Basic Books, 1974).

Nussbaum, M., 'Objectification', *Philosophy and Public Affairs* 24 (1995): 249–91.

_____ , ' "Whether from Reason or Prejudice": Taking Money for Personal services', in M. Nussbaum, *Sex and Social Justice* (Oxford: Oxford University Press, 1999).

_____ , *Women and Human Development* (Cambridge: Cambridge University Press, 2000).

O' Connell Davidson, J., *Prostitution, Power and Freedom* (Ann Arbor: University of Michigan Press, 1998).

Ogus, A. I., *Regulation—Legal Form and Economic Theory* (Oxford: Clarendon Press, 1994).

Oi, W., 'National Service: Who Bears the Costs and Who Reaps the Gains?', in W. M. Evers (ed.), *National Service*.

Parfit, D., *Reasons and Persons* (Oxford: Clarendon Press, 1984).

Pateman, C., *The Sexual Contract* (Cambridge: Polity, 1988).

Perkin, R. and Bennett, G., *Being a Prostitute: Prostitute Women and Prostitute Men* (Sydney: Allen and Unwin, 1985).

Perry, J. and Thomson, A., *Civic Service: What Difference does it Make?* (New York: Armonk, 2004).

Radin, M., *Contested Commodities* (Cambridge, Mass.: Harvard University Press, 1996).

Rae, S. B., *The Ethics of Commercial Surrogate Motherhood* (Westport, Conn.: Praeger, 1994).

Ragonné, H., *Surrogate Motherhood: Conception in the Heart* (Boulder, Colo.: Westview Press, 1994).

Rakowski, E., *Equal Justice* (Oxford: Oxford University Press, 1991).

Rawls, J., *Political Liberalism* (New York: Columbia University Press, 1993).

Raz, J., *The Authority of Law: Essays on Law and Morality* (Oxford: Clarendon Press, 1979).

_____ , *The Morality of Freedom* (Oxford: Clarendon Press, 1986).

Ripstein, A., 'Three Duties to Rescue: Moral, Civil, and Criminal', *Law and Philosophy* 19 (2000): 751–79.

Robertson, J. A., 'Procreative Liberty and the State's Burden of Proof in Regulating Non-Coital Reproduction', in L. Gostin (ed.), *Surrogate Motherhood.*

Rudzinski, A. W., 'The Duty to Rescue: A Comparative Analysis', in J. M. Ratcliffe (ed.), *The Good Samaritan and the Law* (Gloucester, Mass.: Peter Smith, 1981).

Sartre, J. P., *Being and Nothingness* (London: Methuen and Co., 1957).

Satz, D., 'Markets in Women's Reproductive Labor', *Philosophy and Public Affairs* 21 (1992): 107–31.

_____ , 'Markets in Women's Sexual Labor', *Ethics* 106 (1995): 63–85.

Scheffler, S., *The Rejection of Consequentialism* (Oxford: Oxford University Press, 1982).

_____ , *Human Morality* (Oxford: Oxford University Press, 1992).

Scheper-Hughes, N., 'The Global Traffic in Organs', *Current Anthropology* 41 (2000): 191–224.

Schutz, R., 'Surrogacy in Israel: An Analysis of the Law in Practice', in Cook and Sclater (eds.), *Surrogate Motherhood: International Perspectives.*

Sher, G., *Desert* (Princeton: Princeton University Press, 1987).

Shiffrin, S., 'Paternalism, Unconscionability Doctrine, and Accommodation', *Philosophy and Public Affairs* 29 (2000): 205–51.

Shoemaker, S., *Self-Knowledge and Self-Identity* (Ithaca, NY: Cornell University Press, 1963).

Shrage, L., 'Should Feminists Oppose Prostitution?', *Ethics* 99 (1989): 347–61.

———, *Moral Dilemmas of Feminism* (London: Routledge, 1994).

Steinbock, B., 'Surrogate Motherhood as Prenatal Adoption', in L. Gostin (ed.), *Surrogate Motherhood*.

Steiner, H., *An Essay on Rights* (Oxford: Blackwell, 1994).

Swanton, C., 'The Concept of Interests', *Political Theory* 8 (1980): 83–101.

Thomson, J. J., *Rights, Restitution, and Risk* (Cambridge, Mass.: Harvard University Press, 1986).

Thoreau, H. D., 'Civil Disobedience', in H. A. Bedeau (ed.), *Civil Disobedience* (Indianapolis: Pegasus, 1969).

Titmuss, R., *The Gift Relationship*, eds. A. Oakley and J. Ashton (London: LSE, 1997).

Tunc, A., 'The Volunteer and the Good Samaritan', in J. M. Ratcliffe (ed.), *The Good Samaritan and the Law* (Gloucester, Mass.: Peter Smith, 1981).

van Niekerk, A. and van Zyl, L., 'Commercial Surrogacy and the Commodification of Children: An Ethical Perspective', *Medicine and Law* 14 (1995): 163–70.

Veatch, R. M., *Transplantation Ethics* (Washington, DC: Georgetown University Press, 2000).

Waldron, J., 'A Right to do Wrong', *Ethics* 92 (1981): 21–39.

Wall, G., 'The Concept of Interest in Politics', *Politics and Society* 5 (1975): 487–510.

Walzer, M., *Spheres of Justice* (Oxford: Blackwell, 1983).

Warnock, M., *A Question of Life: Warnock Report on Human Fertilisation and Embryology* (Oxford: Oxford University Press, 1985).

Weitzer, R. (ed.), *Sex for Sale: Prostitution, Pornography and the Sex Industry* (London: Routledge, 2000).

Wertheimer, A., 'Two Questions about Surrogacy and Exploitation', *Philosophy and Public Affairs* 21 (1992): 211–39.

———, *Exploitation* (Princeton: Princeton University Press, 1996).

———, *Consent to Sexual Relations* (Cambridge: Cambridge University Press, 2003).

West, D. J., and de Villiers, B., *Male Prostitution: Gay Services in London* (London: Duckworth, 1992).

West, J., 'Prostitution: Collectives and the Politics of Regulation', in R. Matthews and M. O'Neill (eds.), *Prostitution, The International Library of Criminology, Criminal Justice, and Penology* (Burlington, Vt.: Ashgate, 2002).

Wikler, D., 'Paternalism and the Mildly Retarded', *Philosophy and Public Affairs* 8 (1979): 377–92.

Wilkinson, S., *Bodies for Sale* (London: Routledge, 2003).

———, 'The Exploitation Argument against Commercial Surrogacy', *Bioethics* 17 (2003): 169–87.

Williams, B., 'Personal Identity and Individuation', in B. Williams (ed.), *Problems of the Self* (Cambridge: Cambridge University Press, 1973).

———, 'Persons, Characters, and Morality', in Williams, B., *Moral Luck* (Cambridge: Cambridge University Press, 1981).

Wolff, J., 'Fairness, Respect, and the Egalitarian Ethos', *Philosophy and Public Affairs* 27 (1998): 97–122.

Woodward, J., 'The Non-Identity Problem', *Ethics* 96 (1986): 804–31.

Zargooshi, J., 'Quality of Life of Iranian Kidney "Donors" ', *Journal of Urology* 166 (2001): 1790–9.

Index